TO SAVE THE WILD EARTH

To Save the

field notes from

Wild Earth

the environmental frontline

Ric Careless

FOREWORD BY MAURICE STRONG

THE
MOUNTAINEERS

Originally published in Canada in 1997 by Raincoast Books, Vancouver

First published in the US in 1997 by

THE MOUNTAINEERS

1001 SW Klickitat Way, Suite 201
Seattle, WA 98134

10 9 8 7 6 5 4 3 2 1

Library of Congress Cataloging-in-Publication Data
A catalog record of this book is available at the Library of Congress
ISBN 0-89886-567-0 (North America)

PRINTED AND BOUND IN CANADA

For Dona and Sheena

Contents

Foreword

ALTHOUGH OUR EARTH is but a tiny speck in a cosmos of awesome dimensions that defies human comprehension, it would be wrong to take this as a measure of its insignificance. On the contrary, the more we become aware of the infinite vastness and complexity of the universe, the more we can appreciate how unique and distinctive our small planet is. For nowhere else have we been able to discern signs of the richness of life that exists on Earth, and even here the conditions that make life possible as we know it have prevailed for a relatively brief period in the history of the Earth. From this it must be clear that if life on Earth is not unique, at the very least it is a rare and precious phenomenon. And the future of life on Earth is literally in our hands.

The scale and intensity of human activities have reached a point at which we are affecting the conditions on which life on Earth depends. Our fates are inextricably linked with the entire web of life on Earth. We have become the dominant species, and we are a species out of control. Our activities are now creating imbalances that threaten the entire life systems of our planet, although other species are better suited to survive than we are. Yet it is what we do, or fail to do, that will make the difference.

Ric Careless is one of those rare people who have made and continues to make a difference — a profound difference. As the leader and architect of nine different campaigns carried out over the past 25 years to protect some of the most beautiful and ecologically rich wild places in British Columbia, notably the Tatshenshini River, Spatsizi Plateau, and Nitinat Triangle, he has made an immense contribution to the global effort to conserve the environment and natural resources of our Earth. It is an exciting and inspiring story that reveals the deep-rooted values and ideals that motivate him as well as the sophisticated and pragmatic techniques with which he has pursued his mission so successfully.

His experience and success demonstrate cogently the fact that virtually all of the actions required to ensure the security and sustainability of life on Earth must be taken at the level of specific and often local situations. And virtually every success depends on the quality, commitment, and capability of those who lead the way.

This book tells the compelling story of how the leadership of one exceptional, committed person has made a difference. It is examples like those recited in this book that revitalize my confidence that we can make the transition called for at the Earth Summit at Rio de Janeiro to a more secure and sustainable mode of life on Earth.

Maurice Strong
Secretary-General of the UN Rio Earth Summit
NEW YORK CITY
JUNE 1997

Acknowledgments

THESE STORIES are the result of dedicated effort of thousands of wilderness advocates over the past two and a half decades throughout British Columbia, Canada and the United States. To each of you I express my heartfelt thanks in helping to preserve pristine wild places for future generations.

Above all, I am deeply grateful to my mother and father, Betty and Maurice Careless, who gave me the faith to trust in myself; to Dona Reel, my companion in love and conservation who epitomizes for me what partnership means, and to my daughter Sheena for the joy she brings into my life. I also want to thank Karen Careless, who began this conservation journey with me and who is the mother of our child, for her ongoing friendship.

I particularly want to honor my conservation mentors who inspired me to protect wilderness and showed me how this might be done: Ken Farquharson and Brock Evans, my 'grand mentor' Dave Brower, and the man who first kindled my desire to save Nature's creation, John Muir.

Similarly, I thank Maurice Strong for his moral leadership and ongoing conviction that the environment of this world can and will be saved for Nature and humanity.

Over the years I have had the honor to work with visionary politicians who have demonstrated their commitment to the needs of future generations through their environmental leadership. In Canada: Prime Minister Jean Chrétien, former Prime Minister Pierre Trudeau, former Speaker of the House of Commons John Fraser, Finance Minister Paul Martin, Senator Pat Carney, and former Member of Parliament Jim Fulton. In the United States: Vice President Al Gore, Senator Tim Wirth, Congressman George Miller, and Congressman Wayne Owens. In British Columbia: former Premier Mike Harcourt, former Minister of Forests and Parks Bob Williams, former Ministers of Environment John Cashore and Moe Sihota, former Forest Minister Andrew Petter, and Members of the Legislature Tom Perry and Joan Sawicki.

In addition to the foregoing I want to acknowledge those other dedicated individuals at the senior levels of the Canadian, B.C. and U.S. governments, many of whom I have not been able to name for strategic reasons, who have worked against difficult odds over the years to ensure that the remaining wilderness does not disappear. In this respect I especially think of those key individuals in the B.C. Parks and Wildlife Branches who have acted as guardians of the public's wilderness trust.

Since I have not felt qualified to document crusades where my involvement was minor, such as at South Moresby, the campaigns recounted in this book are limited to those ones in which I played a major role. However, whether on the efforts described in this book or others, there is a grouping of conservation leaders who I have been privileged to work with over many years on multiple campaigns. These individuals have provided an extraordinary example of commitment and deserve exceptional appreciation: Mark Angelo, John Bergenske, Bert Brink, John Broadhead, Adriane Carr, Tom Cassidy, Ray Collingwood, Grant Copeland, Ray Demarchi, Bristol Foster, Rosemary Fox, Joe Foy, Maureen Fraser, Paul George, Arlin Hackman, Monte Hummel, Vicky Husband, Sabine Jessen, Harvey Locke, Jerry Mallett, Lloyd Manchester, Ed Mankelow, Elizabeth May, Colleen McCrory, Greg McDade, Kevin McNamee, Pat Moss, Bob Peart, Kevin Scott, Gerry Scott, George Smith, Bill Wareham, and Ed Wayburn.

Additionally, there are many people who have contributed significantly to a specific campaign without whom the individual parks written about here would never have been protected. These include: Alice Albrecht, Allan Askey, Ethan Askey, Robert Ballantyne, Tony Barrett, David Boyd, Pierce Clegg, Reg Collingwood, Jim Cooperman, Dan Culver, Humphrey Davy, Michael Down, Peter Enticknap, Bryan Evans, Jason Faulkner, Rod Gee, Margaret Gerrard, Ian Gill, Lesley Giroday, Kent Goodwin, Mark Haddock, Jim Hamilton, Roger Handling, Juergen Hansen, Neil Hartling, Carol Hartwig, Syd Haskell, Tom

Henley, Ann Hillyer, Eve Howden, Gerry Irby, Bob Jamieson, Trevor Jones, Myron Kozak, Vladimir Krajina, Harry Kruisselbrink, Joe L'Orsa, Carleen Lay, Ken Lay, Nora Layard, John Lindhorst, Katy Madsen, Ken Madsen, Mike Matz, Jay McArthur, Wayne McCrory, Katie McGinty, Margie Jamieson, Marion McNaught, Pepper McLeod, Johnny Mikes, Liz Mitten-Ryan, Fritz Mueller, Dave Neads, John Nelson, Tony Pearse, Juri Peepre, Dennis Perry, Michael Pitt, Gordon Price, Doug Radies, Sally Ranney, Wayne Sawchuk, Paul Senez, Randy Stoltman, Barry Thornton, Art Twomey, Tommy Walker, John Willow, Norma Wilson, Catherine Winckler, Loretta Woodcock, Alan Young, and Ellen Zimmerman.

My thanks to all the BC Spaces for Nature and Tatshenshini Wild board members who have contributed countless hours to enabling the success of my conservation work in so many ways As well, I am deeply grateful to those funders large and small who share my passion to protect nature, and by their generosity make it possible for campaigners such as me to do our work.

I would also like to acknowledge Mark Stanton and Raincoast for their ongoing interest in supporting and publicizing my wilderness work, Michael Carroll, my patient editor, and Dean Allen, book designer extraordinaire.

Finally, my apologies to anyone I might have inadvertently missed - you know who you are and what you have accomplished on behalf of the wilderness. On the other hand, while many people helped to improve this manuscript any mistakes or omissions are mine alone.

Saving wilderness is a collaborative effort that involves activist campaigners, donors, receptive politicians, enlightened media people, progressive companies, workers, and most of all responsible and responsive members of the public. To all of you I give my deepest thanks. Together, we will succeed in passing on the wilderness splendors of Nature to those who come after us.

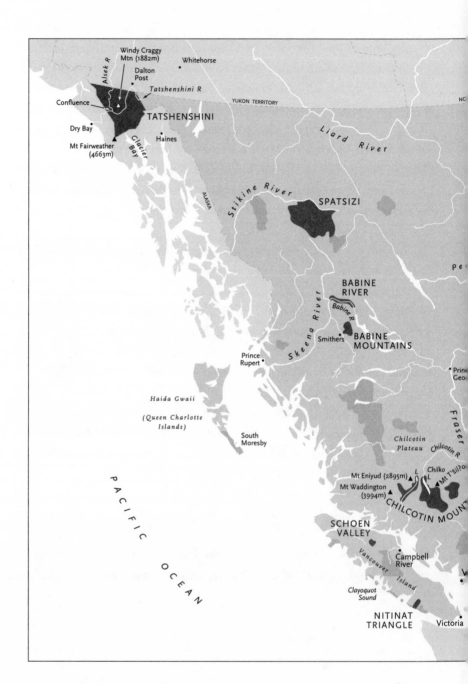

Windy Craggy
Mtn (1882m)

Whitehorse

Dalton
Post

Tatshenshini R

Alsek R

Confluence

YUKON TERRITORY

NO

TATSHENSHINI

Dry Bay

Haines

Liard River

Mt Fairweather
(4663m)

Glacier Bay

ALASKA

Stikine River

SPATSIZI

Pe

BABINE
RIVER

Skeena River

Babine R

Smithers

BABINE
MOUNTAINS

Prince
Rupert

Prin
Geo

Haida Gwaii

*(Queen Charlotte
Islands)*

South
Moresby

*Chilcotin
Plateau*

Chilcotin R

Fraser

*Chilko
L*

Mt Tsi'los

Mt Eniyud (2895m)

Mt Waddington
(3994m)

CHILCOTIN MOUNT

SCHOEN
VALLEY

Vancouver River

Campbell
River

P A C I F I C

Vancouver Island

*Clayoquot
Sound*

O C E A N

NITINAT
TRIANGLE

Victoria

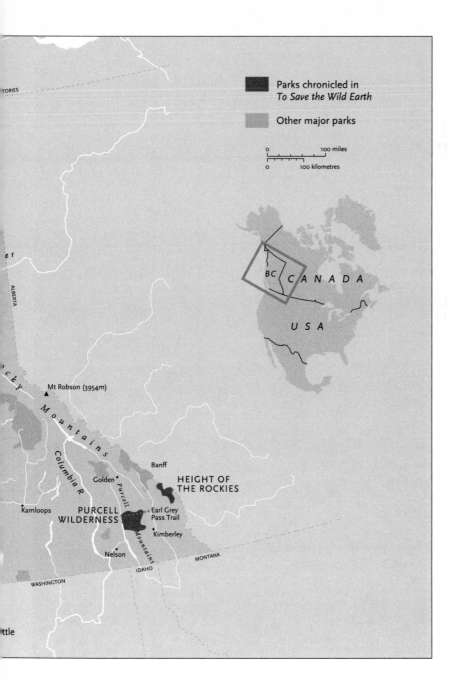

Parks chronicled in
To Save the Wild Earth

Other major parks

0   100 miles

0   100 kilometres

TORIES

BC *C A N A D A*

U S A

ALBERTA

R o c k y   M o u n t a i n s

▲ Mt Robson (3954m)

Columbia R

Purcell

Banff

Golden

HEIGHT OF
THE ROCKIES

Kamloops

PURCELL
WILDERNESS

Earl Grey
Pass Trail

Mountains

Kimberley

Nelson

MONTANA

IDAHO

WASHINGTON

ttle

Birthright

An Introduction to Wilderness

ILDERNESS. It is a place, an experience, a tradition, a remembering, and a future. It is an ancient forest homeland, a living refuge for wildlife, a sanctuary for endangered species and biodiversity. Wilderness is the very archive of life. The essence of purity, it serves as a guarantor for fresh water, clean air, and health. Vast and free, the wilderness provides a wild place to play, a space for solitude. It offers the chance for renewal in Nature, reconnection with the land, reunion with the spirit.

Most important, wilderness is for wilderness's sake. Precious beyond measure, finite, rare, and disappearing too fast, it is all that is left in our world that is un*man*aged. It is where the soul of the planet resides.

For more than 25 years I have fought on the environmental frontline in British Columbia to save the wild earth. I have done this in the company of many fine souls. Together we have dedicated our lives to ensure that Nature's splendor will never be lost for the future.

Living my life for wilderness has been an adventure, an opportunity, an honor. Out of this experience has come my desire to share stories of this work.

How it feels to encounter wild places. What goes on behind the scenes in environmental campaigns. How they are fought. How they are won. And why preserving Creation is crucial for the sake of our children, for life on Earth as we know it, and for human survival.

The stories here are told as they happened, as I lived them. They are one man's firsthand experience of how countless people came together again and again to save Nature. For my part, it isn't that I started off knowing wildness. Quite the opposite, in fact. Rather, I was a city kid who grew up in Toronto in the 1950s. Home was in the downtown core, complete with subways, buses, and the ever-present drone of traffic. But even amid the concrete and asphalt, vestiges of Nature could be found. You just had to know where to look.

My favorite playground was in the wooded ravines of the Don River. Since these were too steep-sided to build on, and with the valley floors prone to flash flooding, they remained covered in brush and remnants of the once-great Carolinean forest. The only development was the network of footpaths we kids had trampled playing hide-and-seek. Here, in waters that surely were polluted, a tribe of young boys got together in spring to make mud dams to hold back melting rivulets. We constructed forts and relived the primitive skirmishing traditions of our species. We smelled the scent of the soil reemerging from winter, stalked squirrels, and scrambled through the bushes.

These were happy, formative times. For it was here in these scruffy Toronto gulches that I first discerned the faintest glimpses of the natural world. And surely this hint triggered a hunger, a yearning to seek something yet unknown to me – the wild earth.

Back then my father would tuck me in at night and tell stories. As a renowned writer and historian, Dad found storytelling part of his calling, I guess. But of all those bedtime tales he told, I liked best the one about a far-off mountain frontier called British Columbia. Here, he said, there were places where no one had gone, places to be discovered that no one knew, places that were wild beyond imagination.

Nowadays, I suppose, many aboriginal Canadians would dispute the accuracy of this story but, as a young child, imagine my wonder, my excitement. As I grew older, the story faded from my everyday life, but it still lingered deep inside me. Always the pictures I drew were of peaks, forests, and oceans. Not surprisingly, when Dad and I built a model train in the basement, I insisted the setting for it be British Columbia. The tracks ran between mountains modeled on western wilderness.

Given that the Careless clan was also carless (oh, how often has my name been so misspelled!), I didn't experience the land until my teens when I first went off to summer camp in Algonquin Park. Here, as I canoed down Opeongo and Happy Isle Lakes, surrounded by the low, mapled ridges of the Canadian Shield, I felt my soul shiver. Paddle dipping into clear water, loons calling plaintively, wind riffling the waves along, I reconnected with my national heritage: "O Canada, my home and native land."

As the coureurs de bois of the fur trade had journeyed these waters 200 years prior, as Native peoples had known this place down through the ages, as the land had ever endured wondrously wild, now I, too, was here. For the first time I sensed the eternal, the infinite, the spirit of the original Earth.

In my 16th summer I finally got my chance to travel west. I was thrilled. My father had accepted a position teaching at the University of Victoria. For days our family rode Canadian National Railways cross-country. The morning the train was scheduled to enter British Columbia I got up at 5:00 a.m. to get a seat in the glass-domed observation car. There, in the silvered predawn light, far off in the distance and still small, I saw them at last — mountains! The purpled peaks of the Rockies. I fairly vibrated with excitement.

The closer we got, the grander the mountains became, more splendid than any picture I had seen, wild beyond what I could ever have dreamed. That morning our train glided up the evergreen corridor of the Athabasca Valley, watched by the gray limestone sentinels of the Front Ranges. Passing through the gateway town of Jasper, we approached the Continental Divide. Then, as our train crossed the invisible boundary and left Alberta, rising above a wild,

3

forested flank stood Mount Robson, the highest peak in Canada's Rockies, massive and snow-clad in a flawless blue sky. It seemed to welcome me, for at last I had come home to my British Columbia.

That fall I started university in Victoria, the provincial capital. Here, given a burgeoning fascination with the natural world, I enrolled in geography and focused on resource conservation. At the university I first encountered the wilderness writings of American visionaries John Muir, Aldo Leopold and, especially, Henry David Thoreau. No other phrase before or since has affected my life more than Thoreau's: "In Wildness is the Preservation of the Earth."

When I began university, taking environmental studies wasn't an option. No such courses existed. Indeed, the word *environment* wasn't really in the lexicon yet. The 1960s were drawing to a close and society's trauma was Vietnam. Nevertheless, I think the nightly news moved the public consciousness. Those appalling images of war showed not just the violence done to people but also the land. The televised footage of napalm bombings and Agent Orange defoliations were the preconditioning for environmental awareness. They probably laid the psychic roots that made Greenpeace such a successful name when the organization was born a couple of years later in Vancouver.

Without question the pictures beamed back by Apollo spacecraft in the late 1960s of a luminous, delicate Earth floating in the black vastness of space awoke humanity to a new reality. This small globe in the void was our home, our means for survival. The environment was what made life on this planet possible. It had to be protected or all existence was threatened.

The summer Neil Armstrong became the first man to walk on the moon was when I discovered true wilderness. Hiking in the Rockies and wandering along Pacific surf beaches south of Tofino, I learned what it felt like to be in a place with no signs of human development. Even Algonquin Park had featured an occasional building, some cottages perhaps or a lodge, but in these British Columbia wildscapes there was a virginal quality. The original Earth as evolved by Nature. A mythic magic.

After that summer, wilderness became my life and my reason for being. Over the years it would become both my vocation and my avocation. But first I had a lot to learn. In retrospect I now see that a key part of my college education was getting a solid grounding in what wilderness was and how it could be kept intact. The leading authorities on the subject at the time were Americans. In 1964 the U.S. Congress passed the Wilderness Act, which defined wilderness as a place

> where the natural community of life is untrammeled by Man . . . where
> Man is a visitor who does not remain . . . [which is] undeveloped land
> retaining its primeval character and not presently occupied by roads or other
> developments . . . [which] generally appears to have been affected primarily by
> Nature with the imprint of Man's work substantially unnoticeable . . . [and
> is] of sufficient size to make practical its preservation and use in an
> unimpaired condition [5,000 acres is the minimum size under this act].

Since then we have learned much about protecting Nature. Still, this definition remains as the foundation of our understanding of wilderness. Of most importance, uses that alter the land, such as industrial logging, mining, roads, dams, and permanently built structures, must be excluded. Otherwise the land is no longer as it was formed. The minimum cutoff size is critical to ensure the integrity of wilderness. Fragmented by logging, highways, or such, the wildness soon vanishes. Grizzlies, for instance, need space; they can't survive in postage-stamp-sized parks. Although small protected spots have their place in the ecology of preservation, they are no substitute for the rapidly retreating great wild spaces. Therefore, these smaller sites need to be called by a name other than wilderness.

While the U.S. Wilderness Act provided the criteria for the identification and protection of wild landscapes, we have also had to learn how to care for them. The clue is to remember that our role is to steward these lands for all who come after. Since it is impossible to make more of the original Earth, the prime directive is to do only what is necessary to keep the land undamaged from illicit human activities, such as poaching, *and no more*. In tending the wild, the Zen governing principle of "least action" applies.

The classroom training I got at university was a good beginning because even before I had graduated I got involved in my initial campaign, which became Canada's first mass public wilderness crusade: the battle for the Nitinat Triangle. In the years and decades that followed, one issue led to another: the Purcell Mountains, the Spatsizi Plateau, the Tatshenshini River, and the other places chronicled here. While I played a leadership role in these campaigns, if I learned one thing, it is that wilderness protection is a team sport, and the larger the team the better.

Indeed, the more people involved, each helping in their own heroic way to protect wildness, the more of the natural world our children will have passed on to them. Therefore, my greatest wish is that these tales will inspire others – perhaps you – to join in and become a wilderness warrior. Hopefully you, too, may decide that despite all the self-serving corporate rhetoric to the contrary, saving the wild earth for tomorrow is not just a possibility but a privilege.

For me the chance to protect the land has given meaning to my life. I have been rewarded for the many tough years of putting myself to the test by a rich sense of aliveness, which flows, I think, from the very essence of wilderness. The wild country is humanity's place of birth and our birthright. So, its preservation is crucial for human kind to always be reminded that we were created and did not ourselves create.

I believe that this is a most necessary remembrance. For were we, in the height of arrogance or disconnection from our worldly beginnings, ever to forget we depend on this planet for our continued existence, then surely the human species would perish. Because ultimately saving the wild earth is about more than protecting the natural environment – after all, life existed before us and will endure with our passing – it is also about the salvation and survival of people, you and me, your child and mine.

In this spirit then, here are some sagas of wilderness won. To me these stories are more than just historical accounts of adventure, struggle, and success;

6

they are a love story. They tell of my caring for the Earth and all the beings, human and otherwise, who share this place. This book has been written as my offering to help ensure that the wonder, the inspiration and, yes, the love that was given humanity by Nature will never be lost.

Perhaps a song written in the heat of the campaign for Nitinat says it simplest:

Here is the birthright of our north country,
The open wilderness, the untouched artistry.
Canada began here in this sweet serenity,
Praise the birthright of our north country,
Praise the birthright that is you and me,
Praise the birthright that is left to be.

Nitinat Triangle
First Battle for the Trees

O N southern Vancouver Island's Pacific coast an enclosure of high ridgelines created a rainforest sanctuary, protecting it from the outside world. Called the Nitinat Triangle because of its geographic shape, this area contained three glistening jewels within its hidden watershed: Hobiton, Squalicum, and Tsusiat Lakes. Their shores were sheltered beneath ancient stands of giant red cedar and Douglas fir.

For millennia a timeless forest had thrived untouched in this secluded valley. Reaching skyward 120 feet and 60 feet in circumference, the individual trees at Nitinat were very old – 300, 500, even 1,000 years of age. From deep-shaded fern floor to the lofty spires where white-headed eagles perched, this was the original Earth as it had evolved since the beginning. Here the primeval energy of creation still resonated from the land – Nature's flow, pure, pristine … sacred.

Since the passing of the last Ice Age 11,000 years ago, life in the British Columbian rainforest had become intricately intertwined. Everything supported everything else. The great trees that had endured here for centuries were fed by nutrients that had accumulated in the deep, wet soils. Their roots soaked

9

up this richness from the forest floor, enabling the great conifers to grow tall and huge. By maturity their crowns reached beyond the canopy into the often misty sky. But nothing is forever, not even rainforest cedars. Gradually, as they got even larger, the beginning of their end was presaged. Decay commenced, and slowly the heartwood of the trees was eaten away. This action was relentless so that eventually a seemingly healthy giant was reduced to a hollow shell of its original self. With the core gone, so, too, was the old tree's strength. Then it would wait through the final seasons for the inevitable end.

One evening, 600 years ago, a massive storm swept in from the Pacific to hammer the mountains of Nitinat. Powered by subtropical energy, the force of the wind was colossal. For hours it wailed through the forest, causing trees to strain in tremendous arcs. And so it was that down on the flats near the outlet of Hobiton Lake a decayed but valiant veteran could resist no longer. First, with a creaking and then a thunderous crash, the ancient cedar smashed to the ground, victim of the gale's fury.

The next day the winds dropped and all was quiet. After a life lived so tall, the fallen monarch now rested in the shadows of the forest floor. Over time its shell of trunk, like the long gone heartwood before, also came to be colonized by fungi and countless microbes and insects. Slowly, over the decades and then the centuries, these life-forms changed the wood into soil, transforming the fallen giant into a foundation for the future.

The years came and went, and with them many winter storms. During one of these tempests, an especially strong gust dislodged a cone from high above. It dropped through the canopy and landed on the decaying cedar. Soon a seed germinated and rootlets extended into the nurse log's soil. The date was October 12, 1492. On the distant side of North America, Christopher Columbus rowed ashore to discover his New World. Stepping out of his boat, he was met by a people who had long lived there. . . .

At Nitinat Native peoples also made their home within the rainforest. Their ancestors were as much a part of the spirit of this place as the cedars. They called themselves Dididat, and they had been there, according to the traditional stories, since Creation. And throughout all these thousands of years of human-forest coexistence little had changed.

Each fall they gathered at the outlet of Hobiton Lake to fish for the spawning salmon that returned upriver. Back behind the camp was a massive tree trunk that the children liked to clamber on. One year small feet running atop the log almost stepped on a little cedar seedling only inches high.

By now, thousands of miles to the east, European traditions were being introduced to the New World. The felling of the great hardwood forests of eastern United States and Canada had begun to make way for first settlements: the Virginia colony, Quebec. These initial clearings of the white man seemed so inauspicious, just tiny, stump-bound openings amid an endless ocean of forest in the North American wilderness.

Yet human "progress" is inexorable and cumulative. So, even as the cedar growing on the fallen log at Hobiton was a mere 20-foot sapling, its young roots embracing the old decaying trunk, the first pioneers on the Atlantic seaboard moved out from their rude footholds to clear more fields and log more trees. The clearings began to converge and increasingly eat into the seemingly infinite forests. Over the decades that followed, the settlements expanded into colonies. Later 13 of these colonies came together to undertake revolution, ultimately forging the United States, a new democracy, out of the North American wilderness.

Subsequently the boundaries of this young nation – indivisible under God – spread incessantly down into the Louisiana country, out across the Great Plains, on to the Oregon territory, up the California coast, and finally all the way to the distant land of Alaska. And with every expansion there was yet another new surge of pioneers, another frenzy of settlement, a further pushing back of the frontier, and an ever-increasing felling of forests.

North of the Forty-ninth parallel, in Canada, the British Empire persisted. But here, too, the trees, the great hardwood forests of southern Ontario and Quebec, fell to the settlers' axes. In Nova Scotia the white pine forests were logged out to provide masts for the British navy.

At Nitinat the Hobiton Cedar reached upward toward the canopy and sunlight. Like a gangly, fast-growing teenager, it was still spindly, perhaps two feet in diameter and 80 feet tall. Now, as it grew, an occasional sailing ship would drift past – explorers and fur traders engaged in discovery, and the first West Coast exploitation.

Decades passed, and the Hobiton Cedar added more height. As the tree approached maturity, its topmost needles reached the canopy and the light, where the vista was a swirling ocean of green washed by winds inbound off the Pacific. Often the air would become quiet as clouds wreathed the arboreal columns and an endless rain descended.

But Manifest Destiny couldn't be denied, and across the continent railways were built. As the steel was extended farther from the Atlantic and closer to the Pacific, more and more people arrived. They joined in the Herculean epic of transforming the landscape to their needs. The eastern hardwood forests retreated from the valleys to the uplands, while the sweeping prairies lost their buffalo, were fenced and rendered into checkerboard squares.

At Nitinat the Hobiton Cedar was now centuries old. Still, with each passing storm, with every welcome interlude of sun, with every season – cool, then warm, then cool again – the big tree added girth, becoming larger and ever more majestic. And still the salmon spawned in the lakes where the Dididat set their nets.

Elsewhere across North America the pace of development quickened. The population grew, technology intensified, and the 20th century dawned. The completion of a new canal across the Panamanian isthmus brought the Old World and New England much closer to the West Coast. Now it became economic to chop down the big trees of the Pacific coast, mill them into lumber, and ship them off to the eastern United States and Europe. The building of the canal was timely, since the great forests of eastern North America, like their once great counterparts in Europe, had become devastated through ruthless overcutting. The infinite timberlands had been reduced to a patchwork of finite remnants. They were wilderness no longer.

Such devastation, such tragedy. The forest lands of the previously wild continent had been ravaged with stunning speed. In only 500 years of European settlement a life system 4.5 billion years in evolution had been ruthlessly exploited, in many places to extinction. All the while at Nitinat the Hobiton Cedar and the other old trees stood oblivious to the destruction suffered across North America during their lifetimes. Rather, in silence, they witnessed another cycle of seasons and stars as the Earth tracked once again around the sun. To the big cedar at Hobiton Lake, eternity and the infinite seemed intact . . . until the morning when the far-off, faint whine of a chain saw first drifted across the guardian ridges.

THE ADVENT OF THE gasoline-powered saw and its ability to allow one man to topple a centuries-old rainforest monarch in minutes wasn't lost on the logging barons. Henceforth, the pace of forest exploitation accelerated. But the use of the internal combustion engine wasn't restricted to driving chain. Horses were replaced by trucks, stationary spar trees by huge mobile metal yarding towers, all of which made for greater efficiency and productivity. Since the pre-eminent desire of forest companies in the 1950s was to grow profits, not trees, they adapted technology developed during World War II to build ever-larger logging trucks and increasingly powerful road-building bulldozers and log-yarding machines. All this mechanization truly ushered in the era of industrial forestry. The speed, style, and impact of logging took an exponential leap into high gear.

Beginning in the 1950s, logging along the West Coast of North America evolved from small bush mills fed by wood from selective cuts to big corporations such as Weyerhauser and MacMillan Bloedel, which built large sawmills and pulp mills to process ever-greater volumes of wood from vast tracts of land. This industrialized logging razed entire forests from bottomland to ridge top, transforming whole valleys into enormous stump wastelands called clearcuts. Unlike earlier forestry, clearcut logging didn't just remove the bigger trees. Everything was felled, all in the name of efficiency, the companies said. But this same efficiency turned once-wild valleys into treeless moonscapes and left no shelter for animals such as elk, a critical issue of survival when winter snows were deep. With valley bottom trees often logged out for miles, wildlife mortality soared.

When the rains fall hard and long as they often do on the West Coast, the exposed mountain soil washes away because the trees are no longer there to hold it in place. Trickles of mud grow to torrents on the journey downhill, and the land slides, leaving great scars. The eroding soil moves at gravity's urging farther and farther downslope until at the bottom of each valley it stops, filling, clogging, and often obliterating the salmon streams that once ran so clear.

The best B.C. forest lands are found on Vancouver Island. Here deep soils and a mild, rainy climate produce a forest of massive proportions. Places such as Clayoquot Sound, Carmanah Valley, and Nitinat grow the greatest amount of living matter per acre of any terrestrial ecosystem on Earth. So, given that the trees get so huge on Vancouver Island, it isn't surprising that this part of British Columbia first caught the attention of loggers in the early 20th century. And because of the prolonged intensity of cutting, it is equally understandable that this area of ancient forest was among the first in the province to face elimination. By the late 1960s, decades of logging had punched roads and clearcuts into virtually every valley on the southern part of the island. British Columbians who, until very recently, had been kept out of their public forest lands – the companies gated and padlocked access roads – had little idea what was happening to the forests.

Suddenly, after centuries of living in solitude, the ancient trees of Nitinat were about to experience something totally new and quite astounding. In contrast to their previous isolation soon they would become the center of attention. Nitinat was where the mass public campaign to save British Columbia's old-growth forests began, 15 years before the protection of South Moresby on Haida Gwaii (Queen Charlotte Islands) and 20 years before the Clayoquot Sound blockades.

14

After ecologically unconscious centuries as northern lumberjacks, at Nitinat, for the first time, Canadians began to take stock of the environmental destruction happening to their True North Strong and Free. They started to realize that their trees weren't endless and that their wilderness heritage was imperiled. For too many decades the logging companies had been given free rein to annihilate the old-growth rainforests, but in the Nitinat Triangle the public finally organized and shouted, "Stop!"

It all started innocently enough. In 1970 occasional small bands of recreationists traveled across the logging roads of southern Vancouver Island to canoe the isolated Nitinat Triangle. Their early reports of the pristine wilderness lakes and the ancient forest piqued interest and concern. In particular, Jim Hamilton, who had lived at the edge of the Triangle for years maintaining the telegraph line along the West Coast Lifesaving Trail, sounded the alarm: B.C. Forest Products (BCFP) was building a road toward the Triangle and planned to clearcut the valley.

Having heard about this special place, Karen McNaught, Gordie Price, and I decided to take some time off from university one weekend to find out more. We left early in the morning from Victoria, crammed into my secondhand Volkswagen Beetle, and drove through the seemingly endless stump lands to a put-in site. Launching our canoe, we paddled a few miles down the long lake toward the entrance to the Triangle.

The mountains here had already been scalped. One high, rounded summit was half shaved in an immense clearcut, with a fringe left on top. This savaging saddened and angered me. But more dismaying was the new road being bulldozed along the lakefront. Blasted rock and side-cast mud had pushed trees into the water, and a long shoreline scar paralleled us as we canoed down the lake. This was BCFP's new logging road, and it was headed in the same direction we were. Still a few miles short of its destination, it was being built fast.

Big cedars stood sentry at the gateway to the Nitinat Triangle. We were young, not yet 20, out on our own. So, as we entered the ancient forest for the first time, we felt like explorers, uncertain about what we would find. Isolated from the rest of the world by high, forested ridges as it is, the passage into the Triangle is up the Hobiton River. Hobiton is a Dididat word that means "the river that snores," probably due to the sound this stream makes in its lower reaches as the water spills gently down and between a procession of soft, moss-covered boulders. It's like something out of Tolkien. To enter this place of wild mystery, the visitor must wade and line a canoe upstream to the lakes beyond. The water is an ideal temperature, which is good, since crossing some of the deeper pools requires swimming rather than wading.

It was early fall. The fullness in the air was spiced with a hint of the cool that would soon come. From somewhere amid the ferns and massive tree trunks a grouse drummed. Clutching the canoe, I pushed it up-current, threading among the boulders. Suddenly something large brushed swiftly between my legs. It was a salmon, a big sockeye, red with the spawning season. I scanned the stream with surprise. The great fish were moving upriver with us. Sometimes one would hang motionless, its back pillowing in the water like a fleshy rock. Then, with an explosive thrash, it would dart ahead.

As we made our way upstream, the current eased. The river's character transformed as the water became more tranquil. Alternating now between chest-deep wading and swimming, we led our canoe across dark, silent pools covered with brilliant green eel grass. A yard in length, these grasses swirled in the quiet current as if part of a jungle waterway fantasia.

Overhead, forest monarchs rose majestically. In places some of these big trees, often seven feet or more in diameter, had toppled across the river, causing us to haul our canoe, heavily laden with packs, up and over them. It was quite the ordeal, but for us it was pure joy. We felt fully alive.

It had been raining all day, and we were entirely soaked. By the time we moved through the upper reaches of the river, we were chilled to the bone. West Coast rainstorms, even in fall, can last for days with great intensity. Knowing this, we felt our spirits flag. Perhaps this wilderness would prove too tough for us.

Around the next twist in the river the current ceased and the water deepened, not just in pools but continuously. We climbed back into our canoe, picked up the paddles, and proceeded quietly. My blade slid through placid water. The air was settled, soundless. We glided through a timeless sanctuary of infinite green beneath a canopy held aloft by massive living columns of Sitka spruce and Douglas fir. The moist air was heavy with vapored incense.

Rounding the bend, we slipped through a portal in the forest. Wider and wider it opened until at last we could make out the lake, its surface shrouded in a dense fog. And even as we gazed, almost spellbound, a glow developed before us. Halfway between the lake and heaven, a radiance expanded within the fog, subtle at first, then growing in intensity as the sun melted through the mist to reveal its brilliant face.

Initially the sunlight penetrated the gloom like a spotlight, then with a gladdening warmth and comfort it began to evaporate the fog. Across the silent lake on the far shore we could now see, as if through a tunnel, a massive slope of ancient forest. Finally whole windows opened to reveal a ridgeline clad in cedar and fir rising thousands of feet above us. The sky emerged clear and vibrant blue. We had reached our wilderness. . . .

The magic of the moment when I first saw Hobiton Ridge and the lake country of the Nitinat Triangle has remained etched in my memory over all these years. The vista of Hobiton Ridge, ancestral trees ascending in endless ranks up its expanse, inspires me now as it did then.

Indeed, Hobiton Ridge was at the heart of the Nitinat Triangle issue. There were just so many big trees on this mountain, so many board feet of fiber, so many dollars in profits. BCFP could hardly wait to log it. That was why the company was building a road toward the Triangle so rapidly. It had plans to slash clearcuts across the ridge's face, just as it had done on countless other lost mountain slopes of Vancouver Island. And since Hobiton Ridge dominated the entire Nitinat Triangle, BCFP knew that if it could despoil the Triangle's beauty before conservationists organized the public, then the battle, and the wilderness, would be lost.

So the race for the future of Nitinat was on. Our imperative was to educate the public about this unknown treasure as quickly as possible. We had to develop compelling public support that would result in a political decision in favor of preservation. As for B.C. Forest Products, its objective was to get its road built into the valley, a mere four miles, and commence logging first. The stage was set for a classic land-use conflict of the type that has gripped so many parts of North America since.

Because Nitinat was the first time Canadian citizens rallied to protect a virgin rainforest watershed, there were no precedents or formulas. Everything would have to be done from scratch. We were a tiny group of University of Victoria students and some older, fervent recreationists who had come together intent on saving the big trees of Nitinat. Idealistic, naive, and enthusiastic, we had no preexisting organization, funding, membership, campaigning experience, public awareness, or government receptivity. Without any script to follow, we would have to improvise.

Early on we launched British Columbia's first wilderness petition, then set up a speakers' bureau and talked to scores of citizens' groups, thousands of students, countless service organizations, and municipal governments. We even went into the logging towns and met with forest workers face-to-face. Out in the Triangle we slashed routes through seven-foot-high brush with machetes to build the first portage trails between the lakes, which would enable recreationists and reporters to see the wilderness and what was at stake. Soon stories of Nitinat were told around Victoria and in the media. We produced our own radio and television spots and got them aired free. When we made a professional documentary film, it was televised nationally. The cost of making it was just $2,000, the price of the film stock. Everything else was volunteered.

As for our meager campaign budget, it was raised by holding raffles. Donations were also received at the display booth that we operated in shopping malls each weekend. We became very adept at stretching precious dollars to pay for essentials such as the bumper stickers that simply said: NITINAT TRIANGLE, PASS IT ON.

More important, we learned to lobby Cabinet ministers, both in Victoria and Ottawa. Since these people were the individuals who had the power to decide the fate of Nitinat, we intuitively realized we had to persuade them if we were to succeed.

While there had been a long tradition of public lobbying in the United States, prior to Nitinat such democratic advocacy, especially for environmental purposes, was virtually unheard of in Canada. There were cultural reasons for this situation, I think. Americans had been taught, often fervently, to believe in the individual and to fight for their rights. By contrast Canadians were more inclined to defer to, rather than try to convince, those who governed them. The roots of these differences were likely historical. Americans threw off England's colonial rule in a revolution and created a checks-and-balances populist government. Canadians never rebelled; instead, they inherited a more elitist parliamentary democracy from the British Crown and aristocracy. Therefore, while Americans expected conservationists to lobby their leaders, Canadians saw this activity as new ground.

My initial lobbying efforts began when I was only 20 and the ministers I tried to convince seemed overwhelmingly powerful to me. Those first times I sat in an ornate, high-ceilinged, oak-paneled Legislature anteroom, waiting for a silver-haired minister of the Crown to grant me a few minutes of his time, I experienced intense fear. I felt insignificant. Once, this anxiety escalated when my fly burst apart mere seconds before the minister's door opened. Throughout that agonizing meeting I strategically covered my lap with a file folder and continued my pitch. But even at times like that one, when I was especially terrified, somehow I would find the means to reconnect with my passion for the Nitinat wilderness and gain strength from it.

In those first ministerial meetings I came to understand just how important lobbying is to advance the environmental cause. After all, it is *the* contact between citizen advocate and politician, the time when an issue becomes a personal interaction. If things go well, more can be achieved in a few key minutes face-to-face with the person who will make the actual decision than months, even years, of protesting or media coverage can accomplish. To this day I am amazed that conservationists, especially in Canada, don't focus more time on top-level lobbying.

Lobbying is an art rather than a science. It isn't just knowing what you need to say, but how to get your message heard and accepted and your agenda acted upon. Since most politicians want to make the fewest decisions possible, and those usually in favor of the status quo, the job of an environmental lobbyist is tough. But learning to lobby so young when ecology was an unknown concept in a logging province like British Columbia was particularly tough. After all, the common wisdom of the day was that "50 cents of every B.C. dollar came from the forest industry."

In any wilderness campaign there is often one person who is the most important individual to convince, who actually controls the fate of the issue. The Nitinat Triangle's future rested with Ray Williston, the B.C. minister of forests and the elected representative for the northern logging city of Prince George. He would be a tough sell. An ex-school superintendent and principal, Williston was fervently pro-development and had become the most powerful minister in the 20-year government of Premier W.A.C. Bennett. Even today he has a legacy that endures in the Williston Reservoir, British Columbia's largest dam impoundment, which flooded out the once-wild Peace and Finlay Rivers. Williston was brutally frank with those who criticized industry, dismissing them as "armchair environmentalists." In response to complaints about the sulfur pollution that spewed out of the pulp mill smokestacks and stank up his hometown with a pall of rotten-egg fumes, Williston famously replied, "Ah, it's the smell of money, my friend!"

So that first morning when I was ushered in to meet Williston, my nerves jangled. After months of trying to get an appointment, I finally stepped into a large office that seemed charged with power. The oak desk in the center of the room was imposing. Behind it, sitting stiffly upright with a no-nonsense air, Williston, his hair as white as starch, peered at me with penetrating blue eyes. "Yes?" he asked, motioning crisply for me to speak.

Suddenly the room seemed even bigger and I felt dizzy. All around me on the walls were countless awards and mementos given to the minister by forest companies. There were pictures of Williston cutting ribbons at sawmill openings, riding in the cabs of bulldozers, and watching as fallers toppled huge trees. I took a deep breath.

"The cedars and firs of the Nitinat Triangle need to be preserved as a park," I began, watching Williston tighten. "Logging has affected almost every valley on southern Vancouver Island, and if we are to save any examples of big trees for the future, we have to do it there." Needless to say, I didn't convince him that day, but it was perhaps a measure of some success that I didn't faint.

Even though Williston didn't give my plans for a park much encouragement, what he did do at the end of the session was to stand and invite me to look at his awards and pictures. With his characteristic terseness he described, one by one, what each memento was about. Perhaps he intended this tour of his achievements to explain in a subtle fashion why it was inevitable that Nitinat must be logged. But as I reviewed his office memorabilia I sensed a slight shift in his attitude. He began to talk in a fatherly manner, not sternly but with an awkward warmth, almost as if I were his son.

Successful lobbying, I now believe, has a great deal to do with psychology, and is not just about the facts presented. Instinctively I went along with this budding father-son dynamic, which continued to tinge our meetings over the months that followed. Each time we met Williston became a little more relaxed and receptive to my message, making the possibility of preservation more likely.

During all those months, my fellow conservationists and I lobbied, held meetings, gave speeches, and worked the media for all the publicity we could get. B.C. Forest Products, meanwhile, blasted its access road closer and closer toward the endangered watershed. We knew time was running out, and the tension built as we wondered who would reach the Hobiton River first: our wilderness crusade or the logging company.

Our core team had all the characteristics of a successful conservation campaign: it was tiny, innovative, dedicated, and persistent. The group included John Willow, a veteran of the World War II Polish resistance movement and a superb strategist; Pepper McLeod, a nurse and the only typist on the team, who showed us how to conduct a professionally rigorous campaign and brought us order, bookkeeping, and administration; Humphrey Davy, an endearing older newspaper reporter who taught us that there was always a new angle to hook the Nitinat story on; Gordie Price, a radio broadcaster who had read Marshall McLuhan and who as an early enviro spin master knew that "with the media, perception *is* reality"; and Karen McNaught, my girlfriend, who became the secretary of the entire campaign and convinced her mother to allow us to convert the family dining room into Campaign Central. As for me, I became chairman of the whole adventure almost by default, mainly because I was willing to forgo all other responsibilities, including university classes, in my desire to save Nitinat.

Over the months that followed, this small band of conservationists worked at a frenzied pace. Outgunned a thousand to one by the giant forest companies, we had to rely on our spirit and the enthusiasm we could engender in the public. So, while we were ridiculously short of cash, we were incredibly strong of heart. And if I have learned anything from my many years of wilderness campaigning, it is that in the end heart will always prevail, regardless of the odds, as long as one keeps faith.

Still, as remarkable as spirit may be, the fact is that without organizational structure, inspiration on its own seldom results in actual change. To protect Nitinat an organization was needed first. In those early days of conservation Greenpeace hadn't been born yet. In fact, there were no Canadian activist wilderness groups to link up with, which meant we would have to become part of some group that had an environmental tradition outside Canada.

At the time I was a third-year geography student who had, through one of my courses, stumbled onto the inspired writings of John Muir, one of the godfathers of the American wilderness movement. In the late 1800s Muir led one of the first preservation campaigns, resulting in the protection of Yosemite National Park. He also founded the Sierra Club, the world's first true environmental activist organization. Headquartered in San Francisco, the Sierra Club became, in time, the leading U.S. environmental organization. By the early 1970s Sierra Club chapters had been established throughout the United States.

Back then several expatriate Americans living in British Columbia – Jim Bohlen, Katy Madsen, Terry Simmons, Irving Stowe, and Gerry Irby – had decided to set up a Sierra Club chapter in Vancouver. I heard about Sierra's new B.C. presence from its president, Ken Farquharson, the man who led the successful 15-year fight in British Columbia to save the transboundary Skagit Valley from being flooded. Ken was a determined Scot who had abandoned engineering to become one of Canada's first environmental consultants. Deeply in love with the land, he eventually established himself as one of the anchors of the B.C. environmental movement and became a very close friend and teacher of mine.

From my conversations with Ken I could see the benefits of the Sierra Club name. Having been stimulated by reading Muir's works, and already in search of an organization to assist us in our fight to save the Nitinat Triangle, I felt the Sierra Club was an ideal choice to link up with. So, after convening a highly successful meeting to launch the Nitinat issue publicly, I decided our next move was to set up a Sierra Club group on Vancouver Island.

The prudent question should have been how, but being young and naive has its advantages. It never occurred to me that the Sierra Club owned its name or had rules and procedures governing the establishment of new groups, or if it did, I didn't think that much about it. After all, the most important thing surely was to save Nitinat, and if that required the creation of a new Sierra Club organization, then so be it.

I found some U.S. Sierra Club letterhead – I was a member at the time – clipped off the logo with the club's name, and pasted it onto a piece of paper. A little Letraset modified the name to "Sierra Club of Victoria," an address was typed on, copies were printed and, voilà, a new Sierra Club group was born in February 1971, or so we thought.

In fact, we were a pirate operation. When the San Francisco Sierra Club office learned about us, they became quite perturbed. Things weren't made any easier for the head office by the fact that we were achieving record growth as we signed up hundreds of new members in just a couple of months. And our holding on to all the membership dues to finance the Nitinat campaign was certainly illegal and of major concern to them. However, there was no malice in our actions, nor were we aware of their implications. We were merely operating in a way that made sense to us. Our goal was to save wilderness, wasn't it, the same objective as the Sierra Club's?

By now we felt we had to bring the Nitinat Triangle issue to culmination soon if we were to win. Just as mountaineers talk about the crux, that most demanding point in a difficult climb where success or failure is determined, wilderness advocates, too, speak of the moment of truth. After months of intense campaigning, we had thousands of people actively backing us, and it was time to focus this support at a public event that would clearly demonstrate our strength. So we set out to organize a mass meeting, which became, in fact, the first wilderness rally ever held in Canada.

As we planned the event, we knew it had to be overwhelmingly successful. Failure to build to a strategic peak now and force government to act swiftly would mean losing the wilderness, since BCFP's logging road was about to reach the Hobiton River. At Campaign Central in Karen's mother's home we mapped out an intricate strategy. The walls of the dining room were plastered with timeline and action items. We booked the largest auditorium in Victoria, with the intention of attracting an overflow audience. To achieve this goal we had to heat up the issue to a fever pitch, so we saturated the media with interviews and articles about Nitinat. Posters blanketed Victoria, and we spoke everywhere — in schools, at churches, in malls, and at the university. As our blitz accelerated, we generated tremendous attention for the Triangle.

On March 8, 1972, the hall easily overflowed. Movies and slides were screened to a standing-room-only crowd, and the speeches were impassioned. Indeed, the rally had the fervor of an evangelical revival meeting. When the federal minister responsible for parks, the keynote speaker of the evening, was introduced, the energy in the hall became electric. Slowly and deliberately he began to read his prepared speech. But with every sentence the expectation of the audience heightened, and in response the emotions of the minister intensified. With a heavy French-Canadian accent and arms waving, he roused the crowd and they him.

Then, suddenly, he paused, pushed his notes to one side, and took a deep breath. With growing resolve he looked up and spoke from his heart. "I commit tonight," he said, "that the Nitinat Triangle will never be logged. It will be preserved as a national park." The crowd exploded into cheering, and the minister's aides were stunned. Obviously this announcement hadn't been part of the intended speech.

There was a greatness in this man's actions that night. After the rally, a few of us met with him in his hotel room. We talked about Nitinat and the future. His words were heartfelt, and I sensed I was in the presence of an exceptional human being that night. Over the years I followed his career closely, and 20 years later I was delighted but not surprised when that minister, Jean Chrétien, became the prime minister of Canada.

The rally and Chrétien's pronouncement were indeed Nitinat's moment of truth. This became clear a few weeks later when I met with Forest Minister Williston once more. Again I entered his large, wood-paneled office, but this time I felt much less intimidated. I was now more at ease with this man and his fatherly aspect.

That morning there was a certain light in his eyes as he greeted me. His formal voice was inflected with a new warmth. I sat down and this time it was me who waited. He leaned forward across his big oak desk and said, "Yesterday I flew the Nitinat. You're right about what you and the others have been saying. This is a special area. So I have ordered B.C. Forest Products to stop building their road and I have told them this valley will not be logged. It will be protected."

It took another month or so until the August 30 announcement in the Vancouver *Province* made it official. Twenty thousand acres of old-growth forest in Nitinat were to remain wild. We had succeeded.

Later some of my fellow campaigners and I returned to Nitinat for a quiet celebration of our own. We camped where the lake empties into the river at the spot where the mist first parted to reveal to me the magic of Hobiton Ridge. One evening I left the others and walked down to the edge of the water. The sun had dropped below the horizon, but golden light still bathed the treetops. The lake was motionless, and the song of a lone Swainson's thrush echoed through the twilight. In this solitude I reflected on the past 18 months. I thought of the

*At Canada's first rally for wilderness, then National Parks Minister
Jean Chrétien boldly commits to protect Nitinat Triangle.*

hard work undertaken by so many, and tried to grasp what it was we had accomplished. But it all seemed too big, too incomprehensible.

Feeling a need to wander, I stepped back from the water and entered the forest. As I walked amid ferns in the diminishing light at the foot of the great trees, I sensed the mystery of this place again. And when I paused for a moment, I found myself standing in a living church of antiquity before what was surely the altar.

In front of me stood the largest cedar I had ever seen. At its base huge, buttressed roots arched in empty embrace, gripping at a once-massive trunk that had long decayed. The newer trunk rose majestically to form the canopy, huge limbs radiating outward and upward into bleached wooden spires. This tree, I thought, was surely the father of the forest, an ancient warrior that had stood here for untold centuries. Staring at this Hobition Cedar, I could only wonder what events it had witnessed.

At that moment the significance of the struggle of the past year and a half became clear. This glorious ancestral tree in this magic place would now have a future. Unlike so much of North America, it would be spared the saw and the clearcuts. Here the legacy of the rainforest would endure. Because in the Nitinat Triangle we had passed it on.

A QUARTER CENTURY later, when I reflect back on the Nitinat struggle, a few postcampaign notes come to mind. Nitinat was protected 18 months after the creation of the Victoria group of the Sierra Club, which probably established a club speed record for success. Nevertheless, the "illegitimate" organization was still a cause of concern for the U.S. Sierra Club. I am certain the head office in San Francisco would have preferred to disband Victoria Sierra, but how could it do so after such a resounding environmental victory?

I am told it took years to sort out the mess. And since I have never been the bureaucratic type, I didn't hang around, preferring to move on to wilderness campaigns elsewhere in British Columbia. Therefore, to those who persevered and eventually ironed things out with Sierra's head office, my thanks and apologies.

In the long run the result of our illicit, if well-meaning, actions wasn't just the saving of Nitinat, but the founding of organized wilderness activism on Vancouver Island. Furthermore, in the decades following the founding of the Victoria group of the Sierra Club, Vicky Husband, the group's dedicated leader, went on to become a key player in many crucial land-use battles, including Clayoquot Sound. Today, 25 years after Nitinat, the Sierra Club thrives on Vancouver Island and is the backbone of the British Columbian environmental movement.

As for the Nitinat Triangle, even though Ray Williston put an end to logging plans in 1972, it took another 14 years of intergovernmental wrangling before the Triangle's forests were finally transferred from provincial to federal jurisdiction and formally preserved as part of Pacific Rim National Park.

And what about Ray Williston? I bumped into him not so long ago at a public slide show. It was the first time I had seen him since that distant day in his office when he told me Nitinat would be saved. He is now in his seventies, lacks the aura of power, and is no longer intimidating, but he still has that crisp white hair and those clear blue eyes. When I introduced myself, he seemed genuinely pleased to see me and easily recalled the Nitinat campaign. Neither of us wanted to miss the start of the slides, so we only had a few minutes to talk before it was time to take our seats. It was a show on wilderness preservation. As I sat down, I couldn't help smiling at how things had changed in 25 years.

Schoen Valley
Graduate Studies in the Wild

A HEAVY coastal rain had drenched the Schoen Valley meadows, and it was pitch-dark outside the tent. But finally, after a day of nonstop pouring, the deluge had ended. Beneath the cloud-bound peaks and amid the tall trees I had been sound asleep until the low growling of my dog Keah roused me. He tensed, alert at my feet. There was something outside. I listened carefully with shallow breath, my concentration probing the deep wildness of the night. A bear maybe, a wolf. What had Keah heard? At first I couldn't make out anything, just the occasional splatter of last raindrops on the tent fly. But again my little retriever growled, yet still I heard nothing.

Suddenly a crash came from the bush. An animal was moving through the 2:00 a.m. forest. It sounded big. Then there was a lot of thrashing and thumping, confirming to me that there was more than one beast out there and they were coming our way.

Keah's growl became fiercer. He bared his teeth while I fumbled with the flashlight. Cautiously I opened the door a crack to peer outside. My light cut a bright shaft through the misty darkness. Even as the tumult increased and the ground beneath my sleeping bag began to shudder slightly, I couldn't see anything. And then I glimpsed the legs, lots of them slicing through the beam. Elk, big heavy Roosevelt elk, a herd of them, each the size of a horse, emerged out of the rainforest into the opening where we were camped, and started to graze.

Instantly my apprehension turned to excitement. Roosevelt elk live only on Vancouver Island and across the border in the Olympic Peninsula of Washington State. Due to destruction of their crucial winter habitat by clearcut logging, there were few of them around in those days. Indeed, they were thought to be endangered. I had never seen even one of these creatures before, and now here was a small herd!

Keah didn't share my enthusiasm. He snarled repeatedly, his hair raised bristling down the length of his back. After a few minutes, as he felt the shift in my mood, he stopped growling. I hauled him beside me to calm him, waking Karen, my girlfriend. Together the three of us lay awake in the early hours, listening, feeling the ground tremble as the big animals moved within a foot of our tent. Another experience of the land, another thrill in the wilderness.

And how appropriate, I thought, given the origin of the word wilderness. It derives from the Old English *wildeorness,* which literally means "the place of wild deer." In the Middle Ages *wildeorness* was the name given to the hunting estates of British royalty. Gamekeepers managed wild animals in these preserves, keeping them safe from poachers and predators. Then, when the king was in a sporting mood, they would scare the deer and other quarry out for him to kill.

It is quite paradoxical that these regal sanctuaries for recreational slaughter gave birth to nature preservation. Yet medieval gamekeepers quickly learned that ensuring numerous targets for their lord meant maintaining the deer's habitat intact. This necessity led to the first awareness of protecting the land to preserve life. It was the birth of the conservation ethic.

A couple of centuries later when the English king's explorers began their great adventure in North America, conservation was the last thing on their minds. Wilderness now took on a New World meaning: an expanse of seemingly endless wild country abundant with animals that anyone, nobles and commoners alike, could hunt. Indeed, they had to. Wild game served as the main food source for the first discoverers and settlers. To them wilderness was no longer a private estate but a public larder. It was central to their need to live off the land.

The wildlife riches of North America made the wilderness a great repository of wealth, especially for fur and most particularly for beaver pelts. In 1670 King Charles II granted a charter for all lands drained by waters flowing into Hudson Bay, thereby establishing the fur-trading Hudson's Bay Company. This charter was one of the largest corporate resource grants ever made by a government in the history of humanity. It bestowed rights to a territory of 1.5 million square miles.

The effect of this act was to establish the economy of the northern half of the continent upon natural resource exploitation. Over the ensuing centuries the Hudson's Bay Company trapped the fur-bearing population toward exhaustion. At the same time the forts built by the company across what would become Canada served as the first outposts of European civilization. Triggering settlement, farming, logging, and mining, they initiated the subjugation of the Canadian wilderness by Westernized people.

Three hundred years after that royal decree my fellow Canadians had so completely assumed their identity as hewers of wood and drawers of water that in the southern part of the nation wild places had become hard to find. Like frontier trappers who finally realized that beavers were getting scarce, some Canadians began to consider that perhaps we had taken the wilderness for granted. The campaign to save the Nitinat Triangle had served as the wake-up call in British Columbia, informing the people that the wild earth was fast disappearing and that it was in dire need of preservation. The fight for the Triangle had also proved that citizen action could achieve results.

In September 1972 Karen and I had come to the Schoen Valley, looking for our next wilderness campaign. We wanted to move beyond our local "backyard," so we had traveled the distance up northern Vancouver Island to this spectacular, little-known valley. Unknowingly we were also taking the first step toward discovering a more strategic means of protecting wilderness.

The morning after our elk encounter the hot sun finally forced us from the drowsy comfort of our sleeping bags. Stepping outside, we found that the antlered visitors had departed. Footprints in the meadow were the only evidence of their passage. The previous day's rain was also just a memory now. The sky had cleared to blue, promising a stunning September day. All about, high, forested ridges saluted the sun's rising. The research we had undertaken in the past months had been correct: this place's ancient trees and wild animals were exceptional. We were convinced the Schoen had to be saved.

AT THE END of the Nitinat campaign, when we realized victory was close, I had begun to wonder what other wild spaces might be at risk. Our work on the Triangle had revealed that it was virtually the last intact watershed left on the southern third of Vancouver Island. If the land had been hit so hard here, what was the status of wilderness farther north? While this question seemed obvious, no one in 1972 could answer it. At that time satellite imagery was nonexistent, so finding out what wildness remained on the rest of the island would require research.

During July and August, several core members of the Victoria Sierra group – Karen, Gordie Price, Pepper McLeod, Rod Gee, and myself – set out to map every logging road on Vancouver Island. This would enable us to identify valleys that had no roads and were therefore unlogged. Since the island had more than 12,000 square miles, this task would be daunting. We accomplished our analysis by closeting ourselves in the University of Victoria library, away from the glorious summer weather, scrutinizing reams of black-and-white air photos. The result was the first systematic assessment of remaining wilderness ever undertaken in Canada.

To our dismay, what we found was that, like the south, much of northern Vancouver Island had also been heavily logged out. The region that offered the largest expanse of intact forest appeared to be the adjacent watersheds of Schoen Lake and the Tsitika River. Our research indicated a biological urgency to achieve protection there. Located in the lee of the island's mountain spine, the forests in Schoen and Tsitika were different from those found on wetter West Coast sites such as Nitinat. They featured grand fir, amabilis fir, and Douglas fir, trees that the logging companies had long preferred and had historically targeted.

By the time of our air photo survey, clearcutting was well advanced in almost every valley bottom in the northeastern portion of the island, except Schoen and Tsitika. Our primary finding was that these forests were now endangered. Unless we moved immediately to preserve some wilderness in this area, any chance to save low-elevation northeast side valleys would soon vanish.

However, library findings are merely "book learning." To be verified, they need field-checking, which meant flying over the island. But how could we afford this? In those days Sierra Victoria's budget at best ran to three figures, and all of it was raised from membership fees and small donations. Certainly paying for aircraft, especially for such a prolonged survey flight, was out of the question until I mentioned our need to Brock Evans. Based in Seattle, Brock was the U.S. Sierra Club's Pacific Northwest field representative. During the Nitinat campaign, he had been inspired by a visit to that rainforest and was now keenly interested in protecting British Columbia's wilderness.

"Let me work on it," Brock said. "I know a pilot. Jim Rausch, the son-in-law of the club's president, Ed Wayburn. Maybe he'll help out." Within a few days the answer came back. Rausch agreed to donate his plane to reconnoiter the north island wilderness. This was a major coup, and I thanked Brock for his help.

The chance to make such a flight was a dream come true. Even all these years later I remember clearly that afternoon when Rausch's twin-engine red-and-white Beechcraft taxied up to the Victoria terminal. With our summer wilderness research charted onto maps, the flight routing was clear. We were out to confirm the best remaining wild places so we could locate our next campaign.

After takeoff the plane winged out over the sad, familiar desecration of the southern island. I had traveled the logging roads of these valleys repeatedly on the approach to Nitinat and knew only too well the abuse they had suffered.

35

The clearcuts stretched for miles, landslides from unstable roads scarred the ridges, and eroded soil and stumps clogged salmon streams.

When we reached the Triangle's virgin green, it was a relief to fly above wilderness, especially since these trees had been officially saved only two weeks earlier. We flew alongside Hobiton Ridge toward the surf beaches of Pacific Rim National Park. Here we turned north, following the shoreline above the West Coast Trail – the world's finest oceanside hike – and then into the Clayoquot Sound country beyond Tofino.

Clayoquot was a place I knew well. During my student days, this area had been the wilderness playground for the University of Victoria Outdoors Club. As students, we had clambered along headlands hammered by surf, and we had traveled the back channels behind Flores Island, hoping to discover abandoned Native village sites. Those were delightful, if different, times than now. Certainly there was no sense then that Clayoquot would ever be threatened. Wedged between Strathcona Park to the northeast and Pacific Rim National Park to the southwest, Clayoquot and its big trees seemed safe, or so the conventional wisdom of the time believed.

Nitinat's recent protection, as well as that of Pacific Rim, made it seem that the preservation of other coastal cedar-hemlock forests was less critical than places up-island, especially those east of the Insular Mountains. Hence, a landscape as extraordinary as Clayoquot wasn't on the agenda for immediate action. Now, as I look back and reflect on all the heroism shown in support of Clayoquot's giant trees during the 1980s and 1990s, all the protests by people who got themselves arrested on behalf of the Earth, I can only wonder how things might have been different. If only in those early times we could have seen what was coming. If only we had had more activists to meet the protection needs of the northern island and Clayoquot simultaneously. But the fact is, just as there are too few conservationists to do all the work now, back then we were even more shorthanded.

Proceeding beyond Clayoquot Sound, we flew past Nootka Island where the earliest European explorers – Juan Pérez, James Cook, and George Vancouver – had first sighted British Columbia in the 18th century. What impacts, I thought ruefully, these encounters had led to in this part of the planet. At the far tip of Nootka, Rausch turned the plane eastward toward the place I was most curious to see. Shortly after we entered Schoen country, we crossed a long, deep lake edged by fine trees. An untouched beach defined the far end, while above the grand, snow-crested peak of Mount Schoen looked on. Banking around the mountain's flanks, we swept into Nisnac Valley. Below, a chain of golden meadows came into view. A small stream wandered through them and into Nisnac Lake, a shimmering jewel.

All around the meadows the firs stood tall, straight, and broad. They marched across the valley floor and without hesitation climbed the steep, surrounding cliffs. Here and there showy waterfalls danced down long rock walls. My airborne entrance into the Schoen was love at first sight. The drama of this inland island sanctuary was enthralling. What was more, I had heard much about this place from government biologists who said the valley provided critical Roosevelt elk habitat and supported a high-quality fishery.

Taking in the Schoen Valley's splendor, and knowing about its wildlife riches, I was even more certain that the valley met the criteria to make it the Sierra Club's next candidate for protection. As I scribbled notes on the maps and took photographs, I made mental plans to come back on foot with Karen. I wanted to experience this place firsthand on the ground before making the final campaign commitment.

For the moment, however, there was no time to linger. Our reconnaissance routing now took us into the neighboring Tsitika Valley. Although less visually spectacular than the Schoen, the old-growth forests found here from headwaters to mouth made this drainage important. Unfortunately, though, things were about to change. Even as we flew into Tsitika, I could see that clearing was under way for the new North Island Highway. Soon that road would transect the upper valley, and once it was completed, the logging of Tsitika would soon follow.

We flew the length of the river until we reached the place where it flowed into the Inside Passage at Robson Bight. This spot, we had been told, was

favored by orcas, or killer whales, not that the fishermen of the time were much impressed. They believed orcas competed for their fish and should be shot. Today it is hard to imagine such an attitude. Work done by scientists since then, especially at Robson Bight, proved that the fishermen's fears were unfounded. The same research also revealed that the Tsitika River's estuary is the most important orca rubbing beach in the world.

After leaving Tsitika, we felt we had surveyed what we had come for. The plane flew south for 30 miles and landed, dropping me off at the town of Campbell River. When I stepped back onto the ground after several hours in the air, I reeled with the images of the fine wild country I had seen. That evening I met with several local Sierra Club members and debriefed. Then, together, we discussed how to protect the best of the northeastern island. In effect, that meeting heralded the beginning of the campaign to save Schoen and Tsitika. Over the next few weeks our Sierra Club core group linked up with several other conservationist leaders, many of whom we had gotten to know during the Nitinat campaign. Most notable was Ed Mankelow, the president of the Vancouver Island Wildlife Federation.

While the federation represented a grouping of local hunting and fishing clubs, a strong conservation thrust had developed under the leadership of Ed and others like him. Not only had the federation been a strong supporter of the Nitinat Triangle's protection, it was now also interested in the Schoen-Tsitika region. Although the federation's primary concern was fish and wildlife, just as it had been with the gamekeepers of old, the membership understood that the survival of animals, especially threatened species like Roosevelt elk, depended on the protection of habitat. The partnership between Ed's wildlifers and the Sierra Club's environmentalists was a potent combination. Furthermore, I found working with Ed a pleasure. Indeed, in the two decades since the early days of Nitinat and Schoen, the two of us have remained good friends.

It wasn't just his cheerfulness that I enjoyed; it was also his enthusiastic, unflagging commitment. Sturdy and energetic, with a friendly English accent, Ed worked in a lumber mill as a sawfiler. His employer was MacMillan Bloedel,

39

British Columbia's largest forest company, not that Ed ever let this fact crimp his activism.

Ed had immigrated to British Columbia on a whim after completing a stint in the Royal Navy. But when he arrived he never looked back. He once told me how he was impressed by the beauty of the land here and the freedom we had to enjoy it. In Britain, he said, recreational access was restricted to those privileged few who owned portions of rivers and forests as part of their estates. By contrast, in British Columbia anyone could fish and hunt. "But what struck me," Ed said, "was how few people here seemed to know how lucky they were. There was almost no one taking care of the land. That's why I got into conservation."

Together, Ed and I, and our respective companions, developed a joint campaign plan for Schoen and Tsitika. While Sierra's conservationists had decided to seek outright wilderness protection of the Schoen as a park, Ed and his federation were particularly concerned about protecting Tsitika's forest, fish, and wildlife values as an ecological benchmark. Despite the fact that, like Ed, many of his members worked for the forest industry, they weren't afraid to criticize the terrible logging practices that had ruined key habitats in valley after valley.

Accordingly the Wildlife Federation and the Sierra Club pooled their efforts. While we knew we wanted Schoen dedicated under the Parks Act, we were less certain how to retain Tsitika's values. We decided to use the province's new Ecological Reserves Act, legislation that was intended to protect sites for scientific research purposes. Initially we aimed for a large eco-reserve, although we understood we might have to accept a series of smaller reserves as an alternative. Years in advance of concepts like biodiversity or conservation biology, we realized we were flying by the seats of our pants. One thing I did know: I wanted to apply lessons we had learned saving Nitinat to Schoen and Tsitika. Certainly there were many similarities between the two campaigns. Most notably, here, too, the logging companies were building roads fast to try to preclude preservation. As had been the case with the Nitinat Triangle, the race for the wild was on.

At Nitinat, with no previous experience, we had proceeded in an ad hoc fashion. In the course of that effort we had developed a set of skills and had some idea which tactics yielded the best results. This knowledge offered us the means to map out the Schoen-Tsitika campaign in advance, determining strengths, weaknesses, and opportunities. The result would be a more effective, efficient effort. In retrospect I now see that Schoen-Tsitika heralded a new style of strategic wilderness campaigning in Canada.

The initial requirement was to assemble our team. By now the Sierra Club and the Wildlife Federation had been joined by the B.C. Federation of Naturalists, the Steelhead Society, and a number of outdoor recreation clubs. Evening meetings of leaders from these groups held in one living room or another built a strong coalition. The effectiveness of what this grouping managed to achieve made a strong impression on me. Since the time of Schoen-Tsitika, I have always believed in *e pluribus unum*, "one out of many." After all, if it works for a superpower like the United States, why not for environmentalism? With activists united we then agreed on our approach. We would push for a development freeze on Schoen-Tsitika on an as-soon-as-possible basis from government. This would remove the imminent threat of losing wilderness values to the logging companies' roads and allow us the necessary time to achieve the best ecological solution for the area.

Since we wanted to control the course of the campaign rather than be forced to react to the logging industry's moves, as had been the case with Nitinat, we delayed announcing our intentions publicly until all informational materials were prepared. We mapped out and sequenced the various actions each organization would undertake during the course of the campaign. Like seasoned chess players, we plotted our moves and countermoves in advance to ensure swift success.

Our planning paid off. In fact, we exceeded our own expectations. Once we officially launched the campaign in November 1972, events proceeded so rapidly that the logging industry was caught completely off guard. It didn't know how to react. Indeed, the decision to seek a park in the Schoen Valley and ecological protection in the Tsitika Valley brought support from strange places.

Several of the fallers at MacMillan Bloedel's Kelsey Bay Division who were assigned to cut trees in the Schoen-Tsitika became covert allies. They tipped us off concerning the company's intentions and built backing among local loggers for what we were attempting. Many of them had also become appalled with logging industry methods. Often forced against their will to fell trees in ways they knew would harm fish or wildlife, they looked for ways to stall company foremen. As well, they believed some places should be left wild. After all, they worked in the woods because they *liked* the outdoors. They were sportsmen and parents also. So, during the heat of the battle throughout the winter of 1972-73, these people provided invaluable intelligence and moral support. We appreciated their phone calls and cryptic messages.

By the start of the new year, we had also enlisted the support of the elected members of the provincial Legislature for the northern part of Vancouver Island. They joined with us to lobby the Cabinet to put a logging moratorium in place. Working at a lightning pace, we soon generated waves of public support in the form of letters, telegrams, and phone calls — with most remarkable effect. On February 20, 1973, the provincial minister of forests and parks announced that resource development would be suspended pending the result of a comprehensive "North Island Study."

The first stage of our strategy had been achieved in only four months. During the following year, Ed and I pressed the case with the commissioner assigned to head the study. These efforts were backed by our coalition partners, by ongoing citizen support, and by strong representations from the B.C. Parks Branch and the B.C. Fish and Wildlife Branch. Reporting back a year later, the study commissioner recommended that the Schoen Valley be upgraded immediately to park status and that the logging moratorium on the Tsitika Valley be extended. These recommendations were acted upon, safeguarding Schoen and giving the Tsitika a 10-year reprieve while Ed Mankelow and the Vancouver Island Wildlife Federation refined the eco-reserve concept.

With the Schoen destined for protection and the Tsitika temporarily safe, my involvement in this campaign was reaching completion. I now had a desire to work on a larger scale, so I began to look beyond Vancouver Island to the other 95 percent of British Columbia on the mainland. Just as I had at the end of the Nitinat battle, I wondered about broader possibilities, in particular, the state of wilderness province-wide and what the priorities should be. As had been the case earlier with Vancouver Island, no one knew the answers, and this time studying air photos wouldn't help. Since British Columbia is equivalent in size to the combined area of Washington, Oregon, and California, the province was simply too large to be assessed this way.

Instead, in the summer of 1973 I set out to travel British Columbia. Living out of the back of my Datsun truck, I met with conservationists, park managers, anyone who knew anything about wilderness. I queried each about what he or she thought the prime regional preservation opportunities were. In turn, they drew lines for me on map sheets, and from these discussions about numerous "backyard wildernesses," I was able to compile a provincial map that proposed a complex of new protected areas.

That fall, I presented this map to the minister of forests and parks, urging that he move beyond one-off preservation efforts and begin a comprehensive approach to complete British Columbia's park system. My presentation had limited effect, though. The time wasn't ripe for such an idea. Actually, it took almost 15 years for the government to realize that only by taking such a sweeping approach could the range of British Columbia's natural endowments be safeguarded before the wild country was irretrievably lost.

This provincial mapping-and-systems-preservation proposal was the first undertaken by the public in British Columbia and, in fact, Canada. And while some time would pass before the concept was adopted, it still provided a vision for the future, a blueprint for activism, and a tool to determine what individual parks should be fought for next. Just as Sierra Victoria's Vancouver Island study had led to the identification and protection of the Schoen Valley, this provincial wilderness systems map would help to select sites such as the Purcell and Babine Mountains and the Spatsizi Plateau to devote my energy to in subsequent years.

All of this campaign work had, of course, started with Nitinat, which had been won as I was graduating from university. In many ways that was appropriate.

Academics aside, what I really learned in my undergraduate years – what all of us in Sierra Victoria learned at the time – was the basics of how to save the wilderness. By comparison Schoen was like graduate school. Here we took the tactical approaches pioneered with the Triangle and refined and linked them together into a strategic effort. As a result, we learned how to configure a campaign and fight it on our own terms. We discovered how to take the long view, to move past the urgent to the important.

In light of how fast and successfully the Schoen was protected, the advantages of working strategically were obvious. The campaign had taught a lot of skills: building coalitions; scoping the issue out prior to going public; and using systems evaluation to identify preservation priorities. Each of these techniques would assist future victories in campaigns ranging from the Height of the Rockies to the Tatshenshini River.

For me, my involvement in the Schoen and Tsitika campaigns had an even more profound effect: it confirmed my desire to move beyond volunteerism and make wilderness activism my profession, not that I was sure how to accomplish this feat. Back then no one in Canada earned a living campaigning for parks. But, perhaps because I was young, this fact didn't worry me. Accordingly I respectfully turned down the job that had been offered to me by the National Parks Service. Instead, I began to look for people to fund me as a wilderness advocate. Before long I found enough money to pay the bills and started my work, intent someday on transforming that map of wilderness proposals into a much-expanded system of parks.

In subsequent years and decades while I worked elsewhere around the province campaigning with people as dedicated as Ed, follow-on conservation action occurred at Schoen-Tsitika. Ultimately Tsitika's preservation values were represented in a series of smaller ecological reserves. In particular, special efforts were taken to protect the integrity of the land near the Robson Bight orca rubbing beaches. But any hope for enlightened forestry elsewhere in the Tsitika wasn't met in a major way. As usual MacMillan Bloedel relied on clearcutting rather than less-damaging alternatives. To make matters worse, the rate of logging, while somewhat modified, was still far greater than what we had wanted.

Eventually environmentalist showdowns were staged to protect more of the lower Tsitika Valley, leading to road blockades by the late 1980s that resulted in increased protection. Still, even with all the various reserves in place, Tsitika wasn't the same untouched area I had flown over in 1972. Because of that, I doubt I will ever return to the valley; the pain would be too much.

By contrast the Schoen Valley, my personal concern, fared well. In October 1977, acting on the recommendations of the "North Island Study," the government designated the valley a provincial park. Years later I returned to those elk meadows beneath the tall peaks among the old trees. They were just as special as ever.

On that revisit I hiked through the ancient firs, now the largest valley bottom remnant of Vancouver Island's once-glorious east side forests, to the beach at the end of Schoen Lake, where I was entirely alone. The sky was cloudless, the sun hot, the water irresistible. Stripping off my clothes, I swam naked in fresh rainforest water and looked up at the peak I had once flown beside. Thank God, I thought, we had sacrificed that long-ago summer cooped up in a windowless library studying air photos. Otherwise we would never have found this wilderness in time to save it.

Three

Purcell Wilderness
Back to the Land

W HEN it came to going back to the land, Art Twomey did it with style. Immigrating to British Columbia from Wisconsin during the Vietnam War, Art didn't just buy valley bottom farm-land to settle on. No, he was a modern-day mountain man, complete with a long, uncontrollable black beard and laughing eyes. The wilderness was in his blood, so he ventured deep into the rugged backcountry of the Kootenay region in southeastern British Columbia. Here, far from any settlement, in the upper White Creek Valley, he built himself a cabin in the subalpine forest amid the peaks of the Purcell Mountains. To grow his vegetables he backpacked soil up above 5,500 feet, likely making Art's garden the highest in Canada.

Art had always felt his home to be in Nature. As a teenager, he had chal-lenged the great rapids of the Grand Canyon in a tiny two-person rubber raft. An accomplished mountaineer, he had climbed Mount Everest, the highest peaks in South America, and Alaska's Mount McKinley. He was also one of Canada's finest wilderness photographers.

With this background Art could have chosen any wild place on Earth to live. But for him the Purcells were paradise. From his little cabin he traveled out to discover these mountains. In the company of his partner, Carol, and his best friends, John Bergenske and Harper Hartwig — who had moved out with him from the United States and were now his closest neighbors, 10 miles down the valley — he hiked, skied, and climbed throughout the range.

In the early 1970s the Purcell Mountains were little known. Very few people traveled in them at the time. Yet, without a doubt, this range was wondrous to explore. Here were found St. Mary's alpine where 20 sparkling lakes perched above the tree line on the edge of a plateau; Dewar Creek, with its hot springs that flowed right out of the ground; the Leaning Towers, 2,000 feet of sheer vertical granite; the raging gorge of Fry Creek Canyon; the Toby Glacier; and the historic 38-mile-long Earl Grey Pass Trail that traversed the range.

On the west side moist winds grew big cedars in the valley bottom of Hamil Creek. East of the Purcell divide, a rain-shadow effect had created smaller, drier forests and the grasslands favored by elk, moose, and deer. In the high country, grizzlies and mountain goats roamed. During summer, passage through the wilds of the Purcell Mountains was on foot. The approach to the alpine meant following old horse or game trails for 20 miles along the banks of fresh-flowing rivers. Once in the alpine, traverses across sharp-edged ridgelines were exhilarating. Many peaks were guarded by cliffs, with serious climbing required to reach their summits. But the vista from up there made it worthwhile: a sea of rugged mountains, steep, forested valleys, untouched wildness as far as the eye could see.

Winter brought deep, dry snow to this range: Purcell powder, feather-light, Canada's best. The result was skiing nirvana. So Art spent the months from December to May playing with gravity in the mountain backcountry. And when groceries ran low, it was six hours by skis out to the nearest road and into town for reprovisioning.

For a mountain hedonist like Art this was quite the idyllic life. He could have probably spent all his years telemarking, rappelling, and backpacking if it weren't for his vision, his sense of duty. Having come to love the Purcells in their

wild state, Art dreamed that they should remain so for others to enjoy. However, settlement, highways, and resource development had already encircled the range. Now plans were afoot to penetrate it. Logging companies wanted to build roads up the Purcell valleys and log the headwaters; prospectors were eager to punch in exploration routes to stake claims with the hope of striking it rich.

Knowing the Purcells well, Art saw what was at risk. He also realized the range's days of wilderness were numbered unless the public could be shown just what beauty and wildlife were found there. So he resolved to photograph and popularize the Purcells. Soon he was touring the Kootenays, giving slide shows and showing his films. Art wasn't just a superb photographer; he was also the ultimate storyteller. Whether a few friends in a bar or a whole auditorium of people, he could hold an audience spellbound. His speeches sounded more often like yarns sprinkled with quips and chuckles. His talks were genuine rather than political, and his eyes twinkled, revealing his warmth, sincerity, and passion.

Art quickly spawned a region-wide concern for his beloved mountains. Groups to save the Purcells sprang up in the towns throughout the range. At Nelson on Kootenay Lake, in the Quaker community of Argenta, in the East Kootenay towns of Golden, Invermere, Cranbrook, and Kimberley, the conservation movement came into being in interior British Columbia.

Of all these communities Golden was the quintessential Canadian mountain town. Situated in the waterfowl wetlands of the upper Columbia River Valley, it is walled in by mountains. To the east, the long, ragged ramparts of the Canadian Rockies soar skyward, marching across the Continental Divide into Alberta. To the west, pyramidal peaks of the much older Purcells act as a barrier to the rest of British Columbia. Golden's connection to the outside world traverses high mountain passes. It was only when this route was finally discovered through these mountains in 1881 that the completion of the Canadian Pacific Railway (CPR) became possible. And it was only when the last spike was driven in 1885 that Canada truly became a nation from sea to sea.

Nevertheless, the railway grades across the mountains there were so steep that steam engines had to double up, their whistles echoing in the canyons.

Even still, great tunnels were required to cross the ranges. In Rogers Pass on the west the CPR constructed what was then the longest tunnel in the British Empire, the five-mile-long Connaught. To get over the Rockies at Kicking Horse Pass two spiral tunnels were built.

For decades the townspeople of Golden lived in considerable isolation amid the wild splendor of high mountains. More so than most Canadians they had a firsthand sense of what wilderness meant. Even after the Trans-Canada Highway was completed in 1962, thereby truly linking the community to the outside, winter snowstorms often returned it to isolation, and avalanches frequently blocked the passes.

Given this history, you would think Golden would be the last place in Canada to hold a wilderness preservation strategy conference. Yet, in fact, it was the first. In December 1972 the Earthwatch Conference was convened there, bringing together wilderness lovers and budding conservationists from throughout interior British Columbia and Alberta.

Perhaps because they lived so close to the wild, the people of Golden were more attuned to what could be lost. In more recent years, especially since the completion of the Trans-Canada Highway, logging activity around the town had accelerated dramatically. The valleys leading into the Rockies and Purcells were hit hard by clearcutting. North of town, 100 miles of Columbia River Valley bottomland were in the process of being drowned behind the new 800-foot-high Mica Dam. The dam flooded several hundred thousand acres of the best forest land in this part of British Columbia, as well as some of the most productive winter range for wildlife.

While the Earthwatch Conference had been organized to talk about mountain wilderness, most of the people attending had been inspired by Art Twomey's presentations and the need to preserve the Purcell Mountains. But during the weekend, discussion expanded to the region as a whole. Height of the Rockies, Akimena-Kishaneena, Kianuko, Top of the World, these were all wilderness areas first identified and mapped at Earthwatch. The strategy discussed at Golden became the foundation for conservation action in the Kootenays over the next two decades. Eventually all these places would be protected as parks.

It was fall 1972. The Nitinat Triangle campaign had just been won and I had graduated from university. Having made the decision to make my living protecting Nature as a conservationist, I set out to find funding. Fortunately I soon secured support from two philanthropists: Catherine Whyte, the widow of Peter Whyte, the famous Canadian artist who had lived all his life in Banff popularizing the grandeur of the Rocky Mountain wilderness through his paintings; and Ed Wolf, an Alberta businessman. Both cared enough about what was happening to the wild country to take a chance on someone so young and allow me to become the first paid wilderness conservationist in Canada. To this day, I thank them for the faith they showed.

I didn't receive much money, $700 per month actually, but it was enough. I wasn't doing this work to get rich; that had always seemed an empty goal to me. After all, if I did things right, I would also get "paid" in parks.

With my funding secured I set out to define my job. Using the title of Western Canada Conservation Representative, I planned to work for wilderness protection in British Columbia (with the B.C. Sierra Club) and Alberta (with the Alberta Wilderness Association). It was a huge territory and there wasn't a precedent for this job in Canada. I intended to emulate the field-office approach used in the United States by the Sierra Club. Given that my mentor Brock Evans was the Sierra field representative for the Pacific Northwest Region based in Seattle, my self-assignment was by no means impossible.

The first requirement was to get out into British Columbia and Alberta to learn where the protection priorities were, what were the most critical places to preserve, and which ones were most imminently endangered. I also wanted to connect with the people working to protect these wild spaces. Not only would they be the most informed concerning individual areas, but they were also the emerging conservation leaders. The Nitinat campaign had shown me that strength and success depended on united action. Therefore, one of my prime goals was to link these leaders across the two provinces and help build the foundation for a grass-roots environmental movement.

While my attention up to now had primarily been focused on the coast, mountains were in my soul. So when it was suggested I meet with a group of conservationists getting together for a weekend wilderness conference on the Kootenays, I jumped at the chance. Within days of becoming the Western Canada Conservation Representative, I got on a bus and traveled through the mountain passes to Golden. Stepping off the bus, I was gripped by the cold air. It was snowing, and the peaks were misted in cloud. I was excited by a pervasive sense of the wild.

The Earthwatch Conference was held in an old-fashioned community hall on the Columbia River. Like so many similar buildings erected in the 1930s across North America, the hall was a wooden structure with a stage up front, the kitchen off to one side, and the dance floor covered by trestle tables for the conference. The toilets were outhouses located across a frozen field.

The gathering was informal, 40 people or so, the energy was enthusiastic, and the potluck meals made by volunteers tasted better than any restaurant fare. All the while the talk was about mountains and wilderness, about how these might be protected, about how we could start to work together.

On Saturday evening after the meeting was finished for the day, we bundled into aging cars and drove out of town to have dinner at a small house by the base of the mountains. The snow was too deep to drive in, so we walked across the field. The clouds had cleared, and diamond-sharp stars flashed in the black sky above the peaks. The air was frigidly still. There was no power to the house – it was too remote – so we had dinner sitting in front of the large, open fire, the flames providing light.

In our group was Doug Pimlott, a legendary conservationist from Ontario and the leading scientific researcher on wolves. His studies were the first in Canada to confront the "evil" wolf mythology by showing that these animals were strongly social and intelligent creatures. He was perhaps the first person to convince Canadians that wolves should be loved not loathed.

Working in Algonquin Park north of Toronto, Doug had discovered that wolves answered back if people howled at them. Using this approach, he had recorded hundreds of hours of wolf calls and had worked to decode the animal's behavior. This stuff may seem old-hat now, but before Doug no one had thought to try to communicate with wolves. And so that night, out in the little house at the foot of the Rockies amid the snow and the stars, Doug howled for wolves in the firelight, and the wintry countryside listened.

The weekend ended too quickly, but not before a rough campaign plan was devised for the Purcells. As the conference broke up, I went out into the parking lot behind the community hall to see people off. I would be taking the late-night bus. Art Twomey, whom I had met only two days prior, was leaving, but already I felt I had known him for years. Helping him brush the snow off his Volkswagen van, I noticed he had an entire engine sitting on his back seat. "Oh, that," he said. "In case the engine dies, I can just replace it."

Then he jumped into the van, stuck his bushy-bearded face out the window, and grinned, looking for all the world like a muppet. "Don't forget about the Purcells. We can work on it together," he said. With that he rolled up the window, headed out onto the highway, and vanished into the falling snow. And so the next two years of my life locked in.

Summer came, and in early July 1973 Karen and I got married. Since wilderness had been so much a part of our life together, and given our desire to see Art's wilderness firsthand, we decided to honeymoon up at Earl Grey Pass. The pass was named after Governor General Earl Grey, the queen's chief representative in Canada who, in 1909, journeyed all the way out from Ottawa to spend a summer in the Purcells, which was quite remarkable considering their remoteness then. The remains of the elaborate cottage built for him in a quiet meadow beside the trail still stand today. Its large, empty window frames, the glass long gone, still look toward the high peaks at the pass, but packrats and porcupines are the only occupants now. Back in that long-ago summer, though, Grey must have been entranced with this place, because when he returned to Ottawa he proposed that the Purcell Mountains be protected as a national park.

In the 64 years between his visit and mine, no action had been taken on his proposal. Inspecting the remains of his old forgotten cottage – the fine masonry fireplace, the hand-adzed wooden beams – only strengthened my resolve to see

54

the Purcells protected. Otherwise the wilderness that Grey had so valued would soon pass into history as surely as his collapsing summer home. Nor was there much time left to act. Earl Grey had ridden in on horseback 25 miles through spruce forests to reach this place. Now the old building stood at the edge of retreating wilderness, and a logging road reached to within a mile.

From this old cottage the eastern section of the Earl Grey Pass Trail heads up Toby Creek to its source in the high icefields. It is easy hiking since the trail is maintained by a local guide outfitter. As for Toby Creek, it is a typical east Purcell stream, alternating between rapids and calmer reaches, with water of a most marvelous green. The river is born as a torrent rushing from the face of Toby Glacier high up in the pass. After a brief, turbulent meander across a gravel outwash, it leaps in a great rumble off a ledge to plummet in froth and mist down 650 feet of cliff.

To reach the Toby headwaters above these falls, the trail takes a roundabout route. Switchbacks climb higher and higher up tree-shorn avalanche chutes. These swaths extend from summit to valley and are the record of winters past. From December to April deep snow, the result of raging storms, accumulates along the alpine crests, forming huge, overhanging cornices. When the snow on the steepest slopes becomes too heavy, it breaks away with a deadly thundering. Then a wall of white roars downslope, its power enormous. Anything in its path is simply crushed, sheared off, or swept away.

Sculpted in colder times by a much larger Toby Glacier, the walls of the valley were left steep, creating especially unstable snow slopes. Therefore, the avalanche tracks up the Toby Valley are broad and numerous. Where the trail traverses these, it runs through a sea of brush, and occasional meadow openings are brilliantly crowded with flowers. Despite such beauty, these places can be scary. Avalanche chutes are favored habitats for grizzlies, since there are many berries on the bushes for them to eat. They forage for succulent flower roots and use their long claws to excavate for ground squirrels. Encounter a meadow where a grizzly has dug and you would think a backhoe had been in action.

I had read that maulings were most likely to happen when a hiker chances

55

on a bear at short distance and surprises it. So here I was, my first time ever in grizzly country, thrashing my way through a jungle of dense bush twice my height. Could it get more dangerous? I felt as if I were crossing a minefield. Adrenaline flooded my veins, my breath was shallow, my heart raced in high gear. The alders on these chutes were so thick that a bear could be three feet away and I would never see it. I constantly thought I saw shapes moving in the leaves just ahead. I was expecting the brush to explode with fury any moment.

And if we were attacked, how could we get help? There was no one else in this valley except us. So we hooted and hollered as we worked our way upslope. We made such a racket that a bear would have to be totally deaf not to know we were coming. It wasn't until we were long clear of the last chute and approaching the crest of the falls that my fear subsided and the hair on the back of my neck settled down.

Over the years I would come to spend a lot of time in bear country. It isn't that grizzlies are blood-lusting man killers. If you know what you are doing, they are actually pretty safe to be around, as long as you give them plenty of warning and keep your distance. With experience I would learn how to be more at ease, but on my first foray I was glad I never saw a grizzly.

Once above the falls, we reached the pass. Here the landscape was dominated by ice. Huge glaciers pooled around the base of Toby Peak and draped the flanks of Mount Hamil. From the divide we surveyed the immensity of this primeval place. Forty miles to the east was the limestone ramparts of the Rockies. Westward, we looked toward Kootenay Lake. Peering over the edge of a 3,000-foot cliff, we glimpsed the secret U-shaped valley of upper Carney Creek. Far below, along its floor, a fine line of water flowed.

The days that followed were pure adventuring. We climbed to high alpine lakes but were forced to beat a rapid retreat when a fierce summer thunderstorm blackened the sky and targeted the peaks with lightning. The sound in the sky was explosive. Another afternoon we set off a huge slide when the track of our footsteps cut the slush surface of a glacier. Later, when crossing Toby Creek on the outwash plain downstream of the ice, Keah, our golden retriever, was swept away by the current toward the falls. Fortunately he was tied to a long rope, and we hauled him to shore just in time. Occasionally we rolled boulders off cliffs, cheering as they bounded and smashed down a thousand feet. And we spent hours watching mountain goats as they picked their way across the huge cliff faces above us.

One evening when the mosquitoes were biting fiercely, we got the twisted idea of fighting back by eating them. Amazingly the little demons didn't taste that bad: crispy and somewhat sweet and sour. More important, once the tables were turned and these predators had become our prey, they seemed to vanish in minutes. Could it have just been our deranged imaginations, or did some message get communicated to the swarm? Later, when we happened to mention to our doctor what we had done, he blanched. "Are you crazy? Do you have any idea how many blood diseases mosquitoes carry?"

Indeed, these were crazy and happy times. But mostly it was the sense of discovery of our first married days together in these mountains. It was the savoring of the alone, the quiet. It was the majesty of the peaks throughout the day: crisp in a clear morning sky; wreathed in afternoon cloud; bathed in soft apricot twilight; silhouetted in the gleam of starlight ...

Upon our return to the low country, we stopped for a short visit with Art Twomey and others in Kimberley. We talked about what Karen and I had experienced and what we all had to do next. I had thought a lot about our task while in the mountains. The Nitinat campaign had taught me that a few key people – the Ray Willistons and Jean Chrétiens – ruled the land, in effect. These individuals were the ones who had the power to decide whether wilderness would endure or not. So it was clear to me that if Art's wish for a Purcell park was to happen, a select group of senior bureaucrats and key Cabinet ministers living 550 miles away in Victoria would have to be sold on the concept.

As Art's passion had excited many in the Kootenays and inspired me, now I took it as my task to do the same in Victoria. For their part the folks in the Kootenays would assemble the pictorial and factual presentation needed to make the case, which I would use to lobby the government. So, with the Purcell

Mountains fresh in my heart, Karen and I headed down the long highway toward the coast. I was eager to begin my new assignment.

Since the Nitinat Triangle campaign, the government in British Columbia had changed. After decades of right-wing rule, Premier Dave Barrett became the first man to lead the left-of-center New Democratic Party to power in the province. Given that the era was dominated in North America by Richard Nixon's conservative presidency, this accomplishment was pretty amazing.

For too long British Columbia had been regarded merely as a natural resource supply house, especially for the United States. The province was a place where large companies exploited the forests for lumber and pulp and the mountains for metal with scant thought given to environmental impact. Since more than 90 percent of British Columbia was public land, the new government had campaigned on taking better care of the land and getting a fairer value for the people's resources. It promised that the corporations would be more tightly reined and development would no longer proceed regardless of the cost. Not surprisingly, the resource companies were nervous. They foresaw their monopolistic grasp on British Columbia's resources being weakened.

The man most disliked by this conservative elite was Bob Williams, the new minister of forests and also parks. He was an especially potent politician and was to become the most influential minister in the new government. A planner by training, Williams had a strong conservation ethic. He thought that too often the corporations took more off the land than could be sustained and returned too little money to the public. He intended to change the status quo.

I first met Williams during my lobbying for Nitinat when his party wasn't in government yet. He was then about 40, with bright, mischievous eyes, a wry smile, and a wide-awake mind. Extremely bright, he was fascinated by new ideas. I found him stimulating and liked him immediately. Publicly some said he projected an image of arrogance, but beneath this persona I saw a man with a core of shyness and idealism. As well, he cared deeply about the land.

Now that Williams was forests and parks minister I found a sympathetic reception. When I met him several times to urge that he take action on the Pur-

cells, he was interested. Increasingly he was hearing about the issue as word per-
colated up to him in letters from Kootenay conservationists. The third time we
met Williams told me he had decided to commission a special review of the
Purcell Mountains, an encouraging development.

More promising still, Williams had decided to reform entirely how British
Columbia's natural resources and environment were governed. Change was
badly needed because the frontier mentality that had swept across North
America in the 19th and early 20th centuries still lingered in the province. The
belief that the land was superabundant and limitless persisted. It was only
because British Columbia was so large and comparatively late to be exploited
that such limits hadn't been obvious before. But now environmental conflicts
were multiplying rapidly due to the fast-increasing industrialized activities of
logging and mining companies competing with other land users.

The government's old way of disjointedly managing the land through separate natural resource departments wasn't working. Too often development was
pitted against environment, with Nature the loser. Therefore, if conflicts were
to be reduced, if exploitation was to be balanced by conservation, then the
needs of different land users had to be considered together. To do this, multi-
agency problem solving would have to replace confrontation.

Williams proposed a new type of agency, a first for North America. Called
the Environment and Land-Use Committee (ELUC) Secretariat, it would serve
as a catalyst bringing existing resource and conservation ministries together to
find lasting, collaborative solutions. The ELUC Secretariat would be a small,
elite staff grouping that worked for the Cabinet through Williams. As such it
would become one of the most influential agencies in the B.C. government.

One morning I was in Williams's office, the same one that had once been
Ray Williston's. The former minister's memorabilia of the forest industry was
gone from the walls; in its place were pictures of big trees, mountains, and
wilderness. Wrapping up a discussion about the Purcells, the minister turned to
me and asked, "Do you want a job? I am going to establish the ELUC Secretariat."

Exciting as this offer was, I didn't give him an answer that day because I wondered if, by saying yes, I would be selling out as a conservation activist. After a few days of soul-searching, I decided to accept but made a commitment to myself that I would limit my term to two years. I didn't want to become a career civil servant. For me, to stay longer would indeed be "buying the system." It would mean putting money and security ahead of being on the outside again as a conservation activist, where I believed I could make the greatest difference protecting wilderness.

Ultimately three years would pass before I broke free of the bonds of bureaucracy. But during those years I learned how the system worked, both at the political and civil service levels. In retrospect the time spent as adviser to the B.C. Cabinet — and I worked for both the left-wing New Democrats and later the conservative Social Credit Party — was valuable training. It was an apprenticeship into the dynamics of power that gave me contacts I would utilize over the next two decades. Looking back on the experience, I have come to believe that if more environmentalists had the chance to spend a couple of years at the upper levels of government, the success rate of their subsequent campaigning would increase dramatically.

I hadn't been in the Secretariat for more than a couple of months when I got a phone call at home one night. It was Art Twomey. We hadn't talked in a while, and I was glad to hear from him. But as he began to speak, his news wasn't good. The logging companies were planning an offensive on the Purcells; they were about to push roads into each of the remaining intact valleys. One by one, these would be extended rapidly to the headwaters, where a small patch of timber would be removed. The intent was clear: preempt any chance for a park by defiling the wilderness, fragmenting it into little pieces. It was the Nitinat Triangle all over again, but this time on a larger scale. And, said Art, Toby Creek would be first. "Can you help?" he asked. The answer was easy.

Coincidences have happened so often in my years of wilderness campaigning that I no longer see them as coincidental. Within a couple of days of Art's call, the Purcell Study was completed. Williams instructed the ELUC Secretariat to review it and then brief the Cabinet. I was the staff person assigned this task.

Upon reading the study, it was clear to me that the central issue had been missed entirely. While the forester who authored the report suggested innovative ways that the old-growth Purcell trees might be logged, he ignored the strong public demand to preserve this region as wilderness. It was obvious to me that this halfway solution of less-intensive logging wasn't going to help the Purcells.

Wilderness is the pristine legacy of Nature. It is the land and life as they have evolved since the beginning of time, free of the development or exploitation of civilization. There is a priceless virginal quality to wilderness: either it remains intact or it is irreversibly lost. There can be no in between. Defile it with roads, cut down trees and, regardless of the logging technology used, the wilderness vanishes. Instead, it becomes just another plot of land managed, more or less, for human wants. And with its passing, the remnant wild estate of the original Earth dwindles further.

Saving the Purcells was always about more than a technological fix; it was about keeping the dream of the wild alive. And so I acted on Art's call by asking Bob Williams if we could meet. When we got together, I explained to him how the Purcell Study had missed the central issue. I talked about what made wilderness special and why so many in the Kootenays desired full preservation. Would he, I asked, be willing to consider such protection for these mountains, and if so, would he let me take charge of the process in government to enable this? He said yes to both questions.

Since the Secretariat's mode of operation involved multi-agency collaboration, I convened a task force of representatives from the appropriate government land-use departments. Together we assembled maps of the Purcell region and charted each of the land-use resource values onto individual transparent plastic overlays: forests, minerals, wildlife, roadless wilderness, and so forth. Then we analyzed conflicts: in this location there were high timber values, over there were significant mineralizations, here there were the key migration corridors used by elk. Today this is pretty routine stuff — in fact, it is often done on computers now. But back in 1974 we were on the cutting edge. Then there were no computers to use.

Thanks to this analysis it quickly became obvious that the conflicts between development and preservation values were much less than had been feared. The timber was more limited, the mineral claims fewer than suspected. Nevertheless, in previous times such an analysis wouldn't have been done. Rather, the resource companies would simply claim that huge revenues were at stake. Then, with no questions asked and without delay, the roads would be built, the best stands of timber removed, the alpine trenched for claims (that too seldom proved economically viable), and the wilderness lost.

The one uncertainty that remained in our work was where the boundaries for the protected area should be. When I had asked the Parks Branch for their ideas, they had drawn two postage-stamp-sized circles, one at Earl Grey Pass (most of the trail was excluded) and the other around the St. Mary's lakes cluster. Both sites were entirely in the alpine. The reason for such caution was understandable. Clearly the Parks staff had too long been bullied into submission by the Forest Service; they had been conditioned to avoid protecting lands that might be wanted by the logging companies. It was apparent that the Parks Branch would be little help in determining how to protect an expanse of wilderness here. So I called Art, the one person who had traveled each valley in the range, the one true expert on the Purcells. He would know where the boundaries should go.

Within days he drove to the coast in his immortal old van. By now the spare engine had been moved from the back seat and installed in the engine compartment. It labored hard, no doubt, as the Volkswagen crawled over the passes.

Upon his arrival, one night he and I stayed up well past midnight poring over the maps on my kitchen table. All his knowledge gained from hiking and skiing the range in past years now paid off. Pulling on his impossible beard, he shared what he knew. "If we run the boundary along this northern ridgeline, the whole of the Earl Grey Pass Trail will be safe. If we want to keep Fry Canyon, the lines have to go up high. To protect the grizzlies, this part of the valley has to be included. Otherwise they're goners."

And so we worked our way around the mountains on paper until at last, when the boundary was completed, it encompassed a mapped space representing more than 300,000 acres of wildness.

"Wow," Art said with excitement. "Just think if we could protect this."

"Don't worry," I said, grinning. "We'll get it."

In the following days I shopped the map around to the various government agencies and made the sale. The Lands Branch required that the boundaries be legally definable for survey purposes: following a contour, a watershed divide, or a straight line linking two peaks. (The latter wasn't ecologically ideal; Nature doesn't work in straight lines.) As well, there were some minor adjustments required, a jog here to avoid a couple of mining claims, a jag to eliminate some noncritical logging values. But when Ray Demarchi, the government wildlife biologist for the Kootenays, phoned urgently to say we were about to exclude some crucial mountain caribou range, we added a lobe that Art and I had missed. It is sobering to think that the failure to make that change might have committed an already endangered herd to extinction.

With agreement reached by the various departments on the boundary, the final question was how best this wilderness could be preserved. Traditionally land in British Columbia had been protected as a provincial park under the Parks Act. But conservationists in the Kootenays were less than pleased with the track record. The bulk of the once-great Hamber Park had been logged and dammed in the 1960s, and mining had been allowed in Kokanee Park. Even in intact areas the Parks Branch focused more on recreation than preservation: building roads for car touring and chairlifts for alpine skiing. At the time the agency seemed to have only limited understanding of what it meant to protect wilderness for wilderness's sake.

So, at the urging of the Kootenay conservationists, I sat down to draft the order-in-council (an administrative document of the Cabinet) that would legally create the preserve. Drawing inspiration from the U.S. Wilderness Act, I used wording, new for British Columbia, that would define what the values of the wilderness being protected were, and how they were to be cared for:

> *Whereas British Columbia is fortunate to be endowed with wilderness*
> *regions of great scenic beauty which are of notable inspirational value to*
> *the public . . .*

... and whereas it is recognized that wilderness is a fragile commodity which is vanishing rapidly throughout British Columbia and which therefore requires preservation to ensure that the values possessed within it are not forever loſt ...

[Therefore this] wilderness area will be maintained as a roadless traſt in which both natural and ecological communities are preserved intaſt and the progressions of the natural syſtems may proceed without alteration ...

And to ensure the most protecion possible, I proposed the use of the province's Environment and Land-Use Act to create, for the first time, a new, sacrosanct type of preserve: a wilderness conservancy, the Central Purcell Wilderness Conservancy.

The final materials were prepared for the upcoming Cabinet meeting: a briefing document, the overlay maps showing resource and wilderness values, the proposed boundary, the draft order-in-council, and a stunning set of Art's Purcell photographs. On the day of the Cabinet meeting the technical brief and maps provided the factual rationale, while the pictures touched the heart. The decision proved to be straightforward. On December 4, 1974, with a stroke of a pen, Parks Minister Bob Williams and Premier Dave Barrett signed the order-in-council, and Art's dream came into being. His mountains were protected.

In the aftermath the public was strongly supportive. From the communities throughout the Kootenays letters of thanks were received by Williams. As the staff person responsible for the file, I had the pleasure of drafting many of the responses for his signature. Still, some logging people griped. They wanted to mill those pockets of big old spruce. Over the next 10 years they pushed to open up the conservancy for logging. But the public rallied every time, often under the leadership of Art. Nevertheless, vigilance was still necessary.

Within government heroic efforts in defense of the conservancy by wildlife biologist Ray Demarchi kept pro-development Forest Service officials at bay during this vulnerable time. As for the Parks Branch, it remained weak compared to the Forest Service and the Mines Branch. Although the order creating the conservancy gave it the mandate for stewardship, its resources were stretched too thin. As a result, its guardianship of the Purcells often needed bolstering from the public.

In 1986, 12 years after the creation of the Central Purcell Wilderness Conservancy, the Social Credit government of the day established the Wilderness Advisory Committee to review wilderness protection in British Columbia. Originally envisioned by some pro-industry, conservative Cabinet ministers as a means to put the brakes on further wilderness protection, particularly in the high-profile South Moresby area on Haida Gwaii, the committee was initially stacked with resource industry proponents. An outcry from the public resulted in more conservationists being appointed to the committee, one of whom was my longtime friend Ken Farquharson.

I hadn't seen Ken in a couple of years when late one night he contacted me. "Ric," he said, "you've got to testify before the Wilderness Advisory Committee. The boundaries of the Purcells are under scrutiny. You're the guy who knows why they were put where they were and why the area shouldn't be opened to logging."

By now I was living in the Kootenays within sight of the Purcells. The evening the committee came to town I went to say my piece. Art was there. and so was a crowd of 500 packing the largest auditorium in town. Their support of the conservancy was fervently enthusiastic, and the speeches were many and eloquent. The committee got the point: it recommended that the government keep the Central Purcell Wilderness Conservancy intact. The government, in turn, acquiesced, and finally the threats of the foresters on the conservancy began to wane.

Yet still the saga of the Purcells' protection was incomplete. On that night in 1974 when Art and I had drawn the conservancy boundaries we had had little understanding how hard the land would be hit by logging and mining in the Kootenays and throughout British Columbia in the coming decades. We couldn't then conceive that it was the intention of industry to develop every acre of land that wasn't in a park, to build a logging road to within 200 yards – a yarding cable's length – of every merchantable tree. Back in the mid-1970s the conservation focus was on those areas of exceptional wild, scenic, recreational, or wildlife legacy values. In those innocent days the extent of British Columbia and its forests still seemed so vast that we simply couldn't imagine a time when the parks would become islands of nature isolated within a wasteland of clearcuts. Yet by the late 1980s it was becoming tragically clear that this would be the future of our province.

For the Purcell Conservancy this meant that despite its seeming size it was too small to ensure the long-term survival of its wildlife populations and wilderness ambience. The 325,000 acres preserved in the conservancy in the mid-1970s within Art's boundaries contained the best of the elk-and-goat summer range and the most spectacular hiking country. Since the forests to the east had been burned out by forest fires, there had seemed little of value scenically or under threat from industry that required protection. Hence, we had assumed the protected core of the conservancy would always be buffered by a 20-mile-wide band of scrub forest.

In the 1990s, though, times had changed. Drastic overbuilding of the local mills relative to the wood supply had created an insatiable industrial appetite for even small trees. A locust mentality had developed where timber of any pos-

Art Twomey, spirit of the Purcells.

sible commercial worth was now stripped from the land. Soon the east side stands would be gone, the conservancy would no longer be buffered, and roads would come to its edge and gnaw at its wildness.

On the west side, part of the thickly forested Carney Valley remained outside the conservancy. Originally it hadn't been a top priority for preservation. After all, protection of Fry Creek Canyon into which the Carney flowed had cut off logging road access in the 1970s. But here, as on the east side, with the intensified hunger of the forest industry, the conservancy was incomplete. Unless its size was increased on both the east and west sides, it wouldn't remain ecologically viable over the long term.

In response the conservation movement spawned at Earthwatch in the early 1970s strengthened itself and reorganized as the East Kootenay Environmental Society. At its core were the individuals who had long loved the Purcells: Art and his new partner, Margie; his old backcountry skiing buddies, John and Harper; and new people, Anne Levesque, Kent Goodwin, Lesley Giroday, and Ellen Zimmerman. Behind the scenes, from within government, Ray Demarchi was as active as ever. This group, along with guide outfitters and many local hunters, refocused concern on the need to complete the protection of the Purcells.

While environmental awareness was truly born at the first Earth Day in 1970, and went into remission 10 years later, by 1990 it was a mainstream concern broadly embraced by the public. This revolution was largely the result of a series of ecological nightmares: the Chernobyl nuclear disaster, global warming, and the enlarging hole in the ozone layer that served to accelerate ecological awareness dramatically. In the mid-1980s the Brundtland Report warned that economic development must become environmentally sustainable or human civilization was at risk. By 1992 the United Nations convened the Rio Conference on the Environment in Brazil. One of the key accomplishments of this session was the creation of the Biodiversity Treaty, which Canada was the first country to sign. This treaty urged nations to act rapidly to preserve Nature's range of ecosystems and life-forms.

British Columbia was again governed by the New Democratic Party under

67

the leadership of Premier Mike Harcourt. More than any other Canadian political leader, Harcourt was committed to taking protective action on the environment. As British Columbia's contribution to the Biodiversity Treaty, he launched a comprehensive land-use review – the Commission on Resources and the Environment (CORE) – to enable the province to double its parks system to 12 percent of its land base by the year 2000.

CORE worked with the local public in regions around the province to recommend how best to reconcile increased protection of Nature and industrial development. Structured as a public negotiation process, it involved a wide range of citizen participants, including loggers, environmentalists, miners, and farmers – anyone with an interest in the land. One of the regions CORE focused on was the East Kootenay.

Through 1993 and 1994 the parties wrangled around the bargaining table. During this time, there were critics of this democratic exercise, especially in the resource companies. They were betting on the failure of the whole process. In particular, they focused their opposition on the Purcell Mountains and the possibility emerging from the CORE table of enlarging and completing the conservancy. It wasn't that there was a lot of wood at stake in the proposed expansion, because there wasn't. What really riled the forest companies was the fact that the Purcell Conservancy represented the first place in the Kootenays where the government had said no to them.

Now, after two years, as negotiations moved toward conclusion, it became increasingly apparent that this table of disparate interests was going to reach substantial agreement. Suddenly the resource industry executives, fearing the status quo that had long favored them was about to erode, decided to take tough action to kill the CORE plan. For the CEOs this was merely about business. After all, their corporate priority was to maximize profits. For them their private, vested interests came before the public good.

Therefore, to counter any chance that the CORE land-use plan might succeed, the resource corporations quickly raised hundreds of thousands of dollars and imported organizers to stir up public opposition. Soon industry-sponsored rallies were held throughout the East Kootenay. Using disinformation and grossly inflated job-loss numbers, the agitators fanned fears. They said the CORE plan would result in whole mills closing down and the collapse of communities. Merchants were pressured into taking a pro-logging stance, while local newspapers became fat with scare-tactics advertising.

The conservationists, instead, took the high road. They stayed grounded, relying on facts, not fear, countering rhetoric with reason. They did the math to show that the job-loss impact would be low, much lower than the industry hysteria trumpeted. And with almost no money, and reliant upon volunteers, the East Kootenay conservationists met the corporate media campaign by talking truth, one-on-one, with their neighbors and friends. They placed their integrity on the line. In the face of such vitriol and threats they remained resolute that the wild nature so beloved by Kootenay people would remain intact for their children without devastating jobs or the economy. There was a quiet heroism here.

Yet still the resource corporations opposed the conservationists vehemently, and the tension of the situation became extreme. Where traditionally this region of British Columbia had long been a place where people of different opinions respected one another, now the fabric of community was stretched excessively taut.

As for myself, I had moved from the East Kootenay to Vancouver several years earlier and hadn't been active at the CORE negotiating table. Nevertheless, given my long history with the Purcells, I monitored the situation closely. I was in touch with the main environmental negotiators: John, Lesley, Kent, and Ellen. Now, as matters moved toward a conclusion, I became involved with them again and began to collaborate on strategy.

In a way I had a sense of déjà vu, of distant days when I had returned to the coast after my Purcell honeymoon to lobby to protect these mountains. But unlike 20 years earlier, the situation was much more embattled now. In the final weeks of the campaign the struggle came down to a very few of us – both in the region and the provincial capital – playing behind-the-scenes hardball with key leaders in the government, the resource industry, and the forest unions. In particular, my assignment was to do what I knew best: put pressure on the premier's office, a couple of key Cabinet ministers, and a corporate CEO or two to get the strongest possible deal for Nature, and for future generations.

Ultimately, against long odds, we succeeded. A land-use agreement was reached, and while it wasn't perfect – we didn't get everything we wanted – we did achieve crucial victories, especially the preservation of an enlarged Purcell Wilderness Conservancy as well as other important parks. So, in March 1995, when the government legally approved the East Kootenay land-use plan, the Purcell Wilderness Conservancy was expanded to 500,000 acres. It was now the largest protected wilderness in southern British Columbia.

The new boundaries encompassed the original core area protected in 1974, as well as those critical sites that Art and I hadn't foreseen would be essential to the long-term survival of wilderness in these mountains. Now within the enlarged conservancy were the connecting wildlife corridors to the winter range, the east side forests, and all of Carney Creek on the west.

As for the conservancy's order-in-council status, it was strengthened to full, legislated protection. The experience of past years in which the logging industry had repeatedly tried to reopen the area to chain saws would no longer be tolerated. Any future attempts to erode the conservancy's protection could not be implemented by simple executive action of the Cabinet. Instead, such a raid on the wilderness would require scrutiny by the B.C. Legislature as a whole and would not likely ever be approved.

At last the campaign for the Purcell Mountains had reached fulfillment. Reflecting back across all the years and the many experiences, I thought of just what an achievement this was. It had entailed a great effort: two long decades of unceasing citizen vigilance and activism. But finally all this persistence by so many had paid dividends. Art Twomey's vision of an enduring wilderness had become reality. The mountains he had explored and championed since his twenties would remain wild. They would be there for future ages of youthful explorers to discover. Tomorrow's mountain men and women would savor the fragrance of timeless forests, glimpse the passage of elk or goat, ford cool, rushing creeks, and traverse the freedom of high ridgelines, looking out beyond vast horizons, their ears ringing with the still, silent solitude of eternity...

The phone call came on an early January morning in 1997. I was half asleep, but I heard the message. Art had been killed. While he was flying into the Purcells to instruct an avalanche course, the chopper he was in crashed only a couple of miles from his homestead cabin. The engine had powered out, and the helicopter had smashed headlong into a cliff, killing everyone aboard instantly.

Stunned, numb, not yet understanding, I kept replaying the words in my mind, but they didn't make sense. Art dead? But no, it couldn't be. He had always been here since I could remember. True, sometimes we didn't see each other for months, even years, but eventually we would get together again, perhaps as I passed through the Kootenays, or when he made trips to the coast. On those occasions we would talk wilderness, as we always did. And each time he was still Art, tall and lanky, with a great grin, bright eyes, and that untamed mountain beard. But now he was dead, and how could that be? Surely he was too young. Why, wasn't it just the other day we were drawing lines on maps together?

Like fog seeping up-valley from the low country, like gray cloud descending slowly from peaks misting softly, the meaning, the reality, of the news reached me. First, the smallest ache began, then it grew into greater sorrow. An emptiness widened in me as vast as the wild Purcells. As my sadness deepened, grief swirled in and obscured everything. Then tears came. Art was gone.

That morning I talked to many of his friends – our friends – the band of wilderness warriors who since Earthwatch had tended the flame of the wild. To all of us, to each of us, the loss was huge, but so, too, was our gratitude. For Art had entered our lives and shown us what was possible through dreaming. And now the dreamer had died, but his dream lived on, enduring throughout the Purcell Mountains as Nature's first song, as life's essential dance, as wilderness.

Today, as I write these words, Margie is skiing Art's ashes back into his mountains. She will leave these reminders of his life near his high cabin among the subalpine fir, below the great peaks in the place that was home, in the place where he was happiest, in his beloved Purcell Wilderness Conservancy, his heaven on earth. Because today Art has gone back to the land forever.

Four

Babine Mountains

Home of the Pioneers

NORTH America was a continent opened up by pioneers. Seeking to break the bonds of an overly civilized and confining Europe, they crossed the ocean to the New World where life on the frontier offered freedom, independence, and self-sufficiency. But there was a paradox inherent in this pioneering. Through their actions of settlement these rugged individualists sowed the seeds that would eventually destroy the very wilderness they sought and loved. So, when increasing eastern settlement pushed the wild country farther back, replacing it with too many people for their liking, again the pioneers headed out. Westward and into the north they went to where wildness still endured. There they could again live on the edge, on the frontier between tamed and untamed Nature.

The wilderness was always testing them. It defined who they were. A misstep and the wilds would claim you: slipping off a mountain ledge to painful death, breaking through midwinter river ice to drown. Yet where else could you know the raw, pure beauty of the land as new life emerged from the melting snows of April? Where else could you glance up to see caribou on the skyline, explore

73

unknown rivers, or plow meadowland for the very first time ever?

There was an honesty in the lives of pioneers. In so many ways they were the masters of their own fates. The challenge of survival, of success, depended on each individual's determination, vision, and ability to do hard work. Through willpower and perseverance their choices became tomorrow's reality. Build the homestead at this confluence and the site for a future town was determined. Cut the trail up that valley and the route of an eventual highway was foretold.

Unfettered by past human ownership or structures, life on the frontier possessed seemingly endless possibilities. But for all its romance, wild British Columbia then was a hard land that required tough people to tame it. So the pioneers who came to settle, although simple and straightforward in their day-to-day ways, now seem larger than life. And currently as humanity passes into the third millennium, in a world grown crowded with rules and obligations, how many of us have looked back on those frontier days and said wistfully, "Oh, if only I could have lived then."

Gordon Harvey was always a pioneer. Born in northwestern British Columbia, he grew up where Driftwood Creek flows down from the Babine Mountains. When Gordon was one year old, his father, big Peavine Harvey, and mother tied him onto a packhorse and together they rode up the Bulkley River, past the new railway tent city of Smithers, and into Driftwood Canyon. The year was 1914. Here, on the choice bottomlands of the steep-sloped valley, amid the aspen groves beside the little creek that danced down from alpine headwaters, Peavine cleared the first fields. He built a small cabin where his little family weathered the winter. The next spring the father rode farther up Driftwood Creek into the Babines to go prospecting. Atop the rolling alpine of the ridge that now bears his name – Harvey Mountain – Peavine got lucky. He discovered copper.

It was hardly a bonanza, rather just a small deposit, barely large enough to support his family. Still, copper was copper, and the possibility of striking it rich was too enticing. So Peavine, his wife, and tiny Gordon moved into the Babine high country to spend the summer at the claim. Frontier realities required that both Peavine and his wife work the ore body to get the mine shaft started. As for Gordon, he was now old enough to walk. To keep him from toddling off and over a cliff, or perhaps encountering a grizzly, his parents tethered him to a tree.

When Gordon got too old to keep leashed, it was decided that he and his mother should spend summers down at the farm while his father went up to the mountains to mine. The problem was, though, that the Harveys were famous for their fights. They were both so strong-minded and stubborn that often they disagreed vehemently, which may have been due to the considerable differences in their backgrounds.

Peavine was a rough-hewn man inhabiting a massive frame who was quite willing to bully. He was so loud and proud that finally his neighbors resolved to take him down a notch. When he decided to enter samples of his prized timothy hay and huckleberries in the prestigious Pacific National Exhibition, they secretly substituted wild peavine vetch and rabbit droppings in his luggage. So arrogant and self-assured was old man Harvey that he traveled the 700 miles to Vancouver, a huge distance in those days, without once checking his gear. It wasn't until he actually arrived at the fair to unwrap his prized entries that he discovered the switch. He must have been furious and embarrassed. Not that the folks at Smithers let him off the hook; from that time on they called him Peavine.

Gordon's mother, on the other hand, was a petite, educated woman raised in Calgary. Indeed, she had once worked as a secretary for future Canadian Prime Minister R.B. Bennett and was a lover of opera. A terrible housekeeper, she nevertheless spent her spare time writing books on home economics. Not surprisingly, they never got published.

With people so different the fights between the Harveys were legendary. Peavine was also unbelievably stingy. Several times he would be so tight in sharing that Mrs. Harvey and young Gordon would run short of food at the farm. Meanwhile, up on the mining claim, Peavine had an abundance of supplies. It was as if he were showing his outspoken wife who was really in charge.

Mrs. Harvey wasn't easily cowed, though. One night, when she and Gordon were literally starving, she sneaked up to the mine site and took some of her husband's food. When Peavine discovered what she had done, he flew into a rage. He went to town and got the police to jail his wife for stealing. But Mrs. Harvey got the final revenge. Once released, she printed up a notice detailing the sordid details of the abuses she had suffered from her husband over the years. She then stood on the main street of Smithers and handed out copies to the townspeople. Of course, they loved it. Gossip didn't get any better than this.

Years of working hard in the mine led to an early death for Peavine, which left Gordon to grow up with his mother in the isolation of Driftwood Canyon. Later, when she, too, died, Gordon was very much alone. There were no neighbors in his valley. Come winter the canyon would clog with snow and he would be cut off from the outside world. In fact, right into the early 1970s he had no power or phone. So each spring one of his friends would drive out from town, up that twisting road high above the creek, to see if he had made it through alive.

Gordon's farming was quite a contrast to modern-day agribusiness. He still forked the mown hay by hand onto his wagon. He only kept 12 cows, but they were reputed to be some of the best in the Bulkley Valley. He had a tame bull named Oscar, in honor of Oscar Mayer hot dogs. As well, he ran a herd of goats, the leader of which had 24-inch-long spiked horns. Gordon sarcastically called him Hermann, after Hermann Göring.

Undoubtedly Gordon was a character and an eccentric, as was so often the case with those hardy enough to endure frontier life. He kept the goats in his one-room log cabin, and when their droppings got too deep, rather than sweep them out, he would just place another layer of carpet overtop. His floor was always soft, warm, and pungent.

This cabin was his third. The earlier ones had burned down because Gordon could never be bothered to cut his firewood to stove length. It was just too much work, he said. Instead, he would shove the overly long logs into the open woodstove, with the ends hanging out. Then he would push them inward as they were consumed by the flames. But on two fateful occasions the fire climbed up the logs right out of the stove and set the house ablaze.

In front of the cabin, bordering the creek, Gordon created a whimsical little park complete with ponds, countless garden-variety trolls, and a pink lawn flamingo or two. He hung empty plastic lemons, the kind juice is sold in, on an evergreen tree, explaining this would be the closest he would ever get to the tropics. He also got a friend to paint him a full-size lifelike deer cut out of plywood, which he placed in the center of Lone Pine Park, his name for his landscaping creation. One fall a couple of half-drunk hunters cruised up Driftwood Road, looking for easy game. They spied the deer and stopped the car carefully so as not to spook the animal. Shouldering their rifles, they blasted it. Imagine their surprise when the thing didn't move despite the gaping holes in its shoulder. At first Gordon was upset when he saw what had happened, but later he had a good laugh.

Like his garden statuettes, Gordon was a delightful little gnome of a man with pronounced nose, watery eyes, thinning straw-white hair, and a nasal voice. He had never had a wife or even a girlfriend, and yet his was the purest of hearts. He loved to spend time with people, but he was intensely lonely living all those years in Driftwood Canyon by himself. That was why he had built his park, hoping that people would stop to look at its curiosities and talk with him. Later, when a fossil bed on his property became known, he donated it to the B.C. Parks Branch to encourage people to drive up the canyon. They did, and at last he got some visitors.

Gordon was just one of the colorful characters who was woven into the fabric of this northwest frontier. There were many others, like Eli Fletcher, another individualist who came to live on this remote place. Fletcher liked the country so much that when he got the chance he bought land close to the Babine foothills and introduced the first sheep to the valley. But this country was too wild for these woolly immigrants. The coyotes took so many that Fletcher was soon forced out of business.

And there was Fort L'Orsa. Arriving in the valley in the 1930s, he was either a late pioneer or an early forerunner of the back-to-the-landers who would reach here in the 1960s. In the middle of the Great Depression, Fort decided

77

his life was being wasted working as a chemist for a pharmaceutical company in Switzerland. So he quit his job, left his birth country, and immigrated to Canada. Across the Atlantic by steamer, then northwesterly on Canadian National Railways, he made his way, 7,000 miles, to the Bulkley Valley. With high mountains all around and good valley soil for farming, this place was like Switzerland. But unlike the Old World, he was no longer condemned to the claustrophobia of city existence and a rigid social system. Here he could live life on his own terms in a beautiful, wild place.

There was no question that Fort had an eye for scenery. The midslope fields he homesteaded looked across the sweep of valley to Hudson Bay Mountain, sheer twin peaks presiding over an amphitheater filled with ice. Behind the farm the alpine domes of the Babine Range seemed always to invite exploration. Indeed, whenever he could get away, which given the demands of hay farming wasn't often enough for him, Fort would head up into the Babines, his home mountains. He would take his horses up Driftwood Canyon, across the little bridge by Gordon's cabin, and onward into the high country.

The route to the Babines followed cascading rapids. At Sunny Point the rounded bulk of Ptarmigan Mountain rose abruptly. Here the trail forked three ways, the left branch arcing north around the backside of Ptarmigan to Two Bridge Lakes, the right-hand path rising quickly onto Harvey Mountain and Peavine's old claim. But Fort preferred to head straight into the heartland to the alpine meadows in Silver King Basin, at the source of Driftwood Creek.

He made a point of going there at least once and preferably several times a summer. Then, sometimes with his young boys, Tony and Joe, he would climb to the pass or perhaps just linger and watch the mountain goats on the ledges far above on Hyland Peak. July was the prime time for flowers. The meadows were drenched with brilliance: crimson Indian paintbrush, purple-blue lupine, golden arnica. In August the black mountain berries were out in abundance. This was a season to be noisy; the bears were as drawn to this feast as the kids were.

When the boys got older, they started to spend time in the Babines on their own. Here was a gentle wilderness, the rolling alpine of Ganokwa Basin, the

78

roaming walks along the soft shoulders of Pitspidela Mountain. Up top in the Babines you could see almost forever, and yet the world seemed far away. Off to the west the forests eased down to the Bulkley Valley farmlands, with Hudson Bay Mountain a sentinel beyond and the Coast Mountains stretching off toward the Alaska Panhandle. To the north the wilderness wandered endlessly across the Interior Plateau, headed for the Arctic. While southward there were no settlements of size until Vancouver, 700 miles away.

Standing high on these mountains was like being in the wild heart of the universe. So while Fort could see his farm from the Babines, and the Babines from his kitchen window, he always knew he lived close to, but not quite at, his spiritual home. "This is the place," he said to his boys, "where I want to be buried."

If the Babines were pure wilderness, the farms down in the valley sat directly astride the frontier. Every night the dogs would bark as wolves stalked moose in the fields. And even into the 1960s most places were without electricity. To speed up the coming of hydro and cut the costs of extending the lines, farmers got together in volunteer teams. They brushed the right-of-ways and prepared the holes in which the power poles would be placed.

One day, as Fort worked with some neighbors on a nearby line, he encountered ground so hard that the holes had to be blasted. One site required two sticks of dynamite. Choosing to be unnecessarily frugal, he short-fused the charges. The first lit easily, but he couldn't get the second one to catch. Instead of clearing the hole, he tried to get the reluctant wick to light. By the time he succeeded, it was too late. Fort L'Orsa was fatally injured when the initial charge exploded. He died within the hour.

Grief rippled throughout the Bulkley Valley like dampened shock waves. The community had lost yet another of its pioneering companions to the risks of frontier life. But in their sadness Fort's friends remembered where he had always been happiest. With horses they carried his body up to his treasured meadows in Silver King Basin and buried him with quiet ceremony, the goats watching from above. And while a simple cross marked the gravesite, the peaks would stand as lasting monuments to his passing.

For Joe L'Orsa these mountains were the shrine to his father's memory and more. Not only had they been a place of happiness when his father was alive, but now he, too, was spending a lot of time up there. He came to know the range intimately, not just Silver King and Ganokwa Basins, but also the hard-to-get-at places like the long meadows on Harold Price Creek. Just as his father had before him, Joe found that the Babines had become the home for his soul.

His days spent in this wilderness recalled pioneer yesterdays: the old abandoned mine workings, not only on Harvey Mountain but at Silver King and Hyland Basins, as well. He walked the routes of an earlier generation: the unyielding climb of the McCabe Trail; the rock cairns that still marked the way over high passes; the trenches left in alpine soil from horses' hooves so long gone by.

But in the intervening decades the world had changed dramatically from those old days. Now broad resource roads pushed up from the low country aimed straight at the range. Already to the east rectangular clearcuts were beginning to scar the Interior Plateau forests. And on Big Onion Mountain a mining exploration road had left a red gash across the peak's western flank.

Joe was ever more mindful of the fast-approaching threat. On his solitary hikes he worried that if something wasn't done soon to preserve the wilderness in the Babines, this living link to the past would be mined, logged out, and lost. There would be no frontier remaining. Instead, the resource corporations would treat these mountains as just one more place to exploit. Increasingly he knew he had to save his mountains; he just wasn't sure how yet.

As FOR ME, I had never heard of the Babines. I was fresh out of university, employed as Western Canada Conservation Representative, and touring the province to meet local environmentalists. I wanted to learn where wilderness was most at risk. Eventually this traveling, which had brought me in contact with Art Twomey and the Purcell folk in southeastern British Columbia, led to the northwest.

At Smithers in the Bulkley Valley I met with a small group of conservationists who had just successfully prevented a pulp mill from being built
upstream. The ringleader was 35-year-old Joe L'Orsa. He was soft-spoken, well
traveled, and intelligent. His words came out in a slow, melodic, almost Southern cadence. We liked each other from the start. After the meeting, he invited
me to spend the night at his farm.

And what a farm he had. To me it was idyllic: 500 acres of hay fields and
aspen groves, with the most spectacular mountain views. Joe had inherited it
from his father. He had eclectic interests for a country type, being both a talented blues guitarist and a dedicated adherent of Eastern meditation. But of
all his qualities it was his love for the land and the past that touched me most.

We stayed up late and talked. I shared with him what I had learned from
the Nitinat and Schoen campaigns, particularly how to work the government
to get wilderness wins. He told me about the history of the Bulkley Valley and
the beauty of his Babines. It was the beginning of a close friendship. That night
I had one of the best sleeps ever on his living room floor. There was a great
sense of peace.

The next day, as I was leaving, Joe suggested I take a quick side trip to a
little picnic site before hitting the road for Vancouver. The spot was up a nearby
canyon on Driftwood Creek at some fossil beds. "It's quite lovely," he said. So
I drove up the winding road that also led to his Babines. I stopped at the picnic
site and explored the fossilized rock outcrops. I found a few impressions of
ancient redwood needles, but I would have loved to have unearthed a piece of
the fossil fish that Joe had said were occasionally found there.

Later I wandered along the creek. The song of its waters echoed in the canyon.
I climbed the grassy slopes to a point on the rim where I could watch the rapids
below and look at the mountains beyond. I was all alone that afternoon, except for
a small, hunched-over farmer who came into sight for a few minutes up on a far
field. He was forking hay onto a wagon by hand, just as the old-timers had done.

This place was magical. Deciding to stay the night, I pitched my tent. After
all, I had been constantly on the road and needed to take a break, if only to write

out the words for my wedding ceremony. Karen and I were getting married in Victoria in two weeks. That evening I lay on my sleeping bag with my tent open on the edge of Driftwood Creek and wrote my vows and intentions for the future. I felt entirely at home and slept deeply again that night. The next morning, unable to delay any longer, I reluctantly drove back down the canyon and headed south.

After our wedding, and honeymoon in the Purcell Mountains, Karen and I found a little house to rent in Victoria and began married life. It was a time of happiness and discovery. She taught school while I became increasingly immersed in saving the Purcells, particularly in my new capacity as an adviser to the B.C. Cabinet in the Environment and Land-Use Committee Secretariat. During this time, I didn't mind being in Victoria. With so much to do and learn I was preoccupied by work. But once the Purcell Wilderness Conservancy was established, I became restless. There was something missing in my life. I was tired of the city. All my years had been lived amid concrete, first Toronto, then Vancouver and Victoria. My recent tour across the province had awakened a desire to be closer to Nature. I found myself longing for the northwest and its wild beauty. Increasingly I wanted to live there on the land, so I phoned Joe and asked if he could help.

"I know one piece you'd love," Joe said. "It's not on the market, but the owner is a special friend of mine. He knew my parents, and I think if I asked him, he'd sell it to you. He still lives in the old ways. His name's Gordon Harvey and he has a beautiful 50 acres of meadowland up Driftwood Canyon with views of the Babines. Right at the fossil beds. I think you stopped there when you were leaving here that time we met, didn't you?"

I was thrilled at the possibility. When Joe confirmed a few days later that Gordon was indeed receptive, I immediately flew up to Smithers. That evening Joe and I drove to Driftwood Canyon to meet with him. It was twilight. Oscar, his bull, nosed gently against me. "Yes, all right then," Gordon said after a bit. "I'll sell to you and you can be my new neighbor." We both grinned.

Later, as the stars came out, Joe and I walked on what was to be my land. I asked Joe what I could do to repay him for his help. Glancing off toward the Babines, he smiled softly. "Ric, I think I've got an idea. Let's talk about it sometime."

The deal that Joe had made possible at Driftwood was perfect. Since Gordon badly wanted neighbors, he had given Karen and me a very good price on the land, one we could afford. In return we were more than happy to agree that he could have agricultural use of the land for as long as he lived. This arrangement would work for both of us. I had no plans to become a farmer — I just wanted to live in the country — and Gordon got to live his lifestyle as a frontier farmer. The wonderful bonus was that I gained the chance to know one of the last of the Bulkley Valley pioneers, a very special person indeed.

But now it was my turn to learn about living on the frontier. Karen and I put up a tiny house on a small bench of land above the road. From our kitchen table we could watch beavers down at the creek and the Babines from our living room. Behind the cabin we fenced in a half acre of land for a garden. I suppose we were overambitious, especially when we discovered that our cool canyon micro-climate only grew cabbages and potatoes. Down by the creek we built a sauna, using old barn timbers complete with a slide that dumped us right into midstream. In winter we plunged through a hole in the ice. And, of course, we lived with an outhouse, which meant scurrying out on minus-40-degree winter nights when the body's summons could no longer be ignored. But in summer, sitting with the door open, watching the fields was a delight, and once a coyote chanced by.

Karen and I lived like modern-day pioneers, simply and in touch with the land. We cut our firewood in summer in preparation for six months of snow, and come winter, we followed the tracks of moose across our fields. When mid-January nights were clear and cold, we snowshoed to the upper meadow and watched the Northern Lights ripple green and purple, washing the heavens in phosphorescent waves. Silent and mysterious.

Spring was a time of cheer. The snow was gone and the birds returned. Days lengthened while the air became warmer. On May evenings I climbed the steep, grassy slopes to the lip of the canyon above our little house, just as I had done that very first time I had camped at Driftwood. Again I would sit, sometimes for hours, listening to the voice of the creek below, watching sunset radiance bathe the Babines in glowing pink.

Then there was the time we held a longest-day-of-the-year party in our top field. We built a large campfire, and everyone sat around it on log benches, laughing and drinking home brew. Since we were so far north, it was midnight before the sky was dark enough for stars to show. By 3:00 a,m. it was dawn. Throughout that short night Joe's mountains kept us company in the distance.

During the years I lived by Driftwood Creek, the Babines were my backyard. Just five miles away, they were easily accessible year-round. In winter I skied from my back door into Silver King Basin and stayed in the old cabins there. In summer, sometimes after dinner, I drove up to the trailhead and hiked into the alpine. Usually, though, I preferred to go out on multi-day backpacks. And many times on these trips there were no other people in the entire range, which was something special.

So the night Joe came to collect on his "debt," I was quite responsive.

Gordon Harvey, the last of the Babine Mountain pioneers, Karen and Keah at a Midsummer's Night campfire in Driftwood.

"One of the reasons I was glad to find you a home up here," he told me, "was because you know how to save wilderness. I thought if you had a chance to live here and see how special the Babines are, you might help me get them protected, just like you've done before."

He didn't have to pitch me hard, because indeed his mountains had already sold me. However, there was a problem. Saving the Babines would require a different strategy than that used in earlier campaigns I had worked on. Preservation of the Nitinat Triangle and the Purcell Mountains had resulted from well-developed public support. By contrast few people knew the Babines the way Joe did or that they were at risk. Furthermore, since these mountains were located so far north in British Columbia, in the limited time available it would be difficult to make this issue a priority for Cabinet ministers in Victoria.

The fact is, each wilderness campaign is different. For some areas, like Nitinat or Clayoquot, high-profile "flagship" campaigning based on extensive public support is the best means to achieve success. For less-contentious or less-known areas like the Schoen Valley, "finesse" campaigning focused on convincing key politicians is the best way to go. Clearly the formula for success varies from campaign to campaign.

Therefore, if the goal isn't just to make noise, which is easy for environmentalists, but to preserve wilderness, then the first requirement is to evaluate the particular issue carefully before any opening move is made. To win wilderness requires a winning strategy. Too often environmentalists engage in action without first mapping out a plan. The result is prolonged protest that only leads to stalemate and eventual failure due to exhaustion.

Accordingly Joe and I discussed the options. We quickly realized neither a mass public campaign nor political lobbying would work for the Babines. Instead, the solution was for me to utilize the influence of my position inside the bureaucracy to invent a process that would result in protection. This strategy would be difficult but not impossible. Although I was still working as an adviser to the Cabinet in the Environment and Land-Use Secretariat, I had been successful in getting posted to Smithers and was now responsible for the northwestern quarter of British Columbia, a territory larger than the British Isles but with a population of only 80,000. It was quite the place for a wilderness lover.

My job description required me to seek multi-agency solutions on regional land-use conflicts, which often meant I had the freedom to identify many of the projects I worked on. Since the Babines were situated a mere 10 miles from Smithers, they were indeed the subject of competing uses: recreation, forestry, wildlife, mining, and now, with Joe's proposal, wilderness. It wasn't difficult, therefore, to convince my superiors that I should be allowed to head a multi-agency review of these mountains.

As I had done earlier with the Purcells, I assembled a team of land-use specialists from the Forest Service and the Mines, Wildlife, and Parks Branches. I asked each to map their particular land-use concerns for the Babines onto plastic overlays.

The Mines Branch was most concerned about access to claim blocks on the eastern and southern edges of the mountains where small lead, silver, and copper mines had operated in the past. The Forest Service was especially interested in stands at the lower elevations adjacent to the mountains but also wanted to log to the head of Silver King Basin, where Joe's father was buried. If this happened, the wilderness would be cut in pieces and the heartland core lost.

The Wildlife Branch's priority was the survival of mountain goats. Originally the Babines had supported large numbers of goats, but overhunting had decimated this herd. Therefore, the agency had plans to restore the population for wildlife-viewing purposes. However, the biologists said that this effort would be wasted if logging, mining, and new resource roads were allowed, since they would cause poaching as well as the destruction of habitat.

The most disappointing input came from the Parks Branch. Overly deferential to the forest and mining agencies, and with too few staff members, it failed to submit a strong documentation of the Babines' wilderness values. As an agency, it remained in a 1960s mind-set, focused on providing camping and picnic recreation along highways. It had difficulty rating the wilderness qualities of the Babine backcountry as a priority.

The Parks Branch's attitude created a major obstacle for Joe's and my desire for a wilderness. Without that agency's willingness to champion the area for protection at the multi-agency table, I had no ground to work from. Unable to stir up a large public campaign in the time available, it looked as if we might be beaten.

Uncertain how to proceed next, I kept the planning process going in hope that some solution could be found. I had looked at the overlay maps, and it was clear to me that the conflicts were less than what was feared. Certainly from a technical standpoint, protection of the Babines was realistic; the forest industry would have to forgo logging in the heartland, but the volumes of wood affected weren't huge.

As for the miners, the small deposits in the range had been depleted already. (The few prospects still with potential were on the perimeter of the area and could probably be accommodated without causing much loss of wilderness.) Otherwise it was unlikely any other claims would ever be viable. The danger, instead, was that the prospectors might build more roads or trench the alpine with bulldozers while exploring claims, which could scar the fragile soil for centuries.

Prospectors have an evangelical faith that they will strike it rich. So, regardless of the long odds – the industry rule of thumb in British Columbia is that only one claim in 5,000 becomes a mine – they still gouge the ground. In fact, to maintain ownership of a mining claim, B.C. law, as elsewhere, then said that prospectors had to spend $100 per year per claim in exploration. Hence, wilderness lands in the Babines, indeed in all of British Columbia, were at risk from this policy. In the mid-1970s, though, helicopter access and diamond drilling provided the technical means to explore without causing irreversible damage, so surely there were other possibilities, I thought.

My problem was that with the Parks Branch essentially sitting on the sidelines, there was no one to carry the ball for wilderness. Obviously, while I searched for an alternate game plan, it was important to keep the current situation quiet. For if word got outside to the development types – those opponents of the wild – that the Parks Branch ranked the Babines as low-priority, the chance to protect the mountain range would be lost.

So I resolved not to talk about the situation, not even to Joe. I was concerned that if he found out about the Parks Branch's position, his frustration might get the best of him. Experienced as he was, he hadn't worked on the "inside," and I didn't know how to explain the nuances of the finesse that was now forming in my mind. I felt that with all the interagency dynamics, and the increasingly risky place I would be in, that I had the best chance of succeeding if there were as few uncertainties as possible. After all, I was certainly not acting as an impartial bureaucrat. For the time being then, Joe would have to trust me and I would have to stay true to my ethics.

There was a price for this decision. It would take almost a year to complete my strategy for the Babines. During this time, Joe saw what looked like inaction. He began to think his wilderness would be lost. His fears were only made worse when he raised the issue and I was circumspect. It wasn't that I was singling him out; I wasn't telling anyone about my plans, not other friends or workers. No one. But keeping quiet with Joe was the toughest. While we had become close, now, understandably, he began to question whether I had caved in to the resource agencies, whether I was selling out the Babines to protect my job, whether I was betraying our friendship.

His comments hurt. They became more painful as other conservationist friends voiced similar sentiments and distanced themselves. As they doubted me, I also began to have doubts. Was I deluding myself? What if I was making a mistake by keeping things quiet? What if I failed to protect the Babines? How would I ever be able to face Joe and the others? It was a lonely time for me. I felt very vulnerable.

So there I was with no one to talk to. Certainly the resource agency staff members were unlikely to be sympathetic. Yet despite this, my task now was to convince them of the solution I had dreamt up. I proposed a completely new type of land-use status for the mountains and called it an integrated management unit or IMU. The name was quite bureaucratic, but it was appropriate since my strategy relied on getting the Forests, Mines, and Parks staff to embrace the concept as their own. If I could achieve this, then it would be a simple matter to present the agreed-upon land-use plan to the Cabinet for approval, especially since the Secretariat's mandate was to achieve such consensus.

Therefore, unlike the Nitinat campaign in which mass public pressure defined the strategy, or the Purcell struggle, which entailed directly convincing the Cabinet, saving the Babines meant the focus had to be on the bureaucracy. For success this strategy required motivating key civil servants to make the case for protection. Clearly I had work to do.

The essence of the IMU was to have the Babine Mountains managed not by one agency (such as Forests or Parks), but collaboratively by all the branches together through a legally mandated committee approach. This procedure had never been implemented before in British Columbia, so appropriately enough we were going to be pioneers. There was some bureaucratic appeal to the approach because increasingly the individual agencies were becoming paranoid that they might lose all control over the area to another department. First, though, a collective vision would have to be agreed to, one that, as far as I was concerned, retained the wilderness quality of the Babines.

To start things off, using the maps the agencies had provided me, I showed the group why I thought the land-use conflicts could be resolved. I outlined how cooperative IMU management by the whole team was surely better than ongoing confrontation. While the response was skeptical, nevertheless there was a willingness to try.

Using their resource overlays, the group began working toward a zoning plan that would identify the core region to be retained as wilderness and those areas that would be available for resource extraction. Initially turf wars flared with much posturing and bickering. Yet, during the months of out-of-sight negotiations, progress occurred. I saw it as my job to prod and steer the group, to replace differences with agreement, especially ones that would enable the wilderness to remain. Eventually consensus was reached. It wasn't perfect and trade-offs were made by all, but from the conservation perspective, these were minor. Joe's mountains would remain wild.

Having agreed to the zones, the team next wrote the rules for managing them. The Babines would be predominantly managed for wilderness. Goat populations would be restored and hiking trails reopened. Logging was to be excluded from the heartland basins like Silver King, and no roads would be built. In some noncritical sites along the perimeter, timber harvesting would be permitted. As for the miners, they would be allowed to explore their claims but only by low-impact helicopter access and diamond drilling. If they found a deposit that could be proven viable, then road building was a possibility. But given the low likelihood of this, I was willing to take the gamble.

The years ahead would be tricky. We would have to rely on this committee of agencies to honor its agreed-upon management rules collectively. But I was cautiously optimistic. A cooperative psychology had developed in the group during the months of deliberations.

What's more, there was no better alternative. Without park status for the Babines, this IMU approach was the only means available to keep imminent logging and road construction out of the wilderness core. During the years to come, I figured this interim solution would give the public time to discover what Joe and I knew: these mountains were a special place. And assuming that the IMU would protect the wildness long enough, I was confident the day would arrive when the Parks Branch could be encouraged to protect the Babines fully.

With the bureaucrats now in consensus, once more I drafted the necessary documents for the Cabinet: the background document, the maps, and the order-in-council. Shortly after, in September of 1976, the Babine Mountains Integrated Management Unit was signed into existence, thereby safeguarding 68,000 acres of wilderness. Indeed, the Cabinet ministers were enthusiastic that this cooperative IMU approach offered a new legal tool for resolving land-use conflicts.

When I was briefed on the Cabinet's decision, a sense of elation and relief flooded through me. Despite long odds, the strategy had succeeded. Now I could talk to Joe. That evening, after dinner, I telephoned and briefed Joe on the news. After all these months of silence, it felt good to tell him what had really been going on. He was delighted, surprised, and somewhat stunned. He had started to lose hope for the mountains.

As for me, while I had managed to keep my faith from faltering, bringing the Babines through hadn't been easy. There had been a lot of behind-the-scenes stress. So, after touching base with Joe, I felt the need to reflect on the events of the past months, to understand what this announcement really meant to me.

I went outside and climbed the grassy hillside to my favorite sitting place. The spring air was fresh, the creek sang, and the mountains were in their glory. Down in the valley the little herd of domestic goats crowded around Gordon as he wandered past the trolls in his park to get drinking water from the creek. As he stooped to fill his bucket, Hermann pretended to butt him from behind with those great horns. I could hear Gordon chuckle and natter at the animals as if they were family. As the sun descended, the sky and peaks were cast in a golden light and an owl called from the cottonwoods. Another Driftwood day was reaching completion. The ritual shared so long by the land and the pioneer lived on. A timelessness pervaded.

Then, from down the valley, I heard the faint sound of a car wending its way along the canyon road. Someone was coming. Around the corner a small red station wagon came into view. It was Joe. He parked by the house and looked up. I waved to him and waited as he made his way up through the meadow to my lookout.

He had a big smile and a warm handshake for me and we made some small talk. Then he paused and looked at me. "After I got off the phone with you, the news started to sink in and I wanted to come up and hear all the details of how you did it. I'm sorry for doubting you. And, Ric, thank you for the Babines."

Those words meant so much to me! After all, saving the Babines had been Joe's vision. He had been the inspiration.

We huddled on the hillside, two good friends talking until well after dark. I shared the inside story with him, and he told me more tales of the pioneer past. With our mountains watching, we savored the thought that the frontier legacy would remain here for the future. Its memory wouldn't be lost.

Over the next several years the IMU strategy proved itself. No logging, mining, or road building occurred in the Babines. The publicity surrounding the protection of the range stimulated local interest, and many more people started to visit on foot or on skis. Within a decade the gamble paid off. By 1984 the Parks Branch had become convinced of the area's importance and took over responsibility for managing it.

This development only served to intensify public allegiance so that by the mid-1990s the value of this wilderness was such that in June 1997 the Babine Mountains Park was increased to 81,500 acres through a citizens' land-use process. While similar in concept to the multi-resource IMU exercise of the 1970s, this measure was a democratic advance. In the two decades since the implementation of the IMU, land-use planning had evolved considerably. It was no longer done behind closed doors by bureaucrats. Instead, stakeholders from all sectors of the public were directly involved.

The expansion of the Babine wilderness occurred just in time, because what had seemed inconceivable in the 1970s had now happened. Tragically the great northwestern forest that had once stretched to beyond the horizon had become clearcut into a patchwork of squares. The only place in the once-wild Bulkley Valley where the frontier landscape still endured was in the mountains that Peavine, Fort, and all the others had called home. But at least the protection of the Babines would keep the memory of their years spent in the wilderness alive. It would also serve as a memorial to Gordon now that he, too, had passed away, the last of his era.

In a sense, Joe and I, and later all the crusaders who worked for preservation in the Babines, had been pioneers, too. Having found a means to keep this splendid wildness protected, we had also broken new ground. The old-timers had relied on their ingenuity and perseverance to prevail despite impossible odds, and so had we. Like them, we also lived on the frontier between wilderness and development. But where they had worked to survive amid the wilds, to carve out a place for settlement, we had sought to ensure a lasting, pristine space for Nature's survival.

The irony of the pioneers was that they were just too successful. Through their individual heroic efforts, the day the first tree was chopped to build the first homestead was the day the wilderness they so loved began to diminish, when the frontier commenced its retreat. Not that this was evident at the time, for how could they have imagined the vast changes of subsequent decades? No, when those pioneers began to break the soil of the Bulkley Valley meadowland in the early part of this century, they could only think about developing the land, not protecting it.

Even up into the 1970s, when Joe and I sensed that something precious was at risk, there were too few people who understood. So few that when the first protection was being secured for the Babines it was important to work with stealth. Today protecting the environment is much more valued, but at the same time the rate of exploitation has intensified exponentially.

The sad reality at the end of the 20th century is that the opportunity to protect wilderness is almost gone. So there is an urgency here and we must work quickly to pass on the untamed treasures of Nature. In years to come the wilderness – the archives of life – will be restricted to those parklands that have been protected. These places will be all that our descendants will have left of the original Earth. Thereafter, just as the memory of the pioneers endures in museum artifacts and pictures, the remembrance of the wild frontier will live on in the Babine Mountain sanctuaries of the world.

The conservation work we do today is of historic consequence. Future ages of humanity will judge us by what we accomplish. And surely in some distant year when the chance for further wilderness preservation is long gone, many will envy the drama of our lifetime when we took on overwhelming odds to achieve the impossible, when we overcame the corporate forces of development, when we prevailed in spite of adversity. They, too, will hear the stories of saving places like the Babine Mountains and say, "Oh, if only I could have lived then."

Spatsizi Plateau

British Columbia's Serengeti

UNDERTAKEN with stealth and speed, Spatsizi was the ultimate finesse campaign. In just 10 months we protected 1.75 million acres, a wilderness larger than Prince Edward Island, making it British Columbia's second largest park. To this day, though, almost no one knows how we did it.

The northern interior of British Columbia is plateau country. A vast shrub-and-meadow upland rolling to gentle peaks, it stretches for hundreds of miles. Frequently this landscape is dissected by steeply entrenched rivers. In keeping with the scale of this place, these rivers are large. Swimming them on horseback can be treacherous, but in a canoe they are a voyageur's delight.

Spatsizi has long been known as British Columbia's Serengeti. The diversity and numbers of wildlife here are of global importance. The high country is the heart of the stone sheep range. A northern thin-horn relative of the Rocky Mountain bighorn, they hang out in bands on the ridgelines where wind keeps the grass exposed throughout winter. Spatsizi's meadowed expanses are also home to 3,000 Osborn caribou, the largest herd in British Columbia.

These marvelous creatures, with their great, sweeping antlers, graze the alpine and retreat to summer snow patches when the heat or mosquitoes become too much for them. The cliffs on the higher peaks and the rims of river valleys are home to mountain goats. Often these animals roll in the rusty dirt on the ledges, coloring their shaggy white fur and providing the origin of the Native Tahltan word *Spatsizi*, which means "the land of the red goats."

In the valleys, rivers meander through wetlands and spruce, creating moose heaven. As a result, this largest member of the deer family is found here in strength. In winter, when the sheltered valleys receive deeper snow, moose can still move around on their long legs. Frequently they are tracked by wolves, whose populations here are also healthy because the Spatsizi wilderness is large enough to maintain Nature's balance between predator and prey, allowing both to thrive.

The other keystone species of the plateau is the grizzly. During winter these bears make their dens high in the alpine. In spring, as the snow recedes, they reemerge to nibble on fresh plant growth in the valleys. Then, in summer, they move higher, foraging on subalpine cow parsley and grasses. Occasionally they tear the ground apart trying to get at ground squirrels or marmots. In autumn they gorge on berries. Of course, grizzly bears are opportunists, and if they can scavenge a dead animal or scare another predator off its kill, they will. Weighing in at 500 pounds or more, especially in fall when layers of fat accumulate in preparation for hibernation, they can still run as fast as a horse.

The wildlife wealth of Spatsizi is legendary among British Columbians who love the land. What makes it so rich is not just the exceptional productivity of the habitat – there is a great deal of food here for grazers as well as for the carnivores higher in the food chain that feed on them – but the great extent of the wilderness. Big animals need lots of space to survive. After all, they require a considerable food supply in the course of a year to keep their body weight up and to endure the hard winter weather. Since plant-eating animals live in herds to reduce the threat from predators, their impact on the land is great. The way Nature prevents overuse of their habitat is to distribute their grazing across a large range. Constantly on the move, the herds roam extensively throughout the year so that the land has time to recover.

As a result, the only places capable of supporting large populations of herbivores and their carnivorous predators are those that offer expanses of territory to forage in. Two major ecological zones on the Earth originally provided this prerequisite: the tropical savannas of Africa and the temperate steppes found in North America and Asia. While the former supported the evolution of the wildebeest, elephant, and antelope, the latter became home to great populations of bison and members of the deer families.

When humans came on the scene, they were formidable hunters. Nevertheless, despite this prowess, they, like other predators, lived in balance with their prey. Later, though, when humanity learned to farm, the impact on wildlife became ominous so that over time humans infringed on the traditional range of large mammals. Increasingly the grassland ecosystems were converted to crop cultivation and domesticated grazing, resulting in the diminishment of available space and wild animal populations.

The destruction of wildlife reached its most shameful extent with the European settlement of North America. Fencing of the Great Plains for grain farming and the associated massacres virtually annihilated the buffalo. Within a century this slaughter eliminated 60 million bison from the central portion of the continent. Soon after the disappearance of the once-great herds, the prairie wolf and grizzly populations also died off. But the devastation didn't end there. Ever-expanding cultivation and cattle grazing competed with and won out over wildlife elsewhere in the New World. Road building (and the access it provided for hunters), settlement, logging, and mining reduced the habitat so drastically that by the middle of the 20th century the domain of the large grazing animals and their predators was forced back to the last wild frontiers of North American civilization.

Not that the grasslands of Africa had fared well. Increasing human population growth on that continent and more intensive farming also endangered the future of spectacular wildlife populations there. However, then something fortunate happened. Just before independence in the countries of East Africa, the British colonial governments set up a series of large wildlife preserves. These "parks" were intended to protect the trophy-animal populations that the English upper class had long hunted on safari. But what started as sporting preserves for British aristocrats evolved into the modern foundation for the international conservation of wildlife and Nature.

The African experience soon inspired similar action in North America. Here, too, protecting the natural world began to mean more than just preserving spectacular landscapes, which had been the conservation tradition of the late 19th and early 20th centuries. Now the focus was to protect spaces extensive enough to ensure the survival of viable populations of large mammals. And while the initial attention was on animals targeted by human hunters — deer, sheep, and mountain goats — unknowingly this strategy also protected the habitat and food of natural hunters.

As protection of intact large predator-prey habitats improved, conservationists inadvertently began to set aside reserves extensive enough to maintain viable samples of whole ecosystems. In effect, what began as a self-serving effort by big-game hunters resulted in sanctuaries capable of maintaining the range of life-forms — the biodiversity — in an ecological community.

In British Columbia the most important large-mammal habitat is found where rain shadow or cooler climates limit tree growth. By the 1960s, in the south of the province, a century of settlement had severely overrun the grasslands. Although wilderness protection of the higher-altitude summer ranges was still possible in places such as the Purcell and Chilcotin Mountains and the Rockies, the winter ranges in the adjacent low country were often lost. As well, since ranching was a dominant land use in the southern interior, predators had been ruthlessly shot, poisoned, and trapped. If large wildlife reserves were to be protected then, they would have to be in the north where the wilderness was still extensive. And of all this territory — 200,000 square miles — the location long noted for its superb wildlife populations was Spatsizi.

For decades Tommy Walker, the guide outfitter who operated in this wilderness, had been pressing the government, and whoever else would listen, to preserve Spatsizi, but to no avail. He knew and loved this place deeply. Yet despite the movies he filmed of the wildlife, or the articles he wrote, he had been unable to get results.

The reason was simple: right into the 1970s British Columbia was hooked on industrial development and mega-projects. The government saw the north simply as a treasure chest to be plundered, so it focused on flooding valleys behind power dams and building railways to open up this frontier. Indeed, the thought of preserving the north seemed absurd to most politicians of the day. To them the wilderness there seemed infinite. Furthermore, they thought the creation of a large park would only lock away valuable mineral and forest resources from exploitation.

Even though Tommy failed to enlist the government in his plan for a game reserve, he did find allies in the emerging conservation movement. Not surprisingly, the first convert was the B.C. Wildlife Federation, a province-wide organization that then represented 30,000 hunters. It already knew of Spatsizi's wildlife values, yet news of the area had also piqued the interest of those conservationists, such as naturalist groups, who traditionally abhorred the killing of animals for sport. They were also sympathetic to the idea of protecting Spatsizi.

Perhaps the idea of hunters and nonhunters working together seems impossible. However, given that the first priority in wildlife preservation is safeguarding habitat, it makes sense for people who care about animals, regardless of motivation, to cooperate. Otherwise, if they can't work together, it is the developers who win. Even as the two conservation groups squabble, logging, mining, and roads cause the wilderness to disappear. And, of course, once wildlife's homeland is gone, arguments about how the animals should be managed become academic. By contrast, when hunters and naturalists place their love for animals first, their combined strength ensures that preservation prevails over destruction. Then, with the habitat and the animals safe, both sides have the luxury to debate and resolve their differences over years, even centuries, if they wish.

Back in those early days when the idea of a Spatsizi wildlife preserve was only a dream, this pragmatic sense of priorities prevailed. The Wildlife Federation and its nonhunting naturalist counterparts came together. Yet despite such coalescence, northern British Columbia seemed just too distant for even this grouping to make the government act.

Nevertheless, the concept of a Spatsizi preserve caught the attention of Vladimir Krajina, a professor at the University of British Columbia. Professor Krajina – Vlad to his friends – was an exceptional man. A leading parliamentarian in the Czechoslovakian government before World War II and then a resistance fighter, he subsequently fled to Canada to become one of North America's foremost ecologists. He invented the system for classifying and mapping British Columbia's ecosystems, and his science became the basis for forest management in the province and elsewhere in the world.

Krajina was British Columbia's father of plant ecology. In 1971 he convinced the B.C. government to establish its ecological reserves system, the first of its kind in Canada. Unlike the recreation-oriented parks of the day, these sites were designed to protect samples of B.C. natural life zones for scientific research. Remarkable as this eco-reserve program was, it did have a shortcoming: it focused almost entirely on plant rather than animal ecosystems. Unfortunately, while a botanical community can be represented by a reserve a few acres in extent, wildlife systems, especially for large mammals, need much bigger areas, something development-oriented governments in B.C. hadn't been keen about.

Undaunted, Krajina was convinced of the wildlife significance of Spatsizi and longed to see at least a portion of it preserved as the first extensive zoological reserve in his protection system. Given his earlier experience as a shrewd and irrepressible politician, he never gave up promoting this personal quest.

I first met Professor Krajina at his research lab soon after I graduated from university and began to work full-time as a conservationist. Having just heard about his new biogeoclimatic zone mapping system, I wanted to learn more. I thought this method of classification could be an important tool to use when deciding which wilderness areas were priorities for protection.

From the moment we shook hands I was impressed. Not only was he an expert in the field, but his passion for ecology and his enthusiasm were inspiring. Yet of all the things we talked about that day, what I most recall was how he waxed eloquently in a heavy Czech accent about a far northern place called Spatsizi, particularly its vast wildness and wildlife.

Not that I did anything about it. At the time I had my hands full campaigning for the Schoen Valley on Vancouver Island. Besides, northern British Columbia felt far away, almost as distant as Antarctica seems today. And while I might have loved to travel there, that seemed unlikely. So thoughts of Spatsizi soon drifted to the back of my mind.

Once Schoen was protected, my horizon expanded to the preservation of the Purcells in the Kootenay region and then next into the central interior where I homed in on the Babine Mountains. During this time, the New Democrats came to power. Knowing their interest in conservation, I had decided to work as a land-use policy adviser. By now I was stationed in Smithers, which served as the regional center for northwestern British Columbia. When the Babines were finally safe, I began to look around for my next wilderness challenge.

Sitting at work one day in March 1975 poring over maps of my region, I noticed a familiar name in the headwaters region of the Stikine River – Spatsizi Plateau. This jogged memories of my meeting with Professor Krajina and his enthusiasm for the place. Studying the topography, I first got a sense of just how large a wilderness it was. Wouldn't it be a coup, I thought, if it could all be preserved?

The challenge of this idea set my mind in gear. I recalled Krajina's mention of Tommy Walker's name and that he lived in Smithers. Why not? I thought. Finding the number in the phone book, I gave Tommy a call. Later that week I met with him at his log house where he showed me footage of Spatsizi and its wildlife. What I saw that night quickly reinforced what I had already suspected: this wilderness would be ideal to protect next.

However, there was one obstacle. Despite Tommy's long-standing love of the country, he couldn't be the partner I would need to make a Spatsizi park happen.

Retired from guide outfitting, he lacked the energy of his younger days, something that would be required to make the government act. As well, he was a conservative sort and made it clear he wasn't very enamored with the new "socialists" in power. While his political leanings didn't greatly concern me, this attitude would make it difficult for him to work with and convince the ministers in power.

So, in need of an ally, I soon thought of my friend Bristol Foster who, as head of the Royal British Columbia Museum in Victoria, had been quite helpful during the Nitinat Triangle campaign. Since that time Bristol had taken a new and even more ideally placed job. He had become the director of the Ecological Reserves Unit. Not only would this position be a natural to push Spatsizi from, but his sense of humor would make working with him a lot of fun.

Bristol had a Ph.D. in ecology and had spent years researching giraffes in the game reserves of East Africa. He was recognized as one of Canada's leading large-mammal specialists. Tall and thin, he moved quickly and with a certain sense of delight, like a white Masai tribesman. But just as with those Serengeti natives, Bristol had a warrior's tenacity, especially when it came to conservation. If anyone would want to join me in pushing to preserve a really large wildlife sanctuary in British Columbia, it would be him.

I remember the night I first suggested the idea to Bristol. I paid a visit to his oceanfront home in Victoria, bringing along my maps of Spatsizi. Together we stretched out on his living room floor in front of the fireplace to study them and to scheme. Because of his involvement with the Ecological Reserves Unit, he, too, had been lobbied enthusiastically by Krajina on Spatsizi. Furthermore, since he was a mammal specialist, he was keen to establish a large eco-reserve for the scientific study of wildlife. Ultimately it took little effort to turn him on to the idea that together we should work to achieve the goal that both Tommy and Krajina sought.

We quickly agreed that our goal would be to protect all of the Spatsizi Plateau, not just a portion. Due to the great size of the area, this objective was very ambitious and something that had never been done before by citizen initiative. Our plan was to protect the core of the stone sheep range as British

Columbia's first wildlife-oriented eco-reserve – hopefully setting an important precedent - and then to encompass it with a much larger wilderness park. With that decided we took a pencil to the maps and drew the boundaries of the preserve we intended to protect. Once completed, we headed off for a session in the sauna.

Now taking a sauna at Bristol's was quite the tradition. Having lucked into his waterfront house in a wealthy Victoria neighborhood at a low price, Bristol celebrated a certain *joie de vivre* that was considered unbecoming by his stuffy neighbors. The sauna he had built of cedar shakes hand-split from beached logs received the most attention. He had a talent for inviting a collection of attractive bodies to indulge in regular get-togethers that included searing steam sweats followed by nude swims in cold saltwater. But controversial as these sessions might be to the neighbors, they were always an experience for the participants.

With his guests perched inside on driftwood benches, Bristol would crouch Stone Age-style before the oil drum stove and stoke it as hot as he could. The beach wood crackled and the fire roared. When the flames had heated the stove pipe to bright orange, someone would spray it with water from a hose. Then we would brace ourselves, eyes clenched and lips pursed, waiting for the wave of steam to hit. We rated each one by its intensity. The game was to see who could survive the A or A+ blasts without wilting or making a dash for the door.

One time Bristol decided to improve things by exchanging the old rusting steel pipe for a new aluminum one. The night we fired the stove up for the first time after its refit, the pipe quickly started glowing. But when we shot a jet of cold water at the pipe, it collapsed in a thick billow of smoke. Instantly, as the rapidly descending cloud choked the space, 10 slick bodies slithered across the floor to get out.

Not that this close call stopped anything. The pipe was replaced with a new steel one and the sauna tradition resumed. However, a few months later in the quest to attain an A++ blast, sparks from the raging fire shot out the chimney and set the tinder-dry structure ablaze. Fortunately everyone escaped safely before it burned to the ground.

But even this mishap didn't deter Bristol. Undaunted, he cheerily rebuilt the place, but this time with a fireproof roof. Much to the chagrin of his neighborly critics who ogled the goings-on with self-righteous disdain from behind half-closed curtains, this mark 2 version proved indestructible. And so the Dantesque tradition of the seafront saunas continued for years.

Bristol's sweat lodge was much more than some mindless pleasure palace, though. In fact, it was a veritable think tank. Sitting around naked for an hour or two, punctuated by quick ocean plunges, offered an ideal opportunity to discuss ideas. Indeed, the sapping effect of the heat stripped away pretense and tended to focus conversation on the topic at hand. Over the years Bristol's saunas attained a notoriety and attracted a range of impressive individuals: scientists, academics, senior bureaucrats, and even a Cabinet minister or two. This mix often led to innovative problem solving and, from time to time, some sweat lodge lobbying. During the course of working on Spatsizi, we used the sauna on occasion to advance our cause with a heavily perspiring key civil servant or politician.

On that first night of the campaign, with our mapping completed, we sat cooking in the hot, humid darkness and devised strategy. The key person we had to get onside was Bob Williams, the minister of forests and parks. By now Bob was the most powerful man in the B.C. government, after the premier. He headed up the Cabinet's Environment and Land-Use Committee to which the Secretariat reported. As such he was my ultimate boss, and Bristol's also. But beyond that he had also become a teacher who had shown me how the top level of government worked and who had been essential in enabling the protection of the Purcell Mountains and the Schoen Valley.

Bristol and I knew the idea of protecting Nature appealed to Williams, so we felt if we could arrange a situation for him to learn about Spatsizi, we might maneuver him into directing us to do what we wanted – get it preserved. The question was how. We weren't outside advocates, but staff. We were supposed to serve our minister, yet here, in fact, we were seeking the reverse.

Our quandary was soon sorted out with a couple of A+ blasts of steam and a cold ocean swim. Warming up again in the sauna, we hit on our plan. The campaign for Spatsizi's protection would be launched at the annual meeting of the B.C. Ecological Reserves Society, two weeks hence. Bristol figured he could get Williams – the minister responsible for the eco-reserve program – to attend and give the keynote speech. To use the meeting for our real objective, we conspired to schedule Williams as the second speaker rather than have him lead off.

In the opening slot we placed Vlad Krajina. When we told him about our plot, he was only too pleased to give one of his impassioned speeches, especially when we asked him to speak on Spatsizi and propose its protection. On the day of the meeting he spoke magnificently with his characteristic Czech political flair. To close his talk, we arranged for him to screen some of Tommy Walker's footage on the Spatsizi wilderness and its wildlife.

Waiting to speak next, Williams sat innocently through this presentation. In a few short minutes he got briefed and turned on to Spatsizi. At the end of his own remarks Williams opened the floor for a few questions and a prominent reporter from the *Vancouver Sun* asked the minister what he thought about Krajina's idea to preserve Spatsizi. Unaware that the reporter and the question were a plant – Bristol had briefed him in advance – Williams responded by saying he thought the idea was a good one and he would be glad to see it advanced.

The next day I presented the newspaper clipping that resulted from the meeting to my boss. Since Spatsizi fell within my region of the province, I asked if I had his approval to head a multi-agency task force to pursue its protection. The answer was: "Given the minister's comments, yes, by all means proceed."

And so I did. The sauna strategy had worked!

Following the customary approach, I promptly convened a group of civil servants from each of the land-use agencies: Parks, Forests, Lands, Mines, Highways, Wildlife and, of course, Ecological Reserves. At the first session I asked Bristol if he would recount the minister's Spatsizi comments at the Ecological Reserves Society meeting for the group. Because of Williams's leadership of the Cabinet's Environment and Land-Use Committee, the staff of the various agencies understood that the question we would address together was not whether Spatsizi should be preserved, but how.

Williams's power notwithstanding, my time with the Secretariat had taught me the importance of resolving land-use issues in advance of finalizing a proposal for the Cabinet so as to ensure bureaucratic support over the long term. Therefore, each agency was asked to map its resource values – again on plastic overlays – and submit these along with a technical report within six months.

This schedule would allow for field research to fill in information gaps, not that a lot of effort was needed. The resource maps showed, as so often happens, conflicts to be minor. Because of the area's northern location and the fact that so much of its terrain wasn't timbered, forestry values were low. In fact, a jogging of the boundary on the northwest corner was sufficient to remove the prime area of concern to the Forest Service.

From a mining perspective the Spatsizi Plateau overlay sedimentary rocks that aren't typically associated with metal deposits. Review of the Mines Branch's files confirmed this. As well, there were no coal and petroleum deposits (which sometimes occur with this geology) in the study area. Still, the agency wanted to sample some stream sediments just in case evidence of uranium ore bodies might be discovered.

As for the wildlife people, they already knew that Spatsizi was a top priority, but they wanted to do fieldwork to get a better fix on where boundaries should best be located. The Parks Branch, on the other hand, in a hesitant style, had initially been the only agency to resist the idea of Spatsizi's protection. "It's so large," the Parks representative said. "If we protect it we'll never be able to add any other parks elsewhere. After all, we already have preserved four percent of the province in parks." How ironic to think that 17 years later British Columbians and their government would set a minimum protection target triple that at 12 percent of the provincial land base. Fortunately a new Parks director was just taking charge of the agency. Bristol met with him and made a convincing case for Spatsizi. As a result, Parks' position changed to one of solid support for protection.

That July Bristol and I made plans to spend time at Spatsizi to familiarize ourselves with the wilderness and monitor some of the fieldwork being done. Finally, after years of hearing so much about it, I was going to see the plateau firsthand.

The trip north took two hours by bush plane through a pre-storm sky. Tossing about in the rough drafts of billowing thunderclouds, we churned our way over wild peaks and alpine. The last quarter of the flight was spent traversing Spatsizi, which was even bigger than I had imagined. Below, we spotted caribou, sheep, goats; we even saw grizzlies. When we finally landed at Hyland Post's gravel strip — Tommy Walker's old wilderness base camp — it was such a relief when the engine shut down. Then, for the first time, I heard the sound of Spatsizi: silence. Immense, remote silence.

We unloaded our gear and put it in the small log cabin where we would be staying. Then I went down and walked beside the gently flowing Spatsizi River. Two thousand feet above, the long plateau skyline beckoned. I was anxious to get up top.

The next day we got our chance when one of the wranglers offered to take us on what he described as a quick two-hour horseback ride. I had never ridden before but figured that a short trip offered a good chance to learn. So we set off, a line of chestnut horses working its way up the winding trail through buck brush. It was good going as long as I didn't inhale at the same time as the horse in front farted.

I should have been suspicious when we took the whole two hours just to reach the plateau, but I didn't care. The view from up here was different from any wilderness I had ever known. Unlike the small ridge-top alpine of southern British Columbia, the meadowlands here seemed endless. They stretched for 50 miles to the horizon and beyond. That day on the plateau I got a new, expanded sense of what wild meant. Here the outside world was a long distance away. There was no chance of walking out, as had always been possible in the south. Here, up top on Spatsizi, I felt like a speck in the vastness of Nature. It was a thrilling, if scary, sensation and I loved it. But we were never alone. Off in the distance, caribou grazed.

Since we had taken longer to reach the plateau than we should have, the guide said he would lead us down a shortcut. Whenever I have heard that word used since I have taken it with a grain of salt. Eight hours later, just before dark, our little party finally reached Hyland Post. Our route had taken us down steep slopes of broken rock where we almost lost two horses and a rider. Thrashing on horseback through trailless bush, jumping streams and bucking through muddy bogs, I got much more of a riding lesson that day than I had intended. When I finally dismounted at base camp, I bowlegged my way across the field, every bone and joint aching. Fortunately there was a log sauna on the premises. It wasn't as good as Bristol's — the blasts at best got to B+ — but at least it unstuck my body and allowed me a good night's sleep.

The next day we left by boat for a three-day trip down the Spatsizi and Stikine Rivers, and I got a whole new perspective of the country. In contrast to the broad vistas we had encountered atop the plateau, now we rode the winding water through large, incised valleys past endless spruce forests. Over the miles the river grew in size and strength. Often we turned the motor off and moved with the current. At one point we came around a bend and encountered a big black timber wolf swimming across the 200-yard-wide river. Despite the force of the current, he was in no danger of being swept downstream. He passed so close to us that I could see his pupils. Never missing a stroke, he showed no fear. Upon reaching the other side, he walked ashore, stopped, and stared intensely as only a wolf can. Then, turning, he vanished noiselessly into the trees.

On the final day our reluctant return to civilization was heralded when we passed beneath a bridge built for a railway to nowhere. Started in the late 1960s, this section was to be the northwest extension of the British Columbia Railway, but it was never finished. Although a roadbed was blasted out along the western edge of the Spatsizi, the tracks hadn't been laid. Now the empty bridge stood as a symbol of the northern boom mentality, a mega-project gone bust. Still, the threat to the frontier and this grand wilderness was clear. Someday the railway might be completed, followed by the roads and resource development

that would carve the vastness of Spatsizi into chunks. The result would be the beginning of the end of British Columbia's Serengeti.

In fact, 150 miles away a mining company was already building the Omineca Road toward the southeastern corner of the Spatsizi wilderness. Using government money, it was pushing bulldozers through blue-ribbon steelhead trout streams and across prime wildlife winter range, intent that this would become the next route to Alaska. If the mining company succeeded, the days of Spatsizi's caribou, sheep, and grizzlies were numbered. Clearly, if the wildness of the plateau was to remain, its preservation had to come quickly. Yet for all my sense of urgency that day as we headed for the pullout point, I could hardly have imagined what little time Bristol and I really had to complete our task.

I had only been back from Spatsizi a couple of weeks when I heard the news on the radio. Premier Barrett had called a snap election to be held in a month. This announcement was bad since all the polls indicated that his government was likely to lose. If that happened, Bob Williams and all the other politicians who had supported wilderness protection would be gone. In their place would be a very different government, the same old development-prone Social Credit Party that had governed British Columbia nonstop through the 1950s and 1960s, the party that had encouraged the industrial logging and mining that had devastated too much of the province. Certainly the Socreds weren't champions of Nature. Once elected, they would finish the railway and complete the Omineca Road, condemning the once-great Spatsizi wilderness to extinction.

It was time for boldness. Ignoring all bureaucratic protocols, I decided to take advantage of my relationship with Bob Williams. Without permission from my superiors I went over their heads and phoned his office directly. Somehow I got through to him. He was surprised but glad to hear from me.

"Bob," I said, "how would you like to have something to announce during the election campaign?"

"What's that?"

"Spatsizi Park. We're almost done the interagency review. I could finish things up and put a package together for Cabinet. It'll be a large park. A crowning glory."

"Great. Have it to me in two weeks. I can put it through Cabinet and we can announce it at the eco-reserves fall meeting."

Achieving that deadline required a frantic pace, but I didn't mind at all. There was a lot at stake for future generations. So one more time I drafted the order-in-council and prepared the technical brief for the Cabinet. By now the Mines Branch had confirmed that its uranium survey had revealed no deposits, so its staff was ready to come onside. The other agencies were already there.

I put together the final map with the proposed boundaries. These were remarkably similar to those Bristol and I had originally drawn, although some alterations had been made. The presentation materials were completed with photographs provided by Tommy Walker.

Cabinet approval came swiftly, with the result that on December 3, 1975, eight days before the election, Spatsizi Plateau Wilderness Provincial Park, with the Gladys Lake Ecological Reserve in its core, became a reality, all 1.75 million acres of it. Making the announcement, Williams looked pleased. He smiled at Bristol and me, almost as if he had known from the beginning what we had been up to. Naturally Vlad Krajina was delighted. The only person missing was Tommy. Despite his years of fighting for Spatsizi, his politics got in the way and he chose not to attend. That seemed sad, since it was his vision that was finally being acted upon.

As for me, it was certainly a good day, but I was also nervous. I knew that Spatsizi was far from secure. After all, while I had used the deadline of the election to get this huge wilderness protected, there was a strong chance that a new antipark government might choose to dismantle it quickly. Having jammed Spatsizi through in the last days of a doomed government, I worried that the new set of ministers might nullify the previous Cabinet's action, stating that the park had only been created as an election gimmick.

Indeed, when the returns came in, the vote confirmed expectations: Premier Barrett's government was soundly defeated. From now on there would be no one at the ministerial level to be an advocate for wilderness protection. So, with great anxiety for Spatsizi's security, I began my work with the new Cabinet.

Day by day I waited to see if the last-minute gamble would hold.

Then, suddenly, fate intervened in an ironic fashion. One morning shortly after the election I read in the local newspaper that a hunting guide licensed to operate in the new Spatsizi Provincial Park had been caught by wildlife officials with a trailer packed with illegally taken heads of moose, caribou, wolverines, and swans. One hundred and sixteen charges were laid for violating the Wildlife Act. Appalling as this incident was, over the next few days the bad news triggered remarkable good fortune. Rapidly a level of outrage seldom associated with a wildlife offense swept the province. Key to this rapidly escalating concern was the media's emphasis that this unlawful slaughter had taken place in British Columbia's newest park, one specifically created to protect the exceptional wildlife populations. And, as each new story showed more pictures of Spatsizi's magnificent landscape and its wildlife, the public's anger only increased.

Although the wildlife abuse was sickening, the issue couldn't have come at a better time. Almost overnight Spatsizi became a household name, an icon of wilderness and wildlife. Quickly the story became the focus of the conservation movement, galvanizing B.C. Wildlife Federation hunters and naturalist groups alike. (The creation of the park had been especially wonderful news for them.) Consequently the new Parks minister, Grace McCarthy, came under great pressure not just to prosecute the offender but to undertake a comprehensive review of the province's wildlife legislation.

So severe was the storm that the new government had little choice but to act immediately. Strongly decrying the despoliation that had occurred in this important new wildlife park, McCarthy, who was to become as powerful in the new government as Williams had been in the old, announced the creation of a Wildlife Review Commission.

The day I heard her announcement I knew that Spatsizi's protection was secure. With the strong, new public concern for this wilderness and its animals, there would be no way the incoming Cabinet could reverse its protection, especially given the minister's announcement. To do so would be politically reckless. Indeed, as the Wildlife Commission proceeded through its high-profile review of the poaching incident over the next year, the public's allegiance to Spatsizi, and thus the park's security, became even more resolute.

The result was that Spatsizi evolved into one of British Columbia's largest and most valued parks. Eventually it received full legislative protection under the Parks Act, making it no longer vulnerable to the future whims of a development-oriented Cabinet. Finally British Columbia's Serengeti was permanently secure.

TWENTY YEARS have passed since those nail-biting days when Spatsizi's fate hung in the balance. Since then so much development has occurred across our planet and especially in the British Columbian north country. In retrospect it is only too apparent that had Bristol and I failed to make that last-minute effort before the election this world-class wilderness would have been lost forever. If that had happened, by now the great wildlife populations of the plateau would be in decline.

Yet such historic action notwithstanding, detailed wildlife research undertaken since the park's creation has determined that the preservation work at Spatsizi is incomplete. Despite the preserve's large size, it is now known that areas of essential caribou habitat remain unprotected. While this was neither understood nor a problem in the 1970s when so much of the northern part of the province was still remote, as development now tightens its squeeze on Nature even in the Spatsizi country, some expansion is required if this large predator-prey ecosystem is to remain viable over the long term.

Furthermore, the new science of conservation biology, which focuses on species and ecosystems survival, reveals that even parks as large as Spatsizi risk becoming islands within a landscape of development unless buffers and connecting corridors to other large wildlife preserves are provided. Particularly, as climatic change threatens our planet, if extinction, especially of large mammals, is to be prevented, wildlife must have routes available to move north and south with the anticipated changes in vegetation.

As well, if natural populations are not to become weakened through genetic inbreeding, animals need to be able to roam not just within large sanctuaries but between them. And while conservation biology doesn't call for outright protection of these buffers and connectors, they will still require careful lower-intensity resource use if viable wildlife populations in the great reserves like Spatsizi are to survive.

In the two decades since Spatsizi's down-to-the-wire protection, human exploitation of the Earth has accelerated so much that we are now facing an extinction rate of 100 species per day. In effect, we are condemning to oblivion life-forms that have been evolving for four billion years. Not only is such destruction Homo sapiens' ultimate selfishness, it is also suicidal. Recently scientists have recognized that failure to stop the loss of biodiversity risks the collapse of the web of life as we know it. And if this calamity happens, scientists say the endangered species will likely be us. Recognizing, therefore, that our survival is also on the line, we begin to see that the large sanctuaries once set aside for wildlife are much more crucial now. In essence, they are biological lifeboats.

And so the significance of those actions taken in the 1970s to preserve one of Earth's great wild spaces is clear. Spatsizi serves as a modern-day Ark to ensure that wild creatures, both predator and prey, will never vanish. And just as Noah saved all in his keeping and gave the planet a future, so, too, must we cherish this wilderness place. The living heritage of Spatsizi belongs to the whole world for all time to come.

Height of the Rockies
Lessons in Power

TEN thousand years ago, when the Ice Age finally released British Columbia from its frigid grip, the southeastern Kootenay region was the first to melt free. Even as the ice retreated from the broad, low-elevation valley between the Rocky and Purcell Mountains, bighorn sheep, elk, and deer moved in to graze the new grasslands. Close behind came humankind, the K'tunaxa, the earliest people to settle interior British Columbia. They traveled north to this region from present-day Idaho.

Preceding other interior Natives by centuries, perhaps millennia, the K'tunaxa were culturally distinct from those who arrived later. Their language was unique and their technology, such as the sloping bow canoe, was different than that of others. They came to live along the banks of the Kootenay River, a major salmon-bearing tributary of the Columbia, where they established a society that has endured to the present.

Such stability was due to the abundant wildlife found in this grassland-and-montane ecosystem. In winter the animals were especially accessible: they came down from the storm-bound mountains to winter where the rain-shadow climate in the Rocky Mountain Trench kept snowfall light. During summer they migrated back to the high alpine meadows, followed by K'tunaxa hunters. In July and August these Natives camped in the higher valleys, often by a streamside opening in the spruce forest. From here the views were superb, because the Rockies, then as now, were exquisitely rugged.

This landscape possessed great power. The mountains were the tortured product of forces within the Earth that jammed immense plates of the planet's crust together, thrusting sedimentary rock skyward. Sometimes the geologic pressure was so intense that strata of limestone or shale thousands of feet thick would be crumpled into radical folds. In places stone that had once lain horizontal was pushed straight-up into sawtooth peaks that tore at the sky. Elsewhere the layering remained level but had been lifted a mile vertically. With enormous cliff faces and flanking abutments, these summits loomed like great castles on the horizon. On the highest sites remnant glaciers continued to sculpt, their meltwaters tumbling down to fill azure lakes. With parallel ranges of peaks reaching above 11,000 feet, this region displayed some of the wildest, most spectacular alpine scenery in Canada, the veritable Height of the Rockies.

The mountains supported the highest densities of mountain goats on Earth and great populations of elk and deer, as well as bighorn sheep and, later, moose, because the passes straddling this part of the Continental Divide were among the first in the Rocky Mountains to emerge after the Pleistocene ice disappeared. Soon lush, lofty meadows evolved, providing excellent grazing for large mammals. These corridors enabled passage over the ranges out to the Prairies, serving as prehistoric highways for migrating animals and humans. Palliser, North and South Kananaskis, Maiyuk, and Pass of the Clouds were the routes across, and the trails created by 100 centuries of footsteps remain today in places trenched two feet deep and eight feet wide into the alpine soil.

From the mid-15th century to the early 19th century the climate of North America cooled during what is known as the Little Ice Age. While nothing like the prehistoric deep freeze that once cloaked the land in continental ice sheets, the Little Ice Age still witnessed the expansion of alpine glaciers. The result was

that many of the alpine meadows in the Rockies were glaciated, causing a
dieback in wildlife populations and harder times for the K'tunaxa. Increasingly
it became important for these Kootenay Natives to travel east across the mountains into the Alberta prairies to hunt. However, these plains were the territory
of the Blackfoot, a people jealously possessive of their wildlife. They guarded
the main low-elevation Crowsnest Pass route through the Rockies from western intruders, forcing the K'tunaxa to take a more arduous backdoor approach
across the Great Divide in the Height of the Rockies region and on to the
prairie buffalo grounds. At Pass of the Clouds they climbed to over 8,600 feet
and then descended a huge, steep rock slide on the other side. Somehow they
picked their way down the dangerous boulder field toward the Elk River. Their
trail is still obvious today, but how they managed to lead horses down it, as they
did, almost defies imagination.

In the mid-19th century European newcomers arrived in the high mountain passes. In 1854 James Sinclair led a party of 28 settlers from Fort Garry
(now Winnipeg) over North Kananaskis Pass en route to the lower Columbia
River in Oregon Territory. At the base of the mountains a baby was born, but
it died within a day. Despite this tragedy, the settlers had little choice but to
press on. Abandoning their wagons, they climbed into the wilderness, fighting
their way through dense forest and tangled brush and over loose shale slopes
and fast rivers. It was September already, late to attempt a high-altitude Rocky
Mountain traverse. By the time they reached the pass, the snow was three feet
deep. But they persevered down the Palliser River and into the Kootenay Valley,
finally arriving on the other side of the Rockies after 30 days of walking.

In 1858 the Palliser Expedition retraced the settlers' route through Height of
the Rockies. Under the direction of Captain John Palliser it explored the southern Rocky Mountains for the British government, assessing the possibilities for
settlement and transportation. However, discovery of the easier Kicking Horse
Pass to the north and Crowsnest to the south soon directed attention elsewhere.

While Height of the Rockies may have been too ruggedly wild to allow
farming or the building of roads, its beauty certainly attracted attention. In

1902 this wilderness was the subject of an article in *National Geographic*. A few years later the B.C.-Alberta border survey of 1916 brought back news of challenging peaks. Three were over 11,000 feet, rising directly more than a mile from the valleys below. Another 18 exceeded 10,000 feet. All were unclimbed.

When word got out as to what lay at the head of the White and Palliser Rivers, mountaineers were quickly attracted. By 1919 the three highest peaks – Mount Joffre (11,210 feet), Mount King George (11,120 feet), and Mount Sir Douglas (11,070 feet) – had been conquered, as were all the 10,000-foot summits by 1930. Notably, eight of the 21 first ascents were accomplished by women, six by Miss Kate Gardiner, a schoolteacher from Banff. Old black-and-white photographs show her climbing high on the cliffs, with simple leather boots and a coil of rope. On her head she wears a 1920s hat. No Gore-Tex, fleece, or ultra-tech climbing gear in those days.

These early mountaineering expeditions were all the more remarkable since the Height of the Rockies country was hard to get to. Located on the southern boundary of Banff National Park, the region required everything to be carried in 50 miles on foot or by horse. Such remoteness notwithstanding, though, news of the exceptional animal populations – among the best in the Canadian Rockies – led to the designation of the White River Game Reserve in 1936. Created by the B.C. government, this reserve was modeled after the great East African preserves. While the intent of such protection was admirable, it wasn't well honored. Over the years logging and roads ate into the pristine wildlife habitat, putting the animals at ever-increasing risk.

By the early 1970s industrial logging had clearcut the forests of interior British Columbia so much that the explorers and Native peoples of the past would have hardly recognized the place. The logging was now well advanced up the White and Palliser Valleys toward Height of the Rockies. The destruction was watched by local recreationists, who realized that park protection was needed if the wildlife and wilderness were to remain. At the 1972 Earthwatch Conference held at Golden, these individuals proposed the area's preservation as the Palliser Wilderness. Unfortunately, at the time, there was no one with the ability of the Purcell campaign's Art Twomey to lead a Palliser offensive. So, for a few years, the forest companies were unopposed as their logging approached Height of the Rockies.

The successful protection of the Purcell Wilderness Conservancy in 1974 freed up people and provided motivation for a focused conservation effort in the southern B.C. Rockies. Before long the Palliser Wilderness Society was founded. By now citizen-led wilderness campaigns across British Columbia were multiplying, especially after such successes as the Nitinat Triangle, the Schoen Valley, and the Purcells. This growing commitment was good news for conservationists, but the logging companies were worried, as was their bureaucratic counterpart, the B.C. Forest Service. While the corporations saw parks as locking up saw logs and profits, Forest Service officials around the province increasingly perceived the new preservation advocacy as a threat to their land base, and therefore to their power.

When Kootenay residents again proposed protection, this time in the Height of the Rockies area, the pro-industry civil servants looked for a counterstrategy that would contain this threatening conservationist trend and render the proposal impotent. They decided to convene a seemingly reasonable and responsive advisory public land-use process in which the range of interest groups would provide input on how best to solve logging / preservation conflicts. But the catch word was "advisory." For neither the Forest Service nor the industry that it championed had any serious intention to allow the public to make land-use decisions, especially one that would result in a park. Instead, the plan was to bottle up and defuse environmentalist energy. Accordingly the Forest Service set up public planning meetings with people drawn not just from the conservation groups but also from the logging industry to discuss options for the Palliser Society proposal, with emphasis on the middle fork of the White River where the timber values were focused.

What the pro-industry officials hoped was that the two sides would battle things out over the negotiation table to a final stalemate that restricted preservation to areas without commercial timber. Put simply, the Forest Service's ideal solution had the industry agreeing not to log above the tree line while the conservationists gave them all the rest. From an environmental standpoint this strategy was a cynical nonstarter. Valley bottoms are where tree growth is critical to wildlife survival, since this is where animals hunker down when the weather gets rough up high. These forest areas are where the web of life is most diverse. They are where so many of the recreational trails are. To protect just the high country while the logging industry gutted the lowlands would tear the heart out of the land. There would be no meaningful future afforded by such a tradeoff, nothing vibrant to bequeath.

But even if the logging companies and the Forest Service couldn't get the public to support such an agreement, they knew the process was still stacked in their favor. After all, while the industry executives and forest bureaucrats attending these meetings were paid, the conservationists were not. They volunteered their time out of a sense of community service. Therefore, all the Forest Service thought it had to do was to drag the process out long enough and the park activists would tire and give up.

The pro-logging forces were wrong, though. The Palliser Wilderness volunteers showed extraordinary endurance. As has been repeated across North America, the commitment of conservationists to give selflessly is surely valiant. Indeed, if this volunteer effort here and elsewhere were ever put into dollar terms, the debt owed by those who enjoy the wild lands they save, and by future generations, would be immense.

Not only did the Forest Service fail to discourage the Palliser defenders, it also didn't achieve a deal that had no impact on timber. Persistence by the wilderness advocates led to a unanimous agreement by the citizens and corporate negotiators to retain the forests in the spectacular upper half of the Middle White watershed. In exchange the conservationists agreed that the companies could log the lower half of the drainage as long as this was carefully done so as not to damage the important trout fishery and wildlife populations there.

The announcement of the agreement was made in the local newspapers by the district Forest Service head John Cuthbert, the man who had overseen the process. There would be future significance to his involvement, for the Height of the Rockies drama was far from over.

However, the Palliser Wilderness negotiators had made a fatal mistake. Too naive in their trust of the government bureaucrats and in the logging industry's goodwill, they had failed to get any legal guarantee for the preservation end of the agreement from the Forest Service. So, while the logging companies busied themselves with felling the pine in the lower portion of the drainage, no protective status was designated in the upper Middle White, nor were its trees ever formally withdrawn from the commercial forest. This meant that the agreement had no legal force, and within a few years it would be disregarded by the corporations and the Forest Service alike.

Soon new multi-mile-long clearcuts were slashed to the very banks of the lower Middle White. They proved to be as bad as anything that had occurred before, creating a war zone landscape typical of industrial forestry elsewhere in the Kootenays and British Columbia. Despite their earlier promises, the companies didn't demonstrate special sensitivity for fish and wildlife values, nor did the Forest Service enforce any. Both industry and government couldn't be trusted. The extent to which this was so became clear in the mid-1980s when the lower half of the Middle White River was cut through and the companies requested permits to log the supposedly "safe" upper valley. Not surprisingly, the Forest Service began to approve their applications.

Despite past agreements, the roads and cutblocks were already marked out. Within months the companies would log the upper Middle White, the last roadless valley in the southern Canadian Rockies. Intact since the Ice Age, this wilderness camping ground of the K'tunaxa, with its magnificent peaks and abundant wildlife, had thrilled the human spirit for 300 generations. Now the essential soul of the Canadian wild earth, the very Height of the Rockies, was at risk.

PERHAPS AT THAT summer potluck dinner in August 1985 I should have known better than to wander innocently over to chat with Art Twomey. Certainly

I shouldn't have been surprised that this simple action would change my life. After all, he had done that to me before with the Purcells.

He shot his trademark grin at me from behind his famous beard, his eyes shining but serious. "I just got back from the Rockies, up in the Middle White country. You ever been in there?"

"No," I replied with naive curiosity.

"It's gorgeous. The grass in the meadows comes right up to a horse's belly. Lots and lots of wildlife there. More tracks than I've ever seen up in Banff Park or Jasper. And the mountains — spectacular! Anyway, I was up there with Bob Jamieson, you know, who helped found the Palliser Wilderness Society. He was some upset. There's flagging tape on the trees right up to the meadows. They're about to log it. Soon."

With that concise comment what had begun as a casual July party was unwittingly transformed into the first moments of my next wilderness campaign. Not that I was looking for one. In fact, I felt reluctant to undertake another issue. But as Art spoke that afternoon about the magic of this place, about the desecration of the lower Middle White, and about the foresters' broken agreement, my passion began to stir. Somehow this conversation with Art triggered interest in a place I knew nothing about. Despite living in the East Kootenay for five years, I had, in contrast with my familiarity with the Purcells, journeyed little in the Rockies outside the national parks. Now I felt the urge to learn more. So, on Art's suggestion, I went to talk to Bob Jamieson.

Bob's life was entirely wrapped up with the backcountry. Raised as a would-be wrangler in Alberta's Rocky Mountain foothills, and a wildlife biologist by training, he ran a wilderness outfitting operation in the summer and carved turns through infinite powder as a ski magazine writer in winter. Of moderate height and balding, he had a smile that glinted like a frontier card shark's. Bob wore cowboy boots, had the swagger down pat, and owned the necessary horses, guiding territory, and pickup truck, but it was to no avail. His quick mind always gave him away. He thought too much about land use, wildlife management, and strategy to be just any cowboy.

From his teenage years on, Bob had spent a lot of time in the Height of the Rockies country. Indeed, one summer he had walked south all the way from Banff, traveling along the Spray, Palliser, Joffre, and Middle White Rivers, a distance of 80 miles. Out of his love for this area he had been deeply involved in the discussions that had led to the first ill-fated agreement. Now he was angry that the logging companies had reneged and were about to savage the place. He wanted to stop them fast.

Perhaps Art and he had hatched a plan when they were up the Middle White together, because almost before I knew it Bob was talking to me, in his typical low-key style, about heading a new campaign to save this wilderness. "You've got the track record," he said, "and I think I could get several of the guide outfitters to ante up some money."

I said I was possibly interested but first I wanted to know that there was real support for this campaign, then I had to see the country myself before I made a commitment.

Within days I was invited to a meeting of the local guide outfitters association which, I thought, would prove to be interesting. I had worked with such folks in saving wilderness elsewhere, at Spatsizi and, of course, in the Purcells. And although I wasn't a hunter myself – in fact, I was a vegetarian – I had always enjoyed their company. Typically they were straightforward, salt-of-the-earth types who cared deeply about the land. While our perspective on the use of wildlife differed, we were of common mind on the need to protect the animals' habitat and the wilderness. Furthermore, most of the guides really walked their talk or, perhaps more accurately, they sauntered their drawl.

When I got to the meeting, I entered a hotel room filled with tables at which were seated a couple of dozen cowboys. They all wore big hats, mostly gray, a couple black, but all were crumpled and worn. (I have come to believe that cowboy hierarchy is determined by hat abuse. The more weathered and hard done by the hat, the greater the owner's status.) Clearly these guys weren't just a collection of urban wannabes who wore the right duds to the mall. They were still living the lifestyle.

The only person in the room that day without a hat, or cowboy boots for that matter, was me. I felt like an outsider, a marked man. But I needn't have worried, because I was introduced to the group by the local wildlife biologist, Ray Demarchi. Ray and I had known each other throughout the Purcell years, during which time he did more to defend the conservancy than any other civil servant. I considered him to be a man of courage and integrity and one of the strongest supporters of wilderness anywhere. He was deeply respected by environmentalists, guides, and bureaucrats alike.

Ray was Italian to the core. When his passions started flowing, his voice rose in lyric charisma and his arms began to gesture. As he became ever more animated and emphatic, his words swelled into a cadence of fervor that was verbally brilliant. Skilled at arguing his case, Ray was a master salesman for conservation who was capable of rousing great feeling and conviction.

As Ray began to make his pitch, I suspected the conspiracy to press me into leading the Middle White campaign included not just Bob and Art, but him, as well, particularly when he painted a picture of my wilderness accomplishments that even impressed me. By the time he finished, the posse of cowboys was thoroughly softened up. Then Bob came in to complete the deed, fixing their wallets sharply in his crosshairs.

He laid out the facts as he saw them: wilderness was disappearing fast in the Kootenays, and they knew it. The Middle White, Palliser, and upper Elk Rivers – the Height of the Rockies country – was the best left to protect in southern British Columbia. There were more animals there than anywhere else in the central Rockies. It would be tragic if the logging companies got away with their double cross. Ric, he said, knew how to do what had to be done but would need to cover his costs, so they would have to contribute. "The question's not if you're going to write a check this afternoon," he told them, "but how much. I expect a minimum of $1,000 from each of you." Everyone paid; several paid double the minimum and more. Suddenly there was enough money to fight a campaign, and if carefully budgeted, sustain it until victory.

Now that my first condition for involvement had been met I had to see if the land itself spoke to me. The demands of wilderness campaigning are huge: extremely long hours; very limited resources against strong, well-financed corporate opposition; constant frontline stress – all of which can go on for years. So I knew from past experience that I could only commit to lead this effort if my heart was fully there. Accordingly Bob passed me on to yet another of his co-conspirators. I can only presume Alan Askey intended to complete my enlistment by giving me a peak backpacking experience in Height of the Rockies.

There were just three of us on the trip: Alan (a local doctor), his wife, Marita, and me. A large man with a shock of white hair, Alan was about 60 and very fit. Both he and Marita, who was in her early forties, were cheerful types and knew these mountains well. I had a sense this trip would be a good one. Carrying a week's worth of supplies, we entered the wilderness by way of the steep Joffre Creek trail. A small, fast river, the Joffre is fed by runoff from the gray limestone summits of the Great Divide. Here, atop mountains such as Warrior Peak, you can stand with one foot on the Pacific side of North America and the other on rock drained by waters flowing east to Hudson Bay. At the base of Warrior, deep in the mud on the trail, I saw a fresh wolf track. This was quite the find for such an elusive animal so far south in British Columbia. All along the 12-mile climb to the head of the Joffre the trail was crowded with tracks of elk, deer, moose and, yes, grizzlies that had passed ahead of us.

By evening we reached Sylvan Pass, having gained 2,400 feet vertically since first hefting our packs. Now, as we took them off, we looked up a massive cliff to the summit of Mount Joffre, another mile above. Golden with sunset, the semicircular form of Joffre's face was reminiscent of Half Dome in California's Yosemite Valley. At the mountain's base we pitched our tents, cooked up stew, and then each of us went for our own after-dinner wander.

Nestled beneath the great mountain, Sylvan Pass lived up to its name: a magical basin where tendrils of alpine larch gave way to flower meadow. The concentration of wildlife use here was astounding. I had never seen such an intensely used site. There were mud wallows each 60 feet across and tracked solid with animal prints. The slopes to the basin were stepped into terracettes by the numerous elk and deer that had grazed here throughout the aeons. These trails over the pass were deep, wide, multi-laned wildlife highways. I followed one upward.

Approaching the pass, I felt the urge to stoop and move carefully. I peeked over the divide into another gentle basin. There, scarcely 200 yards from me, were 35 white-rumped elk the size of horses, the males sporting stately racks. They grazed unaware of my presence as I watched silently. This encounter was made all the more marvelous by the stunning mountains just beyond: it was my first glimpse into the Middle White Valley and the fantastic peaks of the Italian Range. Named in honor of Italy's famed World War I generals – Abruzzi, Cadorna, Swiderski – these peaks of vertical rock rose sheer for thousands of feet from the valley floor to a ridgeline of sawtooth fins. I was spellbound and have no idea how long I sat there. Finally, when it was time to get back to camp, I turned away from these mountains quietly so as not to scare the elk, only to face an equally amazing vista.

Unlike the Middle White, this new view north was a long one. I looked up the Palliser River to the glaciered massif of Mount King George in the Royal Group 15 miles away and then double that distance to the sharp matterhorn of Mount Assiniboine on the edge of Banff National Park. Transfixed, I sat back down and began to watch again: first, the big northern peaks, then behind me, the bold summits of the Middle White, and then above, towering Mount Joffre. I stayed there for hours. Dusk faded to dark, daylight into starlight, the Earth turning beneath the heavens . . .

The next day we awoke early to go exploring. Taking only light knapsacks, we walked easily up a long ridge toward a viewpoint. Once there we looked out across a great amphitheater of rock. Its geology was extraordinary: concentric tiers of limestone stepping back as if they were part of an ancient Roman coliseum. A mile across, the "structure" was built on a scale to accommodate the gods. We clambered down into this huge formation to find that weathering had rendered the rock surface into foot-long, knife-edged pinnacles. In places resistant slabs of stone remained atop the sharp-edged pedestals, obviously the benches in this amphitheater. Sitting on one of these seats and looking across the open-air gallery, I had a sense that a mythic, immortal drama might unfold. It seemed a place to witness the supernatural.

Shamans and mystics throughout history had long believed there were certain exceptional sites on our planet where conscious energy converged. Just as some Eastern religions spoke of such chakras for the human form, so, too, these wise men of antiquity believed that the global body possessed vortices where creative forces focused. Power places they called them. If they did exist, surely, I thought, this was one of them.

Even as I considered this possibility, I noticed that in ascending the terraces the sense of energy grew. Whatever was happening here, I felt as if I were still approaching and hadn't arrived yet, as if the amphitheater were merely the antechamber and not the throne room. Curious, I decided to experiment, to see if I could use my body like some psychic homing device to find the exact place where the creative force seemed to culminate. Cresting the rim and moving beyond the amphitheater, I led myself onward. Finally, when I sensed I was reaching the place of maximum power, I stepped out onto a high peninsula, a pulpit of rock, before an enormous, emerging temple.

Hundreds of feet below me, arrayed all around, was a cluster of alpine lakes, each one a different hue: cobalt, turquoise, emerald. Their shores were crenulated into countless bays. Beyond, the land dropped abruptly a half mile down to the Middle White meadows. The far skyline was torn ragged with the crest of the Italian Range. Behind and encircling this basin of lakes, the perimeter was defined by a grand progression of peaks. High above a golden eagle soared.

It was as if all the glory from this huge parabolic landscape found its focal point in the very spot where I stood. There was a sense of vibrancy. It sparkled off the waters of the lakes, it radiated in the glow of the sun from above, it flowed with the rushing streams of wild wind, and throbbed timelessly from the summits, ridges, and rock. With such concentration of grandeur it was as if a beam of conscious energy were being generated on this high promontory, spinning and swirling with the midday wind, a vast current resonating from deep within the wilderness and shining outward to infinity.

I don't quite know how to explain it, or what words to use, but somehow the power of that place changed me. It was as if something essential awakened within, and suddenly my sense of purpose in this life became clearer, my role more apparent, my will more resolved. Because there in that Rocky Mountain cathedral I touched the Tao of the wild.

How long I stood in that place, my consciousness caught in meditational grace, I can't say. But eventually, if hesitantly, and at first with semidreamlike awareness, I reconnected with the daily me and the place ironically called the real world. Slowly I summoned the will to resume.

When I rejoined Alan and Marita, we retrieved our packs from where we had left them at the pass and headed down into the Middle White. The trail was wide and well used by wildlife. Soon we reached the valley floor and set up camp in the meadow. The view that evening was so different from the previous night's. No longer atop the alpine, we now looked at great walls of rock rising all around us. The climb up the Italian Range to Pass of the Clouds the next day would be tough. That night, though, we were among the old spruce forests in the company of grizzlies. We knew that for certain. We had seen lots of fresh tracks, one and a half times the length of a man's foot, with claws extending two inches in front.

But bears or no bears, that night we went to bed soon after sundown. It had been a long, splendid day. We settled in on the same ground used by generations of K'tunaxa before us and slept with the ancestors, our dreams merely the latest of all those that had accumulated here over time. Mine were of the energy and power at that pulpit above the lakes, at that focal point where mind and matter fused into the divine, a glorification of all Creation.

Sleeping with aboriginal memories is one thing; climbing their steep trails with heavy packs is another. We were right to have been apprehensive. The uphill trek from the Middle White to Pass of the Clouds was exhausting. We chose to break it into two days with a stop halfway up at Wilcox Lake, where we found old tepee poles abandoned in the alpine. Like the people who had left them, we, too, watched the mountains for goats. It was the ideal spot to do so. This part of Height of the Rockies featured the highest number of mountain goats per acre of any place in the world. Bands of 150 animals weren't uncommon.

The next day we pressed onward following the old Native route over the pass. At the top, before heading down into the Elk River drainage, we sat and gazed back one more time into the Middle White and all its wild forests. This place meant so much to Alan. He had spent a lot of time here over the years. As well, he knew about the agreement gained and lost with the forest companies and was only too aware of what was at stake if the loggers weren't stopped soon. And so, with the forested valley as a backdrop, Alan, Marita, and I took a break from hiking and talked strategy. We plotted how to save Height of the Rockies.

Upon my return from the mountains I phoned Bob and confirmed that I would lead the campaign. I got all the back files from him and the key maps from Ray. I wanted to scope out the issue to determine what our strengths and weaknesses were. I had to figure out how we could win.

My research on Height of the Rockies made several things apparent. First, protecting the forests of the Middle White and Palliser Rivers would hardly cripple the forest industry; the timber impacts had been greatly overstated. As well, the superlative wildlife, recreation, archaeological, and scenic values found there were clearly of national, even international, distinction. In fact, the more I learned about the place, the more I was amazed that it was so little known and that it hadn't been protected decades ago. After all, this wilderness adjoined Banff National Park to the north, Alberta's Kananaskis Park on the east, and British Columbia's Elk Lakes Park on the southeast. Protection of Height of Rockies would link all these preserves into one large intact wilderness.

While making the case for preservation would be easy, victory would require much-increased publicity. The fact that the logging industry thought it could renege on past promises and get away with it proved that. Therefore, to help raise the area's profile, the old Palliser proposal was renamed the Height of the Rockies Wilderness, which would better convey the top-quality preservation values at stake. Incorporating the Rockies into the proposal's name would also intensify recognition and enable the campaign to be extended nationally should that be required.

After reviewing the situation, I was convinced that the only way to save Height of the Rockies in time was through renewed negotiations at the bureaucratic level. But unlike the 1970s Middle White talks, this time the conservationists would have to come from a place of strength and engage in power bargaining. Yet I realized as I read Bob's files and thought about other recent B.C. wilderness issues that power was something few conservationists understood yet.

Since the doomed Middle White negotiations in the 1970s, the Forest Service had gone on to convene many similar land-use processes across British Columbia. The agency always retained control and all the power by restricting such forums to an advisory role. The Forest Service also limited the mandate of these processes: the public was asked how, not whether, logging should be done. Clearly the government was intent on defusing citizen wishes for preservation, and its approach was working. Over the next 10 years many conservationists agreed to participate in good faith, naively believing they could save wilderness by negotiating with the logging industry under the rules set by the Forest Service. Since most conservationists back then were volunteers concerned about a local proposal, they had no background in bargaining. Typically they came in with the innocent belief that if they were reasonable, the other side would be, too, and a fair, balanced agreement could be reached. In fact, they might as well have banged their heads against the wall, because in virtually every case they failed.

Over time public frustration developed. For example, in the early 1980s when a process at Clayoquot Sound on the outer coast of Vancouver Island revealed that a compromise deal between environmentalists and the logging industry might possibly be reached, MacMillan Bloedel made an end run to the provincial Cabinet to stop it. The result: the company got approval to start cutting, but its actions incensed the public and led to British Columbia's first forest blockade, in November 1984. Thus began a series of citizen-corporate confrontations that escalated here at Clayoquot over the next decade until at last in the mid-1990s they attracted worldwide attention to British Columbia's logging practices.

On Haida Gwaii, 50 miles off the northwestern B.C. mainland, the home of the Haida of totem-pole renown, Forest Service-led negotiations regarding the South Moresby area started at about the same time as those for the Middle White Valley. Here, too, the agency and the companies obstructed the public by drawing talks out for almost 10 years. All the while logging continued. Citizens there finally lost patience and logging blockades were thrown up jointly by the Haida and non-Natives. Eventually this conservation pressure got so intense that it attracted Canada-wide support and the federal government was forced to declare South Moresby a national park.

The lesson here for conservationists was that mass public protests worked in contrast with the terrible results of endless Forest Service processes. Not surprisingly, environmentalism in British Columbia quickly became more high-profile and radical. Unfortunately for Height of the Rockies a massive show-down approach wasn't an option. It isn't that we couldn't have organized such an action, as had been done at Nitinat years earlier. There just wasn't time to create that kind of campaign. After all, South Moresby took 10 years of simmering to achieve its profile. By contrast Height of the Rockies was hardly known, even in the Kootenays, let alone the rest of Canada. Yet the logging companies were already at the edge of the upper Middle White. Obviously the only choice we had was to wage a fast, low-profile "finesse" campaign rather than the large, populist "flagship"-style one used on Haida Gwaii. Therefore, if the lesson from past wilderness bargaining in British Columbia was that conservationists failed because they didn't negotiate from a position of strength, then this time they would have to learn about power.

Certainly their industrial negotiating counterparts knew how to play this game and get exactly what they wanted. The logging industry was consistent in its intention to keep the cut high, maximize profits, and stop the conservationists dead in their tracks. The fact that environmentalists had yet to learn

what unions had long known was why they continually lost: if you want to succeed at the table, your negotiators have to have leverage, otherwise companies
don't take you seriously. That is why labor leaders rely on strikes to give them
clout. It is the source of their power.

The naivete and lack of real strength of the conservationists meant that
logging companies and the Forest Service could humor, obstruct, and defeat
them without consequence. Hence, the talk-and-log tradition. So, in order
not to repeat history at Height of the Rockies, we had to find the power
needed to win. When we reviewed the background files, we soon found three
strong arguments.

The most potent one related to the fact that John Cuthbert, the civil servant who had headed the Middle White negotiations in the 1970s, had been
promoted to chief forester of the B.C. Forest Service. It was clear he could be
pressed. His integrity and the credibility of the Forest Service could be put
on the line just at the time the agency most needed to hold the public's trust.
Due to the ever more strident outcry for wilderness protection in the 1980s at
places such as Clayoquot and South Moresby, the effectiveness of the Forest
Service's preservationist containment strategy was clearly being challenged
now. To remain viable the agency needed to convince the public that its land-
use processes were undertaken fairly and in good faith. Because of the increasing conservationist statements to the contrary, this task was becoming tougher
for the agency to achieve.

That being so, consider the strategic significance of a front-page clipping
from a Kootenay newspaper that I found in Bob Jamieson's files. In it then
Regional Forester John Cuthbert extolled the land-use agreement that he said
would reserve the upper Middle White from logging. The article went on to
detail the Forest Service's commitment to honor the agreement. In light of
what was actually happening in the Middle White now, imagine if this article
was rereleased to the provincial media, showing that, as the current chief
forester, Cuthbert, and therefore the Forest Service, was reneging on the
agency's word. Just think how this would devastate the Forest Service's land-use

credibility and its means of sheltering the logging industry across the province from environmentalists.

Add to this the fact that my research showed the White River Game Reserve was still in force, which meant that the logging the Forest Service had permitted there over the years was illegal. Surely this revelation would create an even bigger uproar across British Columbia if we chose to publicize it. And as final leverage, consider Native land claims that had never been settled in this part of British Columbia. With no treaty signed, logging in K'tunaxa territory was illegal on this count, as well. The Palliser Wilderness Society had already linked up with this First Nation and it had been clear about its support for Height of the Rockies' preservation. The K'tunaxa wanted to keep the forests and the wildlife of this traditional hunting territory intact.

It was clear to me that these three arguments gave us the power needed to win in negotiations. To strengthen our position, though, we needed to galvanize public support, not just in the Kootenays but throughout British Columbia and beyond. Using tactics drawn from the Nitinat days, we proceeded to photograph the wilderness extensively on the ground and from the air. We then produced a compelling multimedia show, which we took on the road. Over the next few months, assisted by John Lindhorst, a young dedicated biologist, we spoke to countless organizations: conservationists, naturalists, hunters, service clubs, and hiking clubs. We printed up brochures and tabloids and undertook endless media interviews. Quickly the story of Height of the Rockies became known: its wild beauty, its imminent danger, and the duplicity of the forest industry. From all this publicity we fashioned a province-wide public support base that would empower us at the eventual negotiations.

The next step involved advance lobbying in the provincial capital to further determine who our political and bureaucratic allies and opponents were likely to be once we launched the negotiation phase. There were few surprises except for one big one. When I met with the new deputy minister for the environment, he astounded me by saying flat out, "There will be no new parks created in the Rocky Mountains. Parks Branch will not support Height of the Rockies' preservation."

He was so final in his pronouncement that I decided not to bother wasting further energy on him. I suppose I might have been dismayed, but since this man had previously been a personnel director, I wasn't really surprised by his stance. Still, the depressing pattern of the Parks Branch as an obstacle to preservation was repeated yet again, despite the fact that its legal mandate was to protect Nature.

This setback could have posed some difficulty, enough to take two years of lobbying at higher levels to overcome, time we didn't have. Forced to innovate, Bob and I decided to try an unlikely idea that we had been considering for a while. Why not, we thought, follow the lead of the United States and New Zealand by expanding the B.C. Forest Service's role beyond timber harvest to include wilderness protection? While this idea might seem akin to putting the fox in charge of the henhouse, there weren't any better alternatives.

Despite the B.C. Forest Service's pro-development mind-set, I knew that American conservationists had originally faced the same situation. By making individual wilderness areas there so popular, so sacrosanct that they became politically impossible to log, and then by amending legislation to legally require the U.S. Forest Service to protect designated wildernesses, that agency had become a major manager of wilderness. The question was: could we do the same in British Columbia and make Height of the Rockies the first designated Forest Service wilderness area? Surely this was like asking whether we could change a leopard's spots.

Being an optimist, I asked myself: what was the worst that could happen? Certainly nothing worse than would occur if we didn't give it a shot. By contrast, if we succeeded, not only would we protect Height of the Rockies, but in future we would have two agencies in government to play against each other, potentially leading to a place where they would compete to protect wilderness. That was certainly what had happened in the United States. Then perhaps we wouldn't be so vulnerable to the Parks Branch's traditional reluctance to act.

Whether we could pull it off, whether we could indeed preserve Height of the Rockies, would depend on how well we bargained and how well we played the aces in our hand. And so the game began. On a cold December morning Bob and I drove to the District Forest Service office in Invermere to present our ultimatum and set the stage for negotiations on our terms. Just like successful athletes, we had psyched ourselves into a winning space.

We walked into a room containing several Forest Service bureaucrats. The most senior among them was District Manager John Little. They all seemed ill at ease. Bob and I had mapped out our roles, and we now started to work as a tag team. Right off the top we came out tough. We told them that we intended to save Height of the Rockies and that we knew we would succeed. We said we weren't asking them to consider a proposal that would result in some drawn-out process. Instead, we were putting them on notice. We were ready to put intense pressure on the very top of government and they were likely to get caught in the squeeze. Given my wilderness track record, which by then was known around the Forest Service in British Columbia, they knew we were serious.

We told them it was really quite simple. The Forest Service had a choice: did it want a war on its hands – because if so, we had the means and resolve to launch one – or did it want to reach a graceful resolution? To create pressure we then gave them a glimpse of our cards. We showed them the Height of the Rockies publications and multimedia presentation, all professionally designed. We shared with them the resource assessments that confirmed the international significance of the wildlife, recreation, and historic values. We discussed the calculations we had made on timber and the job effects of the proposal, which confirmed that impacts would be low. We shared the tourism economic assessment we had undertaken, which proved that employment to be gained from protecting the area would be substantial.

Next we revealed the scale of the public coalition we had assembled to fight this campaign. We asked them if they were ready for a South Moresby-style fight in the Kootenays. And finally, to maximize the tension, we talked about the Middle White agreement and how the Forest Service had reneged on it. We asked how they thought the B.C. public would react if such a revelation got out at the very time the agency was trying to retain the people's trust. We intimated that they faced quite a credibility crisis, especially if it became known that the current chief forester was the person who had headed the earlier process. Without being overly specific we made it plain that we had the concrete evidence we needed to slam the agency in the public eye. In short, we presented an unbeatable hand and told them we intended to use it to win.

After using the stick, we then offered the carrot. Bob and I said we didn't much care which agency managed the Height of the Rockies Wilderness as long as it was preserved. We knew the Forest Service was worried about losing control of part of their land base to other agencies, such as the Parks Branch, because of the fast-increasing public demand for wilderness. Since territory is power in bureaucracy, we knew the last thing the Forest Service wanted was to give up acreage.

It was a hard-hitting, concise meeting. Having said our piece, we soon took our leave. We weren't interested in having our position weakened. We wanted to leave the Forest Service staff anxious, which we succeeded in doing. They immediately contacted headquarters, and within a couple of days we got a response. Yes, the Forest Service was interested in finding a solution to protect Height of the Rockies as wilderness, particularly if it could become the managing agency. To achieve this, the District Forester was prepared to convene negotiations immediately.

While this development was a good first step – the Forest Service was talking about preservation, not another talk-and-log charade – we still made it clear that we weren't interested in the typical process approach. We repeated that we intended to protect Height of the Rockies, and fast. If the Forest Service could come up with a means to do this, fine. Otherwise we warned them that we would soon move the issue to a much higher profile.

Once more the agency responded quickly. It proposed confidential negotiations that would include Bob and me for the conservationists, a few senior Forest Service staff members, a handful of senior forest company officials, and a couple of key Environment Ministry personnel. Bob and I said we were willing to give it a try, but only for a couple of months. If we didn't get results, we said we would take the issue public. To cover all bases, we immediately went to Victoria and conveyed the same message to then Forest Minister David Parker and the chief forester. Take us seriously, we said, and get to preservation, or there would be a mess. They understood.

Negotiations began quickly, and while the logging companies at first attempted to obstruct, Bob and I were determined not to be blocked. We let them know they would suffer greatly if the talks failed. In order to move things along, Bob and I pursued a negotiating strategy that developed a "can do" psychology around the table. This tactic fostered a group investment in success even as we continued to ratchet up the tension. First, we focused effort on reaching agreement on those easy locations where timber values were least affected. By doing this, the group, including the logging companies, moved quickly off the question of whether to protect Height of the Rockies and onto where to preserve.

With agreement reached on noncontentious sites, the talks increasingly concentrated on smaller and smaller land areas of ever greater timber and protection importance. Just as a child's magnifying glass can focus the light of the sun to a point that it ignites something combustible, so the conflict dynamic around the table heated up. The center of this storm converged on the prized forest of the Middle White Valley.

Bob and I then pulled out all the stops. We sat down with District Forester John Little and his superiors in the executive of the Forest Service and revealed in detail the materials we had on the agency and its past handling of the Middle White. At the same time we reemphasized the potential for resolving the dispute through a Forest Service-administered wilderness area.

Meanwhile, away from the negotiations we began to leak to the public indications of the success of these secret talks. We published a major supplement in the regional newspaper paid for by advertising from Kootenay merchants that not only extolled the wonders of Height of the Rockies but characterized the negotiations as a tremendous land-use achievement in the making. Emphasizing that the two sides were now only in disagreement over a few thousand acres in the Middle White Valley, we turned up the public heat on the logging companies. We gave the process such an intensely positive spin, in contrast with the then concurrent South Moresby road blockades, that the industry would either have to concede on the Middle White or take great public blame if the talks failed.

It was all sheer psychology, as power negotiations always are. It was also about which side could exert the most pressure on the Forest Service. The measure of our effectiveness came one memorable day when again we sat down at the table, forest companies on the other side, Forest Service staff at either end, with Bob and I alone representing the conservationists. As always we were outnumbered but not outgunned. Once more District Forester John Little chaired the session. He opened by stating he had some comments to make.

Little began by saying he had just been in contact with his superiors and they had decided that it was time to finalize things. No doubt they were feeling the heat of the environmental campaign. He said that the minister and the Forest Service executive had decided they wanted Height of the Rockies to be formally preserved by the summer, just two months away. It would be established as the first Forest Service wilderness area, and to enable this the Forest Act would be amended within the month in the Legislature, thus allowing the agency to protect wilderness legally. Secretly, behind show-nothing poker faces, Bob and I smiled to each other.

Little continued by saying that as far as the government was concerned, 95 percent of the area of Height of the Rockies had been agreed to by all parties, and that if agreement couldn't be reached by the group for the remainder of the Middle White, the Forest Service would impose a compromise. It would draw a line between the companies' desire to log all the trees and the environmentalists' desire to save everything. He said that while he believed such a solution could probably work for both sides, it was his preference that the group itself finish what it had started by reaching agreement on this last piece.

And then Little's voice changed. He let go of his objective bureaucratic jargon and began to speak with feeling. He talked about wilderness and why for him personally preserving it was important. He talked about sitting under old-growth trees and watching the stars, how the sense of living in Nature was essential to being a Canadian. He talked of the importance of handing the wild on to the future. Speaking from his heart with a quiet, poetic passion, he sounded like one of the legendary conservationists from the past. In particular, I thought of Aldo Leopold, the visionary in the U.S. Forest Service who had helped found that agency's wilderness protection traditions in the 1930s.

These were extraordinary words for a senior B.C. Forest Service officer. I had never heard anything like them before, nor had anyone else in the room. I began to think that if there were others with his courage within the agency, perhaps there could be a real evolution and the idea of a forest wilderness system in British Columbia could work. After all, it had proved successful in the United States.

Looking around the table, I saw that everyone was listening intently, not just to his words but to the spirit of what he was saying. And then a most amazing thing happened. As John Little spoke, a peacefulness permeated the room, and with it, this group of longtime adversaries — the logging executives, the enviros, and the bureaucrats — were transformed. They changed right before my eyes and became . . . people.

A new ease developed as well as a sense of mutual respect and empathy. For the first time everyone around the table revealed glimpses of their human sides. No longer locked as negotiators, nor even opponents, we just became folks. Suddenly I found myself looking across the table to the man sitting opposite and having some sense of what his world might be like. And I also felt that he could see mine. Because somehow with Little's words an evolution from power to the personal had occurred.

With this shift confrontation became collaboration. Responding to Little's urging, the group addressed how it might overcome the last obstacle dividing us in Height of the Rockies. As ideas were traded around the table, I mused at how this could ever be accomplished. And then a voice drifted into my mind. It whispered, "The Middle White Valley is old enough to take care of itself." A couple of seconds passed before I grasped the meaning, but when I did, I chuckled to myself and thought, Of course. After all, the valley had existed there since long before the Ice Age, long before any of us sitting here, and it would continue to remain long after we were gone. What the message of these words seemed to say was: "Have faith in the possible."

My attention returned to the table. Shortly after, a proposal was put forward concerning where a line might be drawn. And it even looked as if it could work. All the key preservation values of the valley would be protected: the meadows, the viewscape, the key wildlife habitat. Although some area would have to be given up, it wouldn't be a lot, only about 700 acres. Still, I worried over the loss of even those trees, so Bob and I requested a recess in order to caucus. We went off by ourselves to weigh the options.

On the one hand, he and I agreed we could hold out for everything, but if the other side balked, the talks would fail and we would be faced with years of fighting. That is, provided we could hold off the logging companies that long, which was unlikely, and the Forest Service didn't impose a worse compromise. Was it wise to go for all or nothing when we were now so close to getting almost everything we wanted? On the other hand, if we accepted the proposal, would we regret our actions later? Would we give up those last acres that we might otherwise protect?

Try as we might, logic couldn't give us a clear answer, so we went back and forth, caught in a mental deadlock. And then, just when either choice seemed impossible, again those words spoke in my mind: "The Middle White Valley is old enough to take care of itself." With that I realized it was time to allow destiny to assert its own course.

"Why don't we toss a coin?" I suggested.

The tension broke and we both howled with laughter. "If people could only see what all this has come down to, they'd never believe it," Bob said, even as he dug in his pocket for a quarter. He flipped it and the coin told us it was time to settle. We went back in to conclude negotiations. Successfully.

Two months later, on August 22, 1987, the group got together one last time at 7,000 feet in the alpine, right below the glaciers and great cliffs of the Royal Group. It was an extraordinary day accented by a deep blue sky. The Forest Service had arranged helicopter transportation, and now the negotiators, along with a cluster of key conservationists, local mayors, heads of the Forest Service, and B.C. Forest Minister Parker, gathered. Together they officially designated Height of the Rockies as British Columbia's first Forest Service Wilderness Area.

There were speeches and media and a sense of accomplishment. Only nine months after Bob and I had entered that Forest Service office, 140,000 acres of wilderness received official protection as Canada's first wilderness area. Additionally a further 27,000 acres east of the Pass of the Clouds divide, where Alan and Marita Askey and I had stopped to strategize, was also protected as a result of our campaigning. This adjoining preserve was to be known as the Elk Lakes Recreation Area. All of this was the result of intensive conservation power campaigning as well as a final extraordinary effort by a most remarkable forester. By doing what he had done, John Little had enabled us to put Height of the Rockies over the top, and in his own way he had helped to redress the actions of his predecessors.

A few nights after that alpine ceremony the conservationists and the guide

Celebrating the Height of the Rockies preservation cowboy-style with Bob Jamieson (upper left), guide Cody Tegart, his mother Doreen, father Jim, and myself.

outfitters took over a countryside pub to celebrate. It was quite the festive time and cowboy hats were in abundance. Of course, Bob Jamieson was there, as were Alan, Marita, Art Twomey, and Ray Demarchi, as well as the guide outfitter Cody Tegart and his father and mother who had long made their living in Height of the Rockies. And there was someone else I had never met before: a bright-eyed, energetic, attractive brunette named Dona-Lyn Reel. I didn't know it then, but that night at the Height of the Rockies celebration party I met the woman who would become my close partner in life, love, and conservation.

During the past several years, my wife, Karen, and I had grown apart in our style of living and aspirations for life. Eventually, by the time the Height of the Rockies campaign began, we had sadly agreed to separate. While no longer married, fortunately we were able to retain a warm friendship that flourishes even to this day. In the wake of our breakup, the preoccupation of the intense efforts to protect this Rocky Mountain wilderness helped to blunt the melancholy for what we had lost. But it couldn't fill the empty loneliness I endured.

So on that celebratory night when I unexpectedly encountered Dona at the Bull River Inn, I was doubly delighted. In the ensuing years Dona and I began to live together and work increasingly as a close team on wilderness issues throughout the province. The campaign for the Tatshenshini River alone would occupy many years. Although we eventually moved to the small coastal town of Gibsons just north of Vancouver, we continued to keep informed about events in the Kootenays, since Dona's children still lived there and my work on the Purcells and Height of the Rockies had led to many ongoing friendships.

So, in the early 1990s, when the citizen land-use planning process conducted by the B.C. government's Commission on Resources and the Environment (CORE) focused on the East Kootenay to complete the wilderness system there, we monitored the progress. Everything seemed to be on track until one day I learned to my horror that Height of the Rockies was being considered for downgrading from its protection status. Arguing that a Forest Service Wilderness Area didn't fit the full preservation description of a provincial park, the resource industry attempted to split the local conservationists by saying they could have either an expanded Purcell Wilderness Conservancy (which they were seeking) or the Height of the Rockies as park, but not both. This was a classic divide-and-conquer ploy. As well, it looked as if the industry might break a previous negotiated deal for the Middle White Valley a second time. Most of the pressure came from the mining companies, which wanted to build an exploration road up the Middle White Valley into Sylvan Pass and the nearby basin of lakes.

Increasingly it looked as if the conservation position might fracture. Since the Purcell Mountains were located much closer to the major towns in the East Kootenay, they were better known than Height of the Rockies. In fact, it turned out that none of the negotiators for the conservationists had ever seen Height of the Rockies, so they had little idea just how important the forest, wildlife, and biodiversity values of this area were. It was easy to see how this had happened. A small group of very dedicated individuals had put in 18 months of hard effort at the table, working to safeguard the region's environment in the face of tough industry pressure. They had been stretched too thin and hadn't had the time to field-check Height of the Rockies firsthand.

For me the idea that the Purcells might be played off by the resource companies against Height of the Rockies was my worst nightmare. After all, these wildernesses were both my children. As far as I was concerned, there could be no trade here. Both areas had to be held. Knowing that time on the CORE process was running out, I quickly worked to link up with the conservation team, which wasn't easy. Despite my past wilderness work in the Kootenays, it had been eight years since I had moved to the coast. At first I was viewed by some as an interloper. The resource industry had inspired fears that a choice had to be made between the two wilderness areas, which caused some conservationists with a strong allegiance to the Purcells to suspect that I wanted to knock out their extension proposal.

I felt sick that there might be fragmentation in our ranks. I felt even worse that I had to be fighting to save Height of the Rockies after it had already been protected. As the CORE process moved toward a final Cabinet decision, the pressure put on the conservationists by the resource industry became intense. While the official position of the East Kootenay conservationists remained that both the Purcells and Height of the Rockies must be protected, internally the tension to choose one over the other became extreme. My ability to influence matters was limited by my outsider status. So it wasn't until one of the environmental negotiators, John Bergenske (an old compatriot from the early Purcell days and a longtime friend), agreed to fly over both wilderness areas that the two-park strategy finally won out with our people.

When John saw the grandeur of Height of the Rockies, the wildlife ranges, and the old-growth forests of the Middle White, he was able to report after the flight to his co-negotiators that we had to stay the course. There could be no trade-off. Both an expanded Purcell Wilderness and Height of the Rockies had to be passed on to the future.

To their credit and my great relief the other conservationists agreed. Working together in the final weeks, we succeeded in overcoming the resource industry's opposition and convincing the Cabinet to expand the Purcell Wilderness *and* to upgrade Height of the Rockies to provincial park status. Similarly the Elk Lakes Recreation Area also received full park protection. Despite the conviction of John Little, the events of the past few months had demonstrated that, in British Columbia, Forest Service wilderness status wasn't secure enough to guarantee protection over the long term.

That summer in 1995, after Height of the Rockies finally received full protected status, I revisited it for the first time since the alpine dedication ceremony eight years earlier. With great satisfaction I again hiked up the old K'tunaxa trail of the Middle White Valley into the provincial park that I had been told once would never happen. This time I backpacked in with Dona and my 12-year-old daughter Sheena. Thanks to her years of growing up with the Tatshenshini issue, Sheena knew a lot about wilderness and was a strong, enthusiastic backpacker. But although she had heard a lot about Height of the Rockies, she had never been there before.

All day long the three of us walked up through the forest that had been saved in the mid-1970s, lost through reneged agreements in the early 1980s, protected as Forest Service wilderness in the latter part of the decade, almost lost again in the 1990s, and now at last fully protected as a provincial park. Like the climb up the trail to Sylvan Pass, it had been an arduous ordeal.

After camping that night at the pass, the next day I took Dona and Sheena to my mountain temple. Up the ridge, across the ancient amphitheater, and then on toward the promontory, we stepped with reverence out into the sacred whorl of energy. Together we witnessed the presence of Creation, with the lakes below shining.

Across the valley on the rough-edged horizon of the Italian Range I could make out Pass of the Clouds. It carved a gap across the Great Divide just below Abruzzi Glacier, the last remnant of the Ice Age. Caught in the magic of the moment, I thought of those 300 generations of K'tunaxa who had climbed that route to hunt for sheep and goats. I thought of the European explorers who had passed along these valleys, the mountaineers who had made the first ascents, and more recently all those conservationists who had fought to keep this place still wild, still beautiful. And as the energy coursed through my soul, as I stood in this place so special with my closest loves, I wondered how such majesty had come to be and might ever remain.

Then it was as if the land itself spoke to me with those words I had heard years before at the moment of truth: "The Middle White Valley is old enough to take care of itself." And I smiled. Now at last I understood the transition that had taken place that afternoon around the negotiation table. Now I understood the force that had so moved the people in the room. For what had started as a power negotiation over wilderness had, in the end, been influenced by the Power of wilderness itself.

High above where the three of us now stood, wheeling on the column of energy that shone forth from this wilderness place onto infinity, a golden eagle soared. Eternally.

Babine River

The Economics of Preservation

S TEELHEAD are the ultimate North American freshwater sport fish. Thirty pounds of fighting spirit, this sea-run rainbow trout returns to spawn in the waters of its birth like a salmon. Clean, fresh rivers with deep pools to hole up in, that is where steelhead lurk.

They are beautiful creatures: blue-green backs, crimson flanks, silver underneath, strong heads, and oversize tails. Steelhead are built for endurance and strength, requirements necessary to make their long upriver return to ancestral spawning beds. These fish are an elite catch. They don't give up without a fierce, prolonged battle. Once hooked, the muscled, full-bodied males dive deep in the backwater, lashing in a powerful tug-of-war. The females react with a more frenzied leaping, ricocheting off the wave tops to try to break away. And many times an angler will flycast the pools and riffles, hooking into a big steelhead finally, playing the line inward and back out for an hour, only to have the fish escape.

For the river fisherman the experience of catching a steelhead is legendary, something that is only partly due to the animal's feistiness. Steelhead rivers have always been small in number on North America's West Coast. Just getting to a steelhead stream is still no guarantee you will catch your quarry. Both skill and luck are required, which adds to the challenge and the fish's mystique. Indeed, merely finding a steelhead can be tricky. First, you have to get intimate with the river, learning its currents, channels, and pools. Then perhaps you can locate exactly where the fish skulk.

Once you have found them, then they must be enticed, which means figuring what insects they are eating that day and choosing or tying a fly to mimic, to lure. Ultimately it comes down to having the graceful artistry to cast this morsel precisely and present it just so. Then, after a great deal of trying, if you are especially fortunate, a steelhead might bite. Maybe.

But once hooked, there can be no uncertainty. The subsurface strength that yanks and yards is obvious. Your line races out, the reel singing, the rod tip flexing wildly. Then, for as long as it takes, you and the steelhead dance in primal choreography, tethered together by nylon monofilament. Even when you stand with rubber hip waders on in waist-deep water, your legs feel cold. The pulling on your arms is rough and emphatic. Again the fish streaks away with the line, only to be reeled once more carefully inward. Out, then back, out, then back, breaking now to the side and then jumping high. And so it goes, one thrilling minute after another.

The skill required to land a steelhead demands strategy, patience, strength, and finesse. If you have all these talents, and chance is also with you, then you might possibly bring the warrior to shore. Leaning down to stream level, you cradle the grounded giant, now gone quiet from fatigue. Holding the fish close in your arms, you can feel its life force. This is a magical moment, the reason for your passion. And always you never fail to be amazed at how large and vital a steelhead is.

Carefully you remove the barbless hook from its mouth. Ecstatic, your heart still pounding, perhaps you have a picture taken even as your trophy washes in the water. You stroke this river wonder almost lovingly and rock it gently, gills forward to the current. For a moment time stands still. All motion is suspended. But too soon the spell is broken. With a shudder the creature reasserts its life, muscled tension rippling through firm flesh. The great tail thrashes powerfully as you ease your embrace. And then with strength renewed the steelhead rockets forth into pure, fresh waters. Free once more.

Quite simply, river fishing doesn't get any better than matching wits with these prize fighters in wilderness waters. As a result, over the years the steelhead's reputation spread. Increasingly anglers began coming from around the world to the Pacific coast to try their luck. But even as the fame of the great fish grew, its habitat was already being lost. Where originally rivers from Baja to Alaska had supported runs, decades of dam building and development forced the wild populations in the United States and Mexico toward extinction. Only in British Columbia did the species remain strong, making this place the world Mecca for steelhead fishermen.

Yet such distinction didn't remain unthreatened for long. By the 1970s and early 1980s, the tragic pattern of steelhead devastation had crossed the border. With each passing year destruction of the runs crept northward up the British

Steelhead magic: some precious moments of contact.

Columbia coastline. On Vancouver Island the once-famed Cowichan, Camp-bell, and Puntledge Rivers came under assault from mining pollution, urban settlement, and especially logging. With each West Coast rain, soil eroded from clearcuts further clogged spawning gravel and suffocated ever more steelhead eggs. Quickly the runs declined.

Only on the B.C. north coast, and particularly in the Skeena watershed, did the steelhead populations still seem healthy. But even here old-timers said the fishing wasn't what it had once been. The blue-ribbon Kispiox River started to feel the impact of industrial forestry, as did the Morice and Bulkley Rivers. With each passing year the number of cutblocks increased, more miles of log-ging roads were built, and the silt loads entering the waterways rose. As had been the case all up the western seaboard, it was the steelhead that paid the mortal price of such development. The situation continued to worsen until by the late 1980s only one major B.C. steelhead stream remained in pristine wilderness health – the Babine River.

Rising to the east of the mountains I had worked with Joe L'Orsa to pro-tect years earlier, the Babine River is fed by British Columbia's largest natural lake. (Like the river, both the mountains and this lake have the same name.) The upper part of the 60-mile-long river flows across the flat terrain of the Interior Plateau before cutting through mountains to join the Skeena River. From this juncture the Skeena runs a further 250 miles to the sea.

While the Skeena River had become a major communication corridor, with railway, highway, and power lines paralleling it, the Babine remained intact. Here, by contrast, the only travelers were the 13,000 steelhead that swam along with much larger numbers of salmon (1.75 million). In summer and fall, when the run was on, grizzlies came down to fish, and so did people. After all, the Babine River was known internationally for consistently producing record-size specimens that weighed up to 39 pounds.

Like local anglers, the fishermen who came from far and wide based them-selves at three small lodges, the only structures on an otherwise wild river. To protect the Babine's superlative steelhead run, the B.C. Fish and Wildlife

Branch kept the number of anglers low with a limited-entry system. As well, a catch-and-release policy ensured that the Babine would never be depleted through overfishing.

With such care being taken, it looked as if the Babine might be the one world-class steelhead river that would buck the trend of destruction. Given the Babine's famed fish and its pure waters, the hope was that the mistakes made elsewhere might be avoided. However, here, too, the dark day arrived when foresters began to map out clearcuts along the length of this last pristine river.

As if intent on completing the trashing of steelhead streams, in 1987 the B.C. Forest Service prepared a business-as-usual plan to turn the riverside forests into stump lands, which would certainly cause major spawning losses from soil erosion. As well, the access to be created by the logging roads would turn the Babine into a short-lived anglers' free-for-all. The steelhead would get clobbered by overfishing, not that this seemed to matter much to the local Forest Service bureaucrats. Their attitude was: "Trust us, we won't hurt the fish. After all, we just want the trees, not the river."

Yet given the agency's track record elsewhere, it looked as if the days of the Babine steelhead were numbered. In fact, such destruction was imminent. Demonstrating an all too typical lack of regard for values other than fiber, the foresters planned to build a logging road and bridge right across the most important steelhead spawning bed on the river. They couldn't have picked a worse spot to endanger the run.

As soon as the local steelheaders learned of these plans, they were alarmed, as were the Fish and Wildlife Branch and the fish camp guides. Together they appealed to the district forester, but he was unwilling to change plans. Using economics as his justification he said tersely that the Babine trees were too valuable to leave standing and that too many logging jobs depended on "harvesting them."

As appeasement, the agency agreed to a public input process. Lacking any meaningful leverage, though, the conservationists got nowhere. Even as the talking continued, so did the surveying for the road and the permitting of cutblocks. It was bureaucratic belligerence and logging industry arrogance at its worst. Soon

153

a world-renowned sport fishery, the last trophy steelhead wilderness river still intact and one of Canada's premier salmon runs, would be irreversibly devastated.

What made things more tragic was that this type of ruination had prevailed so often before. All across British Columbia, fishing, hunting, rafting, and wilderness guides were finding their livelihood destroyed, along with the wild country, as chain saws slashed in and the trees were hauled out. Horse trails were bulldozed under to make way for logging roads, serenity was lost to the roar of skidders, wild vistas were hacked into squares. As clearcuts and roads advanced, wildlife habitat and the frontier setting retreated. Consequently, in many parts of British Columbia, the animals were getting harder to find and fewer visitors came. Tourism businesses suffered; guides and outfitters lost their livelihood and their lifestyle.

That such damage could be permitted in a place promoting itself to the world as "Super-Natural British Columbia" was astounding. In the wake of Vancouver's Expo 86 world's fair, tourism had become the province's largest land-based employer. It supported 125,000 full-time jobs and was the second biggest source of natural resource revenues. Already British Columbia had the largest adventure tourism industry in North America, offering sport fishing, hunting, wildlife viewing, river running, trail riding, hiking, and backcountry skiing. Furthermore, on the famed Inside Passage to Alaska, 400,000 cruise ship passengers a year came to experience the wild forest coastline. In short, British Columbia's tourism industry relied on a top-quality wild environment to attract visitors from around the world. Given all these facts, it was madness that the province allowed the logging companies to savage irreplaceable natural treasures like the Babine River.

Yet the old reality continued, resulting in Super-Natural British Columbia remaining under siege by an insatiable logging industry. To forge resistance to this threat, a number of adventure tourism operators banded together in mid-1987 to form the Wilderness Tourism Council (WTC) of British Columbia. Its members felt that it was high time for the new importance of tourism to be reflected in land-use decisions.

Co-founding the WTC were Bob Jamieson, a hunting guide and friend from the Height of the Rockies campaign, and Johnny Mikes, a raft operator from Tatshenshini country. Early in 1988 they asked if I would serve as executive director. Funding was very tight, so the offer was far from lucrative. Nevertheless, since it promised to be challenging and might make a difference, I accepted with enthusiasm.

The goal of the WTC was to link the industry together formally in defense of wilderness, which was something new. Even though environmentalists had long pointed out that protecting the land was good for tourism, never before had the operators themselves organized to safeguard the resource they most depended on – wild, natural integrity.

It is strange that such a council took so long to coalesce. Certainly the idea that protecting Nature made economic sense wasn't new. After all, tourism had been the driving force behind the creation of the world's earliest wilderness preserves. Both at Yellowstone – America's first national park – and its Canadian counterpart, Banff, protection of spectacular wild landscapes was seen as the way to attract tourists on the newly built Northern Pacific and Canadian Pacific Railways.

Now, more than a century later, British Columbia's tourism sector was only beginning to realize it couldn't take its natural advantage for granted. Therefore, as the WTC's membership grew, we started to gather the statistics and facts that would help tourism operators make the case to protect themselves from irresponsible logging. We publicized our findings in media interviews, speeches, magazine articles, and lobby sessions. Much to the forest companies' displeasure, the Council's actions began to attract attention. Our message was getting out: protecting British Columbia's environment made good economic sense.

As the WTC became better known, we began to look for a tourism issue we could showcase to increase awareness. Just as we began our search in the fall of 1988, Pierce Clegg contacted me. It was either serendipity or fate. Pierce was in his mid-thirties and owned a small, professionally run fishing lodge on the upper Babine River. Bright, articulate, and entrepreneurial, he had been trying for the past two years to get the Forest Service to abandon its plans to log the river. In so doing he had organized a local group of sport fishermen, rafters, and environmentalists. Despite such citizen concern and endless participation in advisory meetings, nothing had changed. The district forester was as intent as ever on proceeding. The bridge would be built within a few months and then logging would commence. Running out of options fast, Pierce happened to mention his problems to a guide outfitter, who suggested the newly established Wilderness Tourism Council as a place to seek help.

The day Pierce backgrounded me on the issue I sensed it might be the ideal one for the WTC to take on. Soon after, I flew up to take a look at the situation in the field. When I landed at Smithers for the first time in several years, it felt like a homecoming. Off on the skyline were Joe L'Orsa's and my Babine Mountains, looking as special as ever. Meeting with Pierce and others from his group at the airport, I got an issue briefing and reviewed maps. Then Pierce and I got into a chopper to go and see the river firsthand.

There had been a lot of logging in the years since I had last lived up north. The clearcuts were everywhere. There was no question in my mind that these forests were being heavily overcut. As we skimmed along 100 feet above the slash and stumps, the destruction made me sick. Closing in on the river, we could see even more graphically how intensive the logging was. It was clear that the options for protecting a sizable lower-elevation wilderness here were already gone. The best we would be able to do was protect the Babine corridor to keep the fishery and the fishing experience intact. It was far from ideal, but at least we still had the chance to salvage a river of international distinction, provided the logging companies and the Forest Service didn't ruin it first.

It was very late in the game to start a major preservation effort. Until now the district forestry officials had succeeded in keeping public concern about the Babine bottled up at the local level. If Pierce's people had been able to attract provincial public interest a year earlier, we would now have been in a much better position to protect more land. Given this lack of time, it was obvious we had to find a compelling and rapid means to head off the forestry forces.

The flight upstream was impressive. The lower portion carved a canyon through the Skeena Mountains. Here the Babine descended through a procession of fine, full rapids, which explained the river's reputation as a prime site for white-water rafting. Grizzlies lived much of their year in the alpine above. But in fall, when the steelhead and salmon were running, the bears migrated down to the water's edge, where they fished, feasted, and fattened themselves for the coming winter.

We choppered on, weaving our way through the canyon just above the waves. As we reached the midpoint along the route, the terrain changed. We emerged from the mountains and flew onto the Interior Plateau. The river now flowed through a broad country of spruce and pine. The Babine's erosion had notched it down a couple of hundred feet into the plateau. Due to the gentle character of the land, the stream's current now slowed, running clear and easy.

Frequently a riffle would be encountered, causing a brief rush of turbulence. Below were those deep pools and back eddies where steelhead loved to hang out. Whereas the lower river was the playground for rafters, this upper half was a fly fisher's heaven. As we rounded a corner, the first lodge came into sight, a well-kept, rustic cluster of cabins situated on a waterfront opening in the forest. It all looked so appealing, and I asked the pilot if we could land.

Once out on the ground, with the helicopter engine shut down, I got my first real connection with the river. The music of its passing filled the valley with a soft symphony of the wild. The river's waters were so pure, like liquid crystal, with the slightest tint of green. In the depths large fish drifted. Above, a pair of big black ravens cavorted, twirling, spinning, climbing, then diving in close-formation acrobatics through spruce-fresh air. There was a peacefulness here, an all-encompassing calm. It was easy to see why people came to this river from far away and left refreshed, regardless of whether they caught anything.

After lingering for a while, I climbed back aboard the chopper along with the others. Lifting off, we continued upstream, our flight path tracing the luminous bends of the river. Their meanderings became hypnotic, almost dreamlike, as we wound along a passageway edged with cottonwood, aspen, pine, and spruce over waters glinting in the sunlight.

Eventually our pilot gained altitude. Rising above the incised valley, we could look out across the plateau, not that we liked what we saw. Ahead and approaching all too quickly were the stark, disturbing outlines of clearcuts. By the time we reached the upper stretches of the Babine, it was apparent the logging companies were close. In fact, in one spot they had advanced right to the rim of the slopes a few hundred yards from the river. As we hovered over Pierce's camp near the prime spawning beds, I wondered if we might be too late. Already the Forest Service had felled a 60-foot-wide swath to its bridge site. This new road ran within yards of cabins that until recently had been a remote back-country retreat. Seeing such blatant disregard for a wilderness tourism business, let alone the river and its fishery, made me angry and disgusted. I wondered how Pierce could remain calm, given such callous treatment by the Forest Service, especially since the agency claimed it was interested in public input.

Just beyond the lodge and the proposed bridge site, we reached the river's end at Babine Lake. We flew above the lake's surface for a few miles before banking westward toward the Smithers airport and the beginning of the last-ditch effort to save the steelhead's river. Upon landing, Pierce and I were again joined by the other activists. Together we immersed ourselves in strategy. As I saw it, two things had to be done fast. The most urgent priority, especially having just seen the new road, was to get an immediate hold put on the Forest Service's bridge plans. Next we had to build our case for protecting the Babine in order to convince not only local bureaucrats but, more important, their superiors in Victoria.

Acting on item one, Pierce and I went in to see the district forester and a number of other key local civil servants the next day. In each of the several meetings my message was consistent and simple: the Babine River situation had come to the attention of the Wilderness Tourism Council, and since we considered this issue to be of a precedent-setting nature involving an internationally renowned fishery, we were going to fight it at the provincial level. I was explicit that, in our opinion, the way the district forestry office had treated one of our wilderness businesses and a prime tourism resource was deplorable. Accordingly we felt we had no choice but to bring the strength of the tourism industry to bear. I also advised them we intended to mobilize the support of the unionized commercial salmon fisheries, something that was quite achievable.

To emphasize the depth of my concern, I explained that if situations like the Babine River were to go unchallenged, they would spell the beginning of the end for much of British Columbia's environmentally oriented tourism economy. Therefore, I said, the Smithers Forest Service office was being put on notice. The agency was requested to revise its plans or face a firestorm, because the Babine was no longer a local concern. It was my intent, and that of the Wilderness Tourism Council, to turn the fate of this river into a major public issue.

The day's meetings brought results. Thanks to the growing significance of the tourism sector and the potency represented by the WTC, Pierce and I were taken seriously. The Forest Service staff recognized that the Babine River issue was out of the bottle, so they agreed to put a temporary hold on their bridge and logging plans, pending further input from the Wilderness Tourism Council and the Fish and Wildlife Branch. While this was a good first step, it was obvious we had precious little time to build the means to protect the river.

If we were to save the Babine, we had to publicize its plight among British Columbians, and quickly. Considering the caliber of fisheries, wildlife, wilderness, and recreation values at risk, I expected this goal to be straightforward. I figured we would be able to unite sportsmen, commercial fishermen, and environmentalists in support. Concurrently it was critical to assemble immediately the data that would persuade the government to leave the river intact. After seeing the Babine firsthand, I was convinced that to succeed in the time available we had to beat the forest industry at its own game. We would have to use economics to make the case for preservation.

Reviewing the files and technical reports confirmed just how great the conservation values at risk were. They included the world's premier wilderness steelhead river; the most important salmon run on the Skeena River system (worth $11 million per year and supporting 280 jobs); a premier wildlife-viewing river featuring up to 50 grizzlies, as well as moose, wolves, and eagles; and a high-quality white-water rafting run. By contrast the amount of wood affected by protecting the corridor was small.

Although it might be intuitive that saving the river made sense, we would need more quantifiable proof to prevent logging on the Babine. So, just as the Forest Service and the logging industry used economic projections of timber revenues and jobs to justify clearcutting alongside the river, we set out to calculate the nontimber values. In effect, we would determine the dollar-and-employment values of leaving the corridor's forests intact. While such monetary assessments can never account for the actual worth of wilderness – after all, how can you put a price tag on solitude? – still, using conservation economics to counter those of the foresters seemed expedient for such an eleventh-hour effort. We felt sure the preservation values would prove so great and convincing that they would make our case in a manner that no forester, bridge engineer, bureaucrat, or politician could deny.

When economic formulas were applied to the various resource uses of the Babine, the annual revenues associated with tourism, recreation, and fishing were found to be worth four times more than those that would come from logging. Furthermore, while protecting the Babine River could support 350 person-years of employment (especially due to the maintenance of the intact salmon and steelhead fisheries), logging would support a mere 23 jobs. Once all employment gains and losses were calculated, the figures confirmed that logging the wild river's forests would eliminate three times more jobs than would be produced, proving that it made ecologic *and* economic sense to protect the Babine.

In August 1989, with these facts in hand, I again flew up to join Pierce at the latest in the seemingly endless series of Forest Service public meetings. Unlike earlier sessions, though, this one would be different. True to our word, since my last time here, the Babine had gained the attention of British Columbians as well as the wilderness tourism industry. A lot of eyes would be watching what came down at this meeting. With time running out fast for the Babine, the showdown had arrived.

Sensing the importance of this session, the logging companies and the Forest Service came out in strength. Despite the obvious tension, the meeting began in a low-key fashion. As had happened too often before, the public was told it would have the chance to say how, but not if, the river corridor should be logged. Once again, the agency staff and industry ran through the litany of reasons why the trees had to be cut. They acknowledged the steelhead and salmon fisheries, offering the standard but meaningless promises that these wouldn't be affected. And, as always, the foresters emphasized the financial necessity of taking the timber out.

Next it was Pierce's and my turn. Supported by other local guide outfitters and conservationists arrayed around the table, we presented our case in a hardball corporate style. Pierce outlined the quality of the irreplaceable preservation values of the Babine and spoke of how steelhead rivers had suffered from logging elsewhere. I then explained what the Wilderness Tourism Council was and why we, as an industry, saw this issue as a precedent. I told them we were ready to go to the wall to protect the Babine and that the Forest Service was no longer dealing with just local conservationists. After that I listed the coalition of groups we had by now organized to fight for this river.

To cap the presentation and reveal the strength of our position, we laid out the numbers regarding preservation revenue and employment. We stressed there was no doubt that if the foresters relied on economics to decide the fate of this river, the facts spoke irrevocably in favor of protection. From a jobs-and-dollars standpoint, we said, logging the Babine would destroy much more than it would create.

Summarizing our comments, I didn't mince words. I told the group that the WTC intended to publicize these figures extensively. "We're going high-profile on this one," I said. "A whole lot of people are going to be watching what happens to this river. So it's your choice whether things get settled peacefully or explode into an all-out fight."

The response to our presentation was one of considered, if uncomfortable, silence. When the senior Forest Service official finally spoke, he said simply, "I don't dispute your findings. We'll have our people review your data, and if they bear out, then clearly your case is strong and we'll have to revise our plans."

We were confident that our math would hold up. However, due to our low level of faith in the Forest Service, after the meeting we also began to get the Babine economics out through the WTC membership and beyond, just in case. Recognizing the implications of this issue to their own tourism businesses, they, too, lobbied the government. To reinforce all this activity, Johnny Mikes and I met in person with the tourism and forest ministers. Approaching them from a commercial, rather than conservation, standpoint, we found a concern not typical for such pro-development politicians. For while their support for protecting fish or wilderness was limited, once we hooked the issue to economics and employment, they took a solid interest.

Within a couple of weeks the strength of our arguments was confirmed, and our pressure at the provincial level also had an effect. When we met again in that Forest Service boardroom in Smithers, the difference from the previous meeting was pronounced. The agency's position on the Babine had shifted entirely. For the first time in all the many sessions, Pierce heard the government and logging company officials agree that a corridor along the Babine River should and would be protected. He couldn't believe his ears.

During the rest of the session, the group focused not on cutblock locations, but where to set the protected area boundary. It was an impressive last-minute transformation. Even I was amazed at how fast foresters could move when forced. Certainly numbers made quite a difference. On the basis of some figures on a page and a little logic, the Babine steelhead would now have a future.

Our last-ditch surgical strike had hit right on the mark, not that such tactics would necessarily work as elegantly and effectively elsewhere. Due to the Babine River's extraordinary preservation values compared with those for timber, using tourism economics had proved a dramatic success. Indeed, I suspect if we had failed to take a business approach back then to protect the fishery, it would today be in decline.

Currently it seems humanity has come to live in an age when economics has supplanted religion. And while this speaks volumes as to the spiritual impoverishment of our time, the fact is, the high priests of our culture are no longer found in churches, but in accounting firms. Therefore, if it is necessary in these fear-ridden, debt-laden, nature-bashing last days of the second millennium for conservationists to speak in the tongues of economists, then so be it. To live by the rules of our present reality we must use the fiscal tools appropriate to save the essential for eternity. So, even if dollars are but a poor substitute, a fool's creation for Creation itself, still we, too, must use them in our measuring. In doing so we can help society see that it isn't jobs versus the environment, but jobs *and* the environment.

For while 1990s myopia may insist, "It's the economy, stupid," those who take the long view know it is blind stupidity to ignore ecology. Such short-term gain leads only to long-term pain. And although few people may understand it yet, the deficit that will most count for all time to come is the environmental deficit. The way we leave the natural world for our children is what will most determine their future, and their survival, because it is not our standard of living that is at stake as much as it is life itself.

After all, if Nature had only looked as far as the next fiscal quarter, it would never have invented steelhead. If the natural ledger of success had merely been that of the financier's bottom line, wilderness would never have existed. And if money had been the sole criteria for existence, the world would never have been graced with a river like the Babine.

THERE WAS MORE WORK for Pierce and his allies to do before their river was finally safe. It took them many more months of meetings before the details of the Babine River's protection were finalized. But despite such necessary follow-through, thanks to the Wilderness Tourism Council's intervention, there was no longer any doubt the steelhead would have a future.

After my involvement in the campaign, I kept in contact with Pierce to provide support in case any backsliding occurred. Fortunately that didn't happen. Then, once the river was preserved, our contact faded to an occasional exchange of mail. So I was glad when our paths crossed recently and I got a chance to talk to him again.

"How's the fishing?" I asked.

"Great!" Pierce said. "We caught a 39½-pound male this year. It should break the world record. Business has been good, too. And the river was real pretty this past fall with the early frost, bright colors, and all. But you know, the best news is that the steelhead are still here and healthy. Just like always."

Pierce Clegg fishing the waters he loved and saved.

Tatshenshini
Protecting North America's Wildest River

THROUGHOUT the æons the immense tectonic plates of the Earth's crust drifted slowly atop a mantle of molten rock. Carried by convection currents in imperceptible but relentless fashion, in that part of our planet now called the Gulf of Alaska, three great plates jammed into one another, causing the land to rise. During millions of years, under enormous pressure and heralded by quakes, the spectacular St. Elias Mountains were lifted up. They grew to form the highest coastal range on the planet, featuring three of North America's four tallest peaks.

Over millennia cool, moisture-laden winds blowing off the northern Pacific Ocean dropped the continent's deepest snowfalls here. These accumulated into the largest nonpolar icefields on Earth, with grand glaciers that carved and sculpted the land. In one place, and one place only along the 400-mile length of the St. Elias Range, the ice breached the towering mountain barrier, opening a corridor through from the subarctic interior to the maritime lowlands. Fed by glacial melt, a massive flow of water soon traversed the mountains. Tatshenshini was its name, North America's wildest river.

The deeper into the mountains these waters traveled, the more glaciers fed them and the broader they became. At Confluence the river system reached maturity. Here the two great tributaries — Tatshenshini and its sister the Alsek — merged into a mile-wide ocean of roiling, surging waves. This great current swept swiftly onward past a spectacle of glaciers. With each downstream mile the ice descended mountain slopes until finally it reached riverside. Here a frozen face of sapphire-blue, miles across, cleaved into pinnacles that toppled and formed icebergs.

Ever transformed by glaciers, mountain uplift, and downcutting river erosion, the Tatshenshini landscape was raw and youthful. In 1852 a giant ice dam formed by the Lowell Glacier gave way, perhaps triggered by the latest quake. When it ruptured, a 50-mile-long lake that had been impounded upstream was released. Suddenly and violently a half-mile-high wall of water, six times the volume of the Amazon, swept downstream. The forests and soils far up the valley walls were scoured away. Today, high above the river, the flood line remains as evidence of this cataclysm.

The seismic activity in this region was four times that of California's San Andreas Fault, causing the mountains to rise even higher. The largest earthquake recorded in North America (Richter 8.6) occurred just north of the river's mouth in 1899. The U.S. Geological Survey records of the day say that when this event happened the mountains were thrust up 50 feet and glaciers advanced a half mile in just five minutes. Even as recently as 1958 a Richter 7.9 quake caused mountainsides to slide away and the sea floor at the river's mouth to rise and form a new shoreline.

Despite such geological trauma, the great river was rich with salmon. Year after year, century after century, the sockeye and 30-pound chinook returned to the spawning grounds to be feasted upon by an astounding abundance of grizzlies and eagles. Wolves and rare silver-blue glacier bears also came down to the shoreline, while far above, in the steep-pitched uplands, mountain goats grazed. Frequently Native peoples passed along the Tatshenshini. Coastal Tlingit moved upriver, while the Tuchone journeyed downstream from the interior.

Like the bears and the eagles, they, too, fished for salmon and thrived. But for them this place wasn't wilderness; it was home.

And always the waters coursed, broad and braided, wild and incessant. Its banks bordered by forests and shrubs, the river threaded a lowland green ribbon of life through a domain of lofty peaks and icefields.

Tatshenshini. The wildest of the wild, the homeland of the great bear. The place where the mountains shook, where glaciers gave birth to icebergs, and where a tremendous river flowed. The spirit of a vast land.

Preservation in this remote place where Alaska, Yukon, and British Columbia converge began in 1872. That year John Muir, the legendary American conservationist, encountered Glacier Bay. He wrote: "The view is bounded and almost filled by the glorious Fairweather Mountains, the highest among them springing aloft to a height of nearly 16,000 feet, while from base to summit every peak and spire and dividing ridge of the almighty host was spotless white." Unknown to Muir, the opposite flank of these peaks faced an adjoining splendor – the Tatshenshini watershed. Over time Muir's passionate description catalyzed a succession of protective actions that led to one of the most important assembly of parks on the globe: Glacier Bay, first preserved as a U.S. national monument in 1926, upgraded to national park status in 1980, enlarged to include the lower Alsek River that same year; Alaska's Wrangell St. Elias National Park, also preserved in 1980; and on the Canadian side, Kluane National Park, where the headwaters of the Alsek were protected in 1972.

Despite such transboundary conservation, though, the wild core remained at risk. British Columbia's Tatshenshini country, the only place in the St. Elias Mountains where the river ran through and where the biodiversity values were highest, remained unprotected. As the keystone to the surrounding national parks, the preservation of this area was essential to prevent development from penetrating the heart of the transboundary wilderness like a knife.

In the late 1980s this vulnerability became apparent, and the worst fears were realized. Tatshenshini was threatened by one of the most dangerous mining projects ever proposed in North America. Geddes Resources, a Canadian company, had found a major copper deposit on Windy Craggy Mountain in the center of this territory. The mountain was located above the Alsek River, north of Confluence and only 15 miles upstream of Alaska's Glacier Bay National Park. Here Geddes planned to rip the top off the 6,000-foot peak and transform it into an enormous open-pit copper mine. This mega-project would have a monstrous impact. Certainly the proposed 30,000-ton-per-day operation, with its gaping 2.5-mile-long hole, 350-foot-high tailings dam, 500-person town site, 150-mile-long slurry ore and fuel pipelines, as well as a 70-mile-long road, would devastate Tatshenshini's world-class wilderness. But to make matters worse, the mine's massive potential for acid and heavy metal pollution threatened to poison the international river system.

Because the ore at Windy Craggy is 35 percent sulfide, huge amounts of sulfuric acid (the same acid used in car batteries) could be generated if this rock were exposed to atmospheric oxygen and water vapor through mining. Once the acid got into the bedrock, heavy metals could then be leached out. Called acid-mine drainage, this toxic, acid-heavy metal combination is lethal to fish. What is worse, there is no technology that can stop acid-mine drainage once it begins; it is an irreversible chemical reaction that continues for thousands of years. Even today mines that operated 2,000 years ago in Roman England still bleed red acid-mine drainage into streams.

In the case of the Windy Craggy proposal, given the extraordinarily high level of sulfide in the ore, Canadian and American government scientists had confirmed the likelihood that the pristine Tatshenshini-Alsek river system, both in British Columbia and Alaska, could be poisoned for thousands of years. If such a calamity happened, the salmon runs would be devastated forever, as would be the grizzlies, the eagles, and Native peoples dependent on them. In effect, Geddes's project meant risking such perpetual destruction in exchange for a mere 15 years of mining.

To deal with all these apparent dangers, the company proposed to submerge underwater behind huge earth dams the 375 million tons of acid-generating waste rock and mill tailings that the mine would produce. The company said this would stop oxygen in the air from mixing with the sulfide, thus preventing the acid chemical reaction. However, the company's solution was fatally flawed.

The prevention of the poisoning process meant that Geddes's dams would have to operate fail-safe for 10,000 years without allowing the water to leak out and expose the sulfide waste rock and tailings. The idea of a mining company saying that it could plan for a time period twice the age of the Pyramids was absurd, to say the least. Indeed, given the Tatshenshini region's extreme earthquake hazard, no one, and certainly not Geddes, could guarantee that the tailings dam would remain intact for 10 years, let alone 10,000. In short, the company's plans looked dangerously irresponsible.

Quite simply, the Windy Craggy mine had the makings for a transboundary environmental disaster on a monumental scale, one that could result in a major international environmental conflict between Canada and the United States. After all, major American interests were at risk: Alaska's Glacier Bay National Park, the livelihood of the Yakutat and Chilkat peoples, and a commercial salmon fishery worth $50 million each year.

And so in the Tatshenshini region an epic environmental showdown arose. A world-class wilderness faced off against a mining mega-project of catastrophic proportions.

FOR TWO YEARS Johnny Mikes, a rafting guide, urged me to raft the Tatshenshini River. Johnny looked the part of a river runner — fit, tanned, blond hair, and sunglasses — but he was more than that. The wilderness was in his soul. Having spent his teenage summers growing up on the Tatshenshini, he repeatedly lobbied me compellingly about its magnificence, emphasizing the imminent threat the wilderness faced from a proposed mine at Windy Craggy and adding, "I'll give you the trip for free."

Despite the wild appeal of the place, I was reluctant to accept. I suspected that what Johnny really wanted of me wasn't just to raft the Tatshenshini but to lead the effort to save it. At the time I wasn't sure if I wanted to do that. Height of the Rockies had just become a forest wilderness, and I was tired after that effort. Also, I think I subconsciously knew that protecting the Tatshenshini would demand a scale and difficulty of campaigning far beyond any I had done before. Eventually, realizing just how much the Tatshenshini meant to him, I succumbed. In the summer of 1989 I flew north to begin what would become the biggest wilderness adventure of my life.

The put-in point was at Dalton Post, Yukon Territory, just upstream of the St. Elias Mountains. The stunted aspen forest there was typical of the northern interior. On the alpine expanses above were Dall sheep, the bright white cousins of Spatsizi's stone sheep and the bighorn in Height of the Rockies.

Rigging the rafts took some time. We had to make sure we had all our supplies and then lash them down. Once launched on our 12-day trip, there would be no coming back. For 160 miles we would float deeper and deeper into wilderness through Canada's highest mountain range until at last we would pull out where the great river emptied into the North Pacific at Dry Bay, Alaska.

The gateway to the Tatshenshini wilderness is guarded by a tight canyon that contains a sequence of lively rapids. With the river accelerating and the gorge narrowing, I felt both a sense of exhilaration and apprehension as I entered the unknown. The white water took several exciting hours to run. Beyond, the river quieted to a serpentine wander through prime moose country, drifting through a broader landscape of spruce and beaver marshes that was typical of boreal Canada. Even though the mountains here were mild in character, glaciered peaks beckoned in the distance. They foreshadowed the wild drama to come.

The next day we moved faster with the increasing flow. The waters clouded into gray as first silts from an alpine glacier stained an entering stream. Later, after lunch, we bore down on a large, cascading rapid. Shooting its roller-coaster waves, we quickly picked up speed, jetting toward the incoming water of the O'Connor River. Suddenly, just above where the two flows joined, we flashed past orange survey tape on both shores, markers that flagged Geddes's bridge site for its mine road. The shock of seeing this tape was only amplified as the droning sound of development reached my ears. High up, a cargo plane labored across a pristine sky toward the Windy Craggy drill camp. In that moment the reality facing Tatshenshini became stark for me: would this wilderness endure or be lost?

Troubling as this question was there was no time to ponder it. At that moment the O'Connor rushed in with swirling whirlpools, and the size of the Tatshenshini more than doubled. A few minutes downstream the Tkope River also converged, and then the Henshi River, as well. Within the course of a mile the whole character of the flow was transformed. Now the grand spectacle that is the Tatshenshini was revealed. Surging on waters swollen a half mile in width, the rafts tracked an enormous arc past the base of cliffs, then headed due west. As we came about, the first view of the St. Elias ice sheet appeared 30 miles ahead, gleaming white on the horizon.

For the next few hours my heart soared with the oceanic size of this river, its swelling waves, the sweeping veils of dust that blew from the sandbars in the

strong, warm afternoon wind, the commanding peaks that presided above an expanse of alpine. There was such a grand scale to this place. Its vistas exceeded even those found in Spatsizi. Wild beyond belief, it was the essence of wilderness.

That evening I lived the epitome of bittersweet. On the one hand, I watched as the sun descended over the biggest, most spectacular river I had ever known. On the other hand, I mentally traced out the route of the proposed mine road across the base of the mountains opposite. It would scar the landscape for tens of miles. I realized this might be the last summer the great valley remained intact and that I might be one of the last to see its ancient splendor unspoiled. This thought tormented me throughout the long, sleepless night.

The next morning the sun shone once more on my soul. As we continued downstream, Tatshenshini's drama heightened and the ice sheets got closer. When we approached a point where the river swung past a bluff, Johnny looked up from the oars and shouted to me with a big smile, "Get ready! Here we come!" Around the corner a brilliant cascading glacier came into view. Then another. And another. And then a multitude. Before us was the Icefield Range robed in a majestic formation of icy tongues. Everyone on the rafts became silent and stared, transfixed as the river carried us nearer.

Late that afternoon, as Johnny brought the raft to shore, I hopped out onto a 30-yard-long sandbar. While there were no human footprints, fresh wildlife tracks abounded. The moist sand recorded the recent happenings here and could be read like a book. Two sets of grizzly footprints walked the length of the bar, one massive with long claws, the other much smaller – a mother bear with her cub. The sow grizzly had caught a 30-pound chinook salmon. I could see the imprints where the head and tail of the great fish had flailed desperately. Impaled by the bear's claws, the salmon had bled into the sand. After the grizzlies had finished feeding and moved on, a flurry of talons showed that eagles had landed to pick at the remains. Later something else had emerged from the bush, padding across the sand to check out the smell of fish. It was a wolf, a really big one. By the time he had arrived, there was probably little left. Likely he had just sniffed at the ground and continued on his way. And lastly, perhaps only minutes before we landed, hoof prints, sharp-edged and flecked with freshly disturbed grains of sand, revealed that a moose had been there also.

So much life on one tiny piece of riverside! This story of such concentrated activity was repeated wherever we stopped. In southern British Columbia seeing wolf tracks was something special, but here they were common. As for grizzlies, the signs were overwhelming and intimidating. The footprints, much larger than those of their southern cousins, were everywhere, as were the trails through the brush. Often the sites where they had bedded down among the berry bushes were spaced far too close for comfort. Going anywhere in Tatshenshini country meant making a lot of noise.

We spotted grizzlies up on the ridgelines and down fishing on the side channels. One morning as I sat, pants down, in necessary daily vigil, a grizzly stuck his head out of the shrubs 30 feet away. He looked at me for a while, and me at him; there was little else I could do. Then he was gone. As soon as I could hitch my jeans back up, so was I.

But for all the bears we saw, judging by the concentration of tracks, there were far more that watched us unseen from the tangled brush. In subsequent years research scientists would determine the year-round concentrations of grizzlies in the Tatshenshini wilderness to be likely the highest in Canada. They also told us that the silver-blue glacier bears found here were fewer in number than China's giant pandas. All of these splendid creatures lived in the Canadian Tatshenshini and just over the border in the adjoining Alsek-Yakutat region.

One evening in the long twilight of the northern summer I sat alone on the shore. I was at Confluence, the place where the Tatshenshini unites with the even larger Alsek River to form a mile-wide sea of fast water. It was incomprehensibly huge. Yet despite such grandeur, this spot was but the centerpiece within a vast cathedral 30 miles across. Encircling everything were the rugged St. Elias peaks, wreathed in ice. Scanning 360 degrees of grandeur slowly, I counted 25 individual glaciers — frigid blue plumes draping rocky flanks. Central to this glory was the place where I sat. Then, and ever since, Confluence has been, for me, the focal point of my most treasured wilderness.

Tatshenshini. The meaning of the name is uncertain. Some call it the Raven's River; others disagree. This mystery only adds to the magic. Personally I have noticed the coincidence of the word *shen* in the heart of the name. To ancient Chinese mystics this word signified "the emperor," or "spirit." Hence, for me, Tatshenshini has come to mean "The Spirit of a Vast Land." Confluence, as its name implies, is where everything comes together: the waters, the ice, and the mountains. So, just as *shen* was said to reside in the heart, Confluence lies in the very heart of Tatshenshini. Here, where Nature's spirit culminates, is one of the greatest power places on planet Earth.

That night I watched the passing water of a river so few had ever heard of. Sitting quietly, just south of Windy Craggy Peak, I made my pledge: I would commit to protect Tatshenshini. This decision wasn't one to be taken lightly. Intuitively I knew it would rule the next several years of my life.

The days that followed were magnificent. Launching from Confluence, we looked up the Alsek toward Turnback Canyon. This stretch of wild water, one of the roughest on the continent, is where Tweedsmuir Glacier squeezes the huge river into a torturous gorge. In 1972 Walt Blackadar, the first and only person to solo Turnback by kayak, flipped in the class 5 waves and was swept under the ice. Miraculously he emerged downstream and survived.

By comparison our passage downstream was much safer. Crossing the border into the United States, we arrived at Walker Glacier. This glacier extends right down to the valley floor where it splays out into a gently sloping 200-foot-thick tongue. At its terminus we easily walked up a ramp of rock moraine to get on top. From there careful route-finding was important because the surface was fractured by crevasses. We peered carefully down into these, their blue walls melted slick by streams that vanished into the depths. Hiking onward, we eventually reached the base of some ice falls and could go no farther. Instead, we gazed up at the frozen cascade. Beyond, for thousands of vertical feet, the ice cloaked steep slopes up to the summit spires.

Returning to the rafts, we resumed our journey downriver. On and on the tremendous, irresistible current of meltwater took us past more glaciers and into new reaches guarded by resolute peaks. We lost track of the days and the outside world ceased to exist. For us the only reality was wilderness and the endless flowing. Existence distilled into the essential. Life centered on the now, the purest state of being.

Until the moment came when we made the turn into Alsek Bay. Ahead, a mythic scenery appeared. Icebergs. Everywhere there were icebergs — colossal sculptures of frozen azure and white, some eight stories high. A silent flotilla drifting in tranquil waters. Glacial glory so sublime.

Along with bergy bits that slurried the cool green water, these ice monuments were the final statement of the huge ice sheets that pressed down all around from 15,000-foot peaks to the water's edge. Ten miles wide, the glaciers presented a 150-foot-high wall of sheer blue cliffs and columnar seracs to the river. With sacrificial patience they waited for waves to lap a sufficient undercut. Then, with a sharp, startling crack, an overhanging slab fractured free. As it toppled into the water, thunder rang across the bay and huge waves radiated outward as yet another iceberg was born.

All through the afternoon, evening, and next day this primeval spectacle recurred with random precision. Like a glacial gun salute confirming that even ice couldn't freeze time's passing, the rumbling resounded. Presiding over this drama, Mount Fairweather, in its pure white majesty, floated above the clouds. Sheathed in ice and three miles high, this paramount ruler reigned supreme. From its castle astride the Alaska-B.C. boundary, Fairweather afforded us with unwavering attention for the days we spent among the icebergs. And even when it came time to depart Alsek Bay, the monarch — British Columbia's tallest mountain — watched our progress from on high.

Now we traveled the final leg of the trip. Emerging from the St. Elias ranges, we floated out onto a wild coastal plain lush with bright green shrub growth and secretive Alaska brown bears. After a few last hours of travel on the great river, it finally carried us into Dry Bay and the take-out point. We brought all our gear ashore, deflated the rafts, and packed up for the next day's bush flight out.

That evening we went to the river's mouth where the combined flows of the

Tatshenshini and the Alsek entered the cold North Pacific. Our mood was melancholic. Here was journey's end, for us and also for the wilderness waters that had come all the way from distant Yukon. As the huge, fresh river finally reunited with the sea, mixing into saltwater surf, Mount Fairweather maintained its skyline presence. But while that evening signaled the trip down the river was over, I knew my involvement with this wilderness had only just begun.

The flight home, first beside Fairweather's summit and then down the length of the Alaska-B.C. coast, gave me a lot of time to think about the coming campaign. As always, the conservationists would have little time. Geddes Resources had already spent $50 million exploring Windy Craggy. It had excavated a 13,000-foot shaft, built a large camp, and had applied to the B.C. government for approval to proceed. Due to Tatshenshini's remoteness and the fact that it was an entirely unknown place to British Columbians, this issue would be an extremely tough one. In fact, when I returned, several leaders of the environmental movement advised me that Tatshenshini was unwinnable. However, having been on the river and knowing what was at stake, I wasn't going to give up before we even started.

Thinking about the road survey markers I had seen at the O'Connor River, I knew we had to fire a fast shot across Geddes's bow to slow it down. Johnny had learned that the company was slashing its road survey line into Tatshenshini country without permits. Therefore, in my role as executive director of the Wilderness Tourism Council, on August 30, 1989, I wrote a letter of complaint to the ministers responsible for mines and the environment. Quickly the Wildlife Branch supported our position that this unauthorized action would create all-terrain-vehicle access, which could enable poachers to hunt Tatshenshini's grizzlies.

We got a fast response. The ministers agreed that Geddes's actions lacked approval and stopped the company's slashing into the main valley. Geddes was annoyed at this obstruction, but if it had known what our action presaged, it would have been much more concerned. We were intent on protecting Tatshenshini and stopping the mine.

Not long after my return I sat down with Dona and asked if she was willing to help save Tatshenshini. "It's going to be hard," I told her.

"Sure," she said gamely. "Let's do it." Several arduous years later at the end of the fight, she admitted she hadn't known what her words would get her into. However, even in the toughest moments she never relented.

With Dona on board, and Johnny already there well before me, we moved into overdrive to slow and derail Geddes's proposal before it received a permit. We immediately set up Tatshenshini Wild as a nonprofit organization to champion the issue in Canada.

At this embryonic point in the campaign we had the good fortune to attract the help of two young conservationists who would work tirelessly during the next few years. The first was Ethan Askey, the son of Alan Askey, who had backpacked with me on the memorable hike through Height of the Rockies. Kevin Scott was the other one. On his own volition he decided to move from Vancouver to Gibsons in order to work as a full-time volunteer and help with day-to-day logistics. Ethan and Kevin were in their twenties, about the same age I was when I had started out to protect the Nitinat Triangle. Now, with the years gone by – as had been the case for Brock Evans – it was time to begin acting as a mentor and to benefit from their enthusiastic energy.

Preparing for a major public offensive, we then developed all the needed materials: an evocative poster to put an image of this unknown wilderness into the public mind, slide shows, tabloids, briefs, and a broadcast-quality video. We also found the tag line to hang the campaign on: "Tatshenshini, Protect North America's Wildest River."

With this prep work completed, we hit the media with a blizzard of print and electronic stories. The result was that Tatshenshini's profile rose so quickly that within a couple of months we were organizing standing-room-only public meetings across British Columbia and beyond. Quickly this wilderness gained recognition and support as the campaign blossomed. A variety of leading B.C. organizations – Western Canada Wilderness Committee, Sierra Club B.C., Canadian Parks and Wilderness Society, British Columbia Outdoor Recreation Council, and many more – became collaborators. As for Tatshenshini Wild, we were building an exceptionally high-caliber team of professionals.

Several directors were leading Canadian mountaineers, two of whom had climbed to the summit of Mount Everest. It was the quality of people on our board that gave Tatshenshini Wild the daring, disciplined style needed to take on a seemingly impossible campaign.

We were out to stop one of the largest, most dangerous mines ever proposed in North America, something that had never been done before. Certainly there had been countless large forestry campaigns, but no one had ever taken on the hard-rock mining industry on this scale. We wouldn't let that stop us, though. To prevail, first you have to believe. Like mountaineers starting up an unclimbed peak or paddlers entering treacherous rapids, we knew that success meant seeing the win and then going for it, completely. Saving Tatshenshini was all about mind-set, all about will.

Despite such a go-for-it psychology and fast-rising public support in British Columbia, the size of the Windy Craggy project – the company claimed there were billions of dollars of copper under the peak in Tatshenshini's heartland – meant we had to develop more strength than any Canadian wilderness issue to date. Early assessment of Johnny's files revealed Geddes's Achilles heel. Since British Columbia's Tatshenshini region was landlocked behind the Alaska Panhandle, the company required a U.S. port site for the mine to proceed. At the same time Windy Craggy's potential to cause massive environmental damage to a transboundary salmon river clearly put major U.S. interests and territory at risk, in particular Glacier Bay National Park. Therefore, winning at Tatshenshini would entail pressuring not just B.C. legislators but also the government of the United States. Assuming we could make Tatshenshini an issue in Washington, a binational strategy offered the best means of success. This international approach would also require lobbying the Canadian federal government as well as those in Yukon and Alaska. With so many fronts to work on, a large and complex effort would be required. Indeed, Tatshenshini would become the first continent-wide wilderness campaign.

Given our chosen approach, the initial requirement was to find champions on the U.S. side. I immediately thought of Brock Evans who, since the Nitinat

Triangle campaign 18 years earlier, had tutored me in the art of wilderness campaigning. Brock was now the vice president of the National Audubon Society in Washington, D.C., and was recognized as one of America's most experienced and toughest environmental leaders. After I contacted him in late April 1990, we spent a few minutes bringing each other up-to-date in our lives and then I briefed him on Tatshenshini. By the end of the call, Brock agreed to help out. "All right, buddy," he said, "I'll write to Geddes and let them know they face opposition from U.S. enviros."

Brock's letter to Geddes was sent the next day. It was timed for public release by Elizabeth May of the Canadian Sierra Club at the company's annual shareholders meeting in Toronto. Elizabeth, one of Canada's leading environmentalists and a veteran of the South Moresby National Park campaign, was a wizard with the business press that day. The story went national, and the fight against Windy Craggy truly began.

When Brock and I had talked, I also asked him if he would give me introductions to some of the other power types in the U.S. conservation movement. Again the answer was yes. Within days I was in touch with Ed Wayburn, past president of the U.S. Sierra Club and the national leader on Alaskan affairs. Ed had rafted the Tatshenshini-Alsek years before and was the person most responsible for getting the lower portion of the river on the U.S. side included in Glacier Bay National Park. Not surprisingly, he was quick to offer his support.

And so it went. Stepping from contact to contact, I made my way across the top of the American wilderness movement, enlisting assistance from the leaders of the Wilderness Society, the National Wildlife Federation, National Parks and Conservation Association, American Wildlands, and many more. In Canada similar connections were made with the key Canadian national-level conservationists: Monte Hummel of the World Wildlife Fund; Kevin McNamee of the Canadian Nature Federation; Harvey Locke, president of the Canadian Parks and Wilderness Association; and Gary Blundell of the Canadian Wildlife Federation.

It was the classic bootstrap operation. One leg up leading to the next until we eventually compiled endorsements from a formidable grouping of the most effective environmental leaders across North America. But while securing moral support was one thing, converting it into campaign activism was another. To achieve this we had to replicate what Johnny had done with me. The various leaders had to experience Tatshenshini firsthand in order to bond with its wilderness. Then they would surely commit fully to save it.

Thus, one of the crucial elements of the Tatshenshini campaign was born. We invited these leaders to raft the river for free, using trips donated by Johnny and other white-water operators. It also occurred to me that we could fast-track the publicizing of the Tatshenshini issue by inviting select media people to journey down the river. If we could get a blitz of coverage, I thought, especially highly illustrated magazine stories, then the public would soon understand what was at stake in this remote part of British Columbia.

What followed was an intensive marketing effort. Dona, Ethan, Kevin, Johnny, myself, and others from Tatshenshini Wild began to pitch the river trips to a strategically targeted list of influential writers, photographers, and television camera people from across North America. Making cold calls to the likes of *National Geographic* and CNN was tough, but our persistent enthusiasm paid off. We quickly started to book an impressive list of visitors to Tatshenshini. To ensure that there was supply to match this demand, Johnny and I also sought the necessary raft trips from the 16 outfitting companies that ran the river. Their response was most generous.

In the summer of 1990, just six months after the campaign's launch, the first in the stream of journalists and environmental leaders arrived to see Tatshenshini for themselves. As Sally Ranney, a leading conservationist from Denver said to me one day as we made the turn downstream of the O'Connor River, "I've spent my life fighting for wilderness in the United States, but I realize now this is the first time I've ever actually experienced it."

The "on-river program," as we called it, was successful beyond our wildest dreams. In fact, we continued it as a centerpiece of the campaign for the following summers until Tatshenshini was finally safe. Within months a series of photo articles, many of them cover stories, began emerging in magazines such as *National Geographic, Life, Omni, Outside, Sierra, Equinox,* and *Canadian Geographic,* to name only a few. As well, major illustrated articles were published in newspapers from New York to Los Angeles and Halifax to Vancouver, while national television networks in both countries did features and news pieces.

Quickly word of this river spread. Like a successful chain letter, what started with a small group of people radiated outward to a larger and larger audience. So appealing was the issue, so dramatic were the images, that once the public was exposed to Tatshenshini, the wilderness sold itself.

But for all the preservation work we had initiated in British Columbia, unknown to us a parallel effort was under way in Alaska. In retrospect this makes sense, since the river runs through two nations. But it was a complete and delightful surprise the day a letter arrived from Peter Enticknap. It came complete with a database of Alaskan environmentalists he had organized to stop Windy Craggy. Peter lived in Haines, the town where Geddes wanted its port site. When he heard about Tatshenshini Wild, he reached out to make contact. And thank goodness he did, because he was to become one of the leaders on the U.S. side. Not only would he work tirelessly to achieve congressional and White House opposition against the mine and for Tatshenshini, he had already done crucial spadework in Washington, D.C.

Peter had started working with American Rivers, a national U.S. conservation group based in that country's capital. In particular, he had convinced Tom Cassidy, a leading campaigner with the organization, that Tatshenshini was an issue his organization should champion. On Peter's recommendation Tom accepted an invitation to raft the river. He had an exceptional trip and became an ardent convert to the cause, which was more good news for us.

American Rivers was noted for its Ten Most Endangered Rivers list, which was announced annually at the National Press Club in Washington. Upon his return home, Tom worked to get Tatshenshini onto the list in April 1991, a first for any Canadian river and a breakthrough for the issue. The resulting publicity enabled Tatshenshini to jump into the forefront as a conservation concern in Washington, thus gaining the campaign support it urgently needed there.

Over the next couple of years Tatshenshini's profile would continue to rise as it climbed American Rivers' top-ten list. Tatshenshini's recognition in the U.S. capital received another key boost when Jerry Mallet and Sally Ranney, both of Colorado-based American Wildlands, convinced their senator, Tim Wirth, to first raise the issue on the Senate floor. This opening step was crucial in developing U.S. congressional opposition to Windy Craggy.

Meanwhile, even as the conservation campaign was organizing, Geddes was working hard to get a permit for its mine. However, the escalating public concern had thrown a monkey wrench into its plans. The B.C. government now instructed the company to hold a series of hearings throughout British Columbia and Alaska. Such a degree of input had never been required of a mine proposal before. The politicians called for these hearings no doubt hoping they would defuse the opposition. In fact, the opposite happened.

Working the phone lines overtime, Peter and I drummed up so much interest in each town where hearings were held that conservationists packed these meetings. The results were that Geddes experienced a setback and Tatshenshini became a solid grass-roots concern. No longer would the responsibility to organize in local communities be just Tatshenshini Wild's and Peter's (through his Southeast Alaska Conservation Coalition). Now there were citizens' groups across British Columbia and Alaska intent on saving Tatshenshini.

The call that came in from Ken Madsen one morning was an example. Living in the Yukon near the Tatshenshini headwaters, Ken was one of Canada's most talented white-water paddlers and one of the few people with the courage and skill to paddle Turnback on the upper Alsek. For quite some time he had been worried about the mine proposal and wanted to help stop it. Out of our phone conversation that day came the idea that Ken would kayak all the rivers at risk from Windy Craggy: the Tatshenshini, the Alsek, and the Chilkat (along which Geddes planned to ship ore to Haines). Then he would write a book and take a slide show on Tatshenshini across Canada.

Such public shows were already proving themselves an important campaign tool. Johnny, myself, and Michael Downs, one of Tatshenshini Wild's directors, had undertaken a first tour across the country and then into the United States. We found that even in eastern cities, thousands of miles from the St. Elias Mountains, support was high, especially on the day the three of us presented our show to an all-party grouping of federal Members of Parliament in Ottawa. After we finished the presentation, John Fraser, Speaker of the Canadian House of Commons, stood and spoke with eloquence. Summing up, he said, "The Windy Craggy project is a tragedy waiting to happen. If the B.C. government is smart, it will move to protect Tatshenshini fast."

Like the great river itself, the campaign was now flowing with unstoppable momentum. The profile of Tatshenshini and the threat from mining this wilderness were becoming well known in Canada and the United States. Extensive grass-roots networks were developed throughout British Columbia, Yukon, and Alaska. A central team of skilled campaigners – Johnny, Peter, Tom, Sally, Michael, Ethan, the Tatshenshini Wild board members, Dona, and myself – operated together in a leadership capacity. Nevertheless, we still didn't have the capability to knock out Geddes. Actually we were just completing the first stage of the campaign, that of marshaling our forces. To succeed we now needed to knit together the many groups and their leaders into one coordinated strategy. We had to enlarge the campaign's structure. Only then could we focus all our continent-wide strength to stop the mega-mine.

To achieve this goal, invitations were sent by Tatshenshini Wild across Canada and the United States, proposing a weekend strategy conference in Vancouver. To our delight the response was excellent. During those two days in November 1991, leaders from all over North America convened with common purpose. The skill level of the campaigners in that room was extraordinary, and I felt privileged to work with a group that possessed such creativity, commitment, and experience. Together we weighed our strategic options and assessed Geddes's position as well as our own. We also formulated the actions each group would contribute to the winning of Tatshenshini. But while a sequence of tactics became clearer, envisioning how to put the issue over the top wasn't evident yet.

The weekend's single biggest achievement was our agreement to establish

Tatshenshini International, or TI for short. What we conceived was something new and definitely not a coalition. Since coalitions require formal ratification of a common platform, strategies, and tactics by the boards of member organizations, they often result in a "lowest common denominator" campaign mode. As had been the experience of many of the leaders attending that weekend conference, coalitions too often operate in a clumsy, fractious manner. Obviously none of us wanted to go that route. Nor did we want to set up a super group in which all organizations subsumed their independence and identity to an overall controller. Of course, such a development wouldn't have been possible, given the stature and size of the various groups involved. Together the 50 groups linked as Tatshenshini International represented a combined membership of more than 10 million North Americans.

Instead, we designed TI to operate as an ecosystem. This setup meant that each organization would proceed in its own style and in pursuit of its particular mandate to achieve Tatshenshini's protection. Like organisms in an ecological community, individual groups would operate collaboratively in their particular niches. Together these actions would contribute to the overall campaign.

For example, American Rivers, whose mission was to publicize and lobby in Washington, D.C., for endangered rivers, would use Tatshenshini as a focal issue and take advantage of its Top Ten Rivers list. Similarly Western Canada Wilderness Committee, which under its founder Paul George had come to excel in producing mass-circulation wilderness tabloids, agreed to perform this function for the benefit of everyone in Tatshenshini International.

As for Tatshenshini Wild, our role would be to keep the lines of communication open and the information flowing. Just as a healthy organism can only function if all its neural links are functioning well, our responsibility was to make sure the actions of each part of Tatshenshini International were known by everyone. In this manner the organism, the campaign ecosystem, would come to function by itself, with no one group controlling or being more important than another. For conservationists this structure was new and beyond the older styles of hub-and-spoke or hierarchical command. It was a network campaign – and a continental one at that – in advance of the public Internet era. With the World Wide Web not yet in place, we relied on fax and telephone instead.

Later in the campaign, when events moved to a fever pitch, it was this ecosystem structure that ensured success. Eventually so much was happening around North America that saving Tatshenshini meant no one was, or could, direct the show. The organism came to life and functioned on its own accord with its own collaborative mind. The thrill of being part of this process was extraordinary.

After the inaugural Tatshenshini International conference, the various leaders dispersed to take up their agreed-upon tasks. With his paddling complete and the book written, Ken Madsen and George Smith of the Canadian Parks and Wilderness Society set off on a national speaking tour. And what a committed effort these two made. They were on the road for months. Meanwhile, coordinated lobbying programs were simultaneously stepped up in the key capitals: Ottawa, Washington, Victoria, Whitehorse, and Juneau. In the summer of 1992 the on-river program moved into a new stage. Now we invited not just more influential journalists and environmentalists but political leaders, as well.

Soon numerous influential Canadians and Americans – Pierre Trudeau, Canada's former prime minister; Paul Martin, Canada's current finance minister; John Cashore, British Columbia's environment minister; and a number of U.S. congressional staffers – made the trip into the canyon gateway and on down North America's wildest river: One particular government aide, Katie McGinty, was so impressed by her time in this wilderness that she returned to Washington determined to make a difference. She urged her senator to help stop Windy Craggy. After Katie detailed to her boss how this project threatened U.S. interests, Al Gore agreed to help out.

In the spring of 1992 Tatshenshini reached the number two spot on the Endangered Rivers list, and the senator from Tennessee was at the American Rivers Press Conference to speak on behalf of its protection and against the Geddes mine, saying, "The development of a huge open-pit copper mine in the midst of one of the world's most pristine regions is an environmental nightmare that threatens the river and every living thing in the region." The next week, on April 8, Gore launched legislative action in the U.S. Congress, and support for his initiative grew quickly. Within a few weeks I went down to meet with the senator and work with the American members of Tatshenshini International to develop congressional support for his action.

Meeting Al Gore for the first time was one of the highlights of the campaign for me. Along with Tom Cassidy, I was ushered into his office on Capitol Hill. On one wall was an enormous photo of the Earth from space. Environmental mementos and photos were arrayed all around. After years of meeting with development-fixated politicians, it was refreshing to shake hands with someone of Gore's political stature who felt so fervently about the environment.

Talking with the senator about Tatshenshini, I found that he was concerned and well informed on the issue. Katie had briefed him skillfully. There was a personal warmth and style about the man. In all my years of lobbying I had never before met a person with such a sense of power *and* humanity. At the time of our meeting there was no indication that Gore was headed for the White House. The conventional wisdom then was that his time was past after his showing in the 1988 U.S. presidential primaries. Still, of all the political leaders I had met over the years, he was the first one who seemed truly presidential in manner to me.

Our meeting was excellent. The senator reaffirmed his strong, active support for Tatshenshini. After that session, Tom, others from the TI environmental groups in Washington, and myself undertook a battery of congressional, White House, and agency meetings – the most demanding lobbying I had ever done. Compared with Canada's, the American democratic system provides easier access for the people to meet with elected officials. However, this accessibility, and the sheer size of the U.S. populace, results in these invidivuals often being swamped by public contact. Consequently, in Washington, there are far more issues and lobbyists competing for the attention of politicians. I found that in any meeting I had 30 seconds to hook the interest of the person I was with or the opportunity was lost.

For a Canadian who only dimly understood the mechanics and subtleties of the U.S. system, this assignment was tough. Thank goodness I had top-flight environmentalists to work with. The fact that Tatshenshini was located across the border in another country made the selling all that more difficult. Nevertheless, the immense and irreversible threat of the Windy Craggy project to U.S. interests, as well as the superlative transboundary preservation values of the Tatshenshini-Alsek river system, aroused strong concern and support. Consequently, within a few short months, congressional hearings were scheduled on the Tatshenshini issue.

Perhaps it was a weird aspiration for a Canadian, but ever since my University of Victoria days, when I had studied public land policy by reading the transcripts of landmark U.S. congressional hearings, I had always had a secret wish to testify. So it was a memorable day when I helped to present Tatshenshini's case before the House Interior Committee. Included among the presenters were representatives from American Rivers, Peter Enticknap, and a Native woman, Caroline Powell, from Yakutat, Alaska. Her words were especially moving, probably because her people felt so threatened. Since time immemorial they had lived and fished at the mouth of the great river. Speaking to the congressmen, Caroline was blunt: "Windy Craggy's proposed man-made lake, which will hide the mine tailings, is an imminent lake of genocide to the Yakutat Tlingit people of the gulf coast of Alaska." The committee members listened closely to her and to all that was said.

By now our conservation campaign was in high gear in both nations. Concurrent with the activities in Washington, Tatshenshini International members were lobbying heavily in the Canadian, British Columbian, Yukon, and Alaskan legislatures. While the people involved are simply too numerous to list, each person's effort brought Tatshenshini's protection a step closer. I particularly remember some of the final sessions in which Johnny and I, along with a range of B.C. environmental leaders, pressed Cabinet ministers in the provincial government hard. My experience in Washington proved invaluable, and we got to apply it in the B.C. Legislature where the final land-use decision would ultimately be made.

Not that we were unopposed in our efforts, here or elsewhere. For, in fact, we had never been. Everywhere we had gone in North America, but especially in Victoria, our efforts had been countered by mining industry promoters. As we pressed for preservation, they urged mining. Nation by nation, capital by capital, we engaged in a lobbying tug-of-war. In the middle were the officials whom both sides were intent upon convincing.

In some respects the two adversaries were mismatched. Geddes's side had million-dollar budgets to pay hired guns and push the company's vested interests, while we championed the public good with frugal funding, all donated. But despite such disadvantages, the fact that we were focused on passing on the legacy of a living river rather than merely maximizing shareholder returns gave us a strong edge. From a moral standpoint the force was with us.

As the campaign continued, groups of conservationists and mining representatives crisscrossed North America's cities and corridors until one mid-October 1992 afternoon both parties unknowingly came in two different doors of the same office simultaneously. It was the office of Anne Edwards, the B.C. minister responsible for mines, the one person in North America who, more than anyone else, was at the center of the continental storm. For an hour Johnny and I faced off in fierce debate with the president and chairman of Geddes, while the minister, as if watching a world tennis final, sat in between.

After that meeting, Johnny and I debriefed with the others. We had a strong sense that the match had gone our way. Increasingly this kind of feeling was reinforced by reports coming in from across North America. Many months earlier, Geddes's initial mine proposal had been rejected as too environmentally dangerous by government agencies in British Columbia, Canada, and the United States. This rejection had not only confirmed that the environmentalists' fears were real, but had sent the company back to redesign a safe mine. The expert advice we now received from sources inside government agencies, as well as secret sympathizers within the mining industry (who also felt this project was too dangerous), confirmed for us there was simply no technical means of mining Windy Craggy's sulfide-rich ore safely.

On the U.S. side the company had failed to get beyond square one on any of the 31 permits it needed to transport its ore to Alaskan tidewater. As well, in Victoria, in September 1991, a new, more environmentally responsive B.C. government had been elected. Incoming NDP Premier Mike Harcourt had campaigned on a platform that promised better stewardship of the land. Soon after taking office, he announced a review of land-use options for Tatshenshini. In the United States, in November 1992, Al Gore was elected vice president. And early in 1993 Katie McGinty took up her new job as President Clinton's top environmental aide.

With all these developments, and after four years of setting up the continental chessboard, it was clear that checkmate was close. So, in January 1993, the TI leadership came together once more to map out the endgame. A complex, multi-prong strategy was devised that would involve all TI member groups. To coordinate actions a target win date was agreed to: the beginning of summer, six months hence. From that moment on lobbying activity increased by a quantum leap everywhere. This was made easier by the B.C. government's just-released Tatshenshini land-use report, which reconfirmed that massive and perpetual toxic pollution would occur if the mine proceeded.

When Prime Minister Brian Mulroney and President Clinton met for the first time in the spring of that year, TI people worked hard to ensure that the Tatshenshini issue surfaced. Indeed, word out of Washington was that the president had come to ask his staff regularly about the progress of the Tatshenshini issue in British Columbia. This was significant, since lawyers retained by Tatshenshini International had now determined that Canada would violate four different international treaties if British Columbia continued with the Windy Craggy project. Obviously the potential existed for this issue to trigger an international environmental incident. For a trading nation like Canada, and especially British Columbia, the long-term consequences of such a situation could be very serious. Certainly the protest storm and market boycotts that had flared up in Europe when the B.C. government had made its ill-advised decision to allow logging of old-growth timber in much of Clayoquot Sound was proof of what could happen. After all, the proposed mine directly threatened American territory, fisheries, Native populations, and a first-class national park.

As the campaign moved toward culmination, help came from one of the leading environmentalists on the planet. Maurice Strong, the person most responsible for making the 1992 United Nations Conference on the Environment in Rio de Janeiro a reality, weighed in directly with Premier Harcourt. He told him that if British Columbia allowed the Tatshenshini wilderness to be mined, he would come to the steps of the B.C. Legislature and publicly protest the action. Because of Strong's top-level international public profile and stellar environmental reputation, his message stunned the premier and ultimately reinforced the international significance of protecting Tatshenshini. Strong also offered the premier an enticement to do the right thing. If the province moved to preserve Tatshenshini, he said he would personally ensure that the premier and the B.C. government would get the positive recognition they deserved from the world community.

Despite this groundswell of support for Tatshenshini in senior places, the ferocity of the mining industry's campaign intensified. From my vantage point at the communication node of Tatshenshini International, I was constantly apprised of the industry's activities as it lobbied across North America. But everywhere these adversaries went, our people rose to meet them, engaging them in relentless dogfights. Higher and higher the fever of encounter became, even as the B.C. Cabinet entered final deliberations. Every day was ablaze with campaigning activity. All across the continent our people went full out in close coordination. Tough as this work was for everyone, there was a sense of history about it.

And then at last the moment of truth arrived: the campaign crossed the finish line. At a morning press conference in downtown Vancouver Premier Harcourt announced his government's decision: Tatshenshini would be preserved as a park, all 2.4 million acres of it. In speaking to the crowd and the media, Harcourt said:

This million-hectare park, which is twice the size of the Grand Canyon,
will ensure the permanent protection of an area internationally recognized
for its unique wildlife, biodiversity, and wilderness recreation values.

It will protect one of the last strongholds of North America's grizzly bear
population, protect the rare glacier bear, and sustain the Tatshenshini-
Alsek as one of the three major salmon-bearing rivers on the northern
Pacific coast.

This is one of the most spectacular wilderness areas in the world, and today
British Columbia is living up to its global responsibility to keep it that way.

With those words the premier had a lot to be proud of. There was no question that we all felt pride concerning his actions and those of members of his government, especially the environment minister. After his time on the river, John Cashore had returned home to support its protection strongly. Additionally Harcourt announced that in response to requests from the prestigious World Conservation Union, application would be made by the B.C. government to designate Tatshenshini as a United Nations World Heritage Site.

What the B.C. government's decision meant, of course, was that the Windy Craggy project was dead. The day was June 22, 1993, the first official day of summer. We had hit Tatshenshini International's targeted deadline bang on.

Not that we had the luxury to celebrate our long-sought, hard-fought victory. We still had work to do concerning the mining industry, which reacted to the government's decision with anger. Trying to intimidate Premier Harcourt into reversing his decision, the companies protested absurdly that the loss of Windy Craggy would spell the end of all mining in British Columbia. In the ensuing month, it fought the World Heritage Site application every step of the way, but without success.

A year and a half after becoming a B.C. park, Tatshenshini received its United Nations designation, thereby completing the greatest complex of World Heritage Sites on Earth. After 125 years of activism in Canada and the

United States, 23 million acres of St. Elias wilderness was now fully protected in Alaska, Yukon, and British Columbia. At last a conservation effort spanning generations had reached culmination. Finally the world's largest international park was complete, with Tatshenshini at its core.

Only then did Geddes and its allies stop complaining. Perhaps they finally realized they had lived in denial for too long. They had never acknowledged the extreme environmental danger of the Windy Craggy proposal, nor had they accepted the fact that the Americans ultimately had a veto and would have stopped the project sooner or later. After all, Vice President Gore's strong opposition had been based, in large part, on the strong technical reports from U.S. agencies and scientists. Their work repeatedly confirmed that America had everything precious to lose and nothing to gain.

Therefore, it was only right that at the conclusion of this first-ever continental wilderness campaign the two leaders who had made the protection of Tatshenshini possible — Vice President Gore and Premier Harcourt — should finally meet each other in Washington, D.C. To enable this encounter to occur, American Rivers organized a celebration dinner in Washington to honor the two men and the key conservationists who had worked hard to save Tatshenshini.

Dona and I were invited to attend. When we flew into Washington's Dulles Airport on November 5, 1993, we were met by Harriett Crosby, who worked with Katie at the White House. She took us on a late-evening tour of the capital, which Dona had never been to before. For both of us the chance to visit the Lincoln Memorial, the Capitol, and the Washington Monument at this moment of Tatshenshini's triumph was especially moving.

For me, to be in Washington at the campaign's end seemed especially fitting. I reconnected with the many times I had hustled from office to office among the marbled buildings of Washington, D.C. Always I had felt as if I were walking through the 20th century's equivalent of imperial Rome. This capital was the political hub of the modern world. There was such a sense of potency here. Yet working in Congress and the White House had been both exciting and bizarre for me. Pennsylvania Avenue had seemed incredibly far from Confluence, yet the fate of the river and its wilderness had become so connected to this city. And while the form of power each place possessed couldn't have been more different, each was of global stature.

The next night at the celebration dinner I presented the Tatshenshini slide show one last time. Standing at the podium, the vice president on one side, the premier on the other, I looked out across the hall at 1,200 people, many of whom had worked for years to protect this world-class wilderness. Only then did the magnitude of what we had accomplished together begin to sink in for me. In that audience were my co-warriors, environmental superstars all: my mentor, Brock, as well as Tom, Peter, Sally, Katie. And beyond that room were countless more across the continent.

The focus of the evening occurred when Vice President Gore rose to speak:

> We meet tonight to celebrate a success story. It is a story that involves courage. It is a story of activism. It could have been a story of environmental disaster. For, if we had done nothing, we would now face the open-pit copper mine at Windy Craggy. Acid-mine pollution would be devastating the waters of the Tatshenshini. Birds and fish would be dying all the way down to Glacier Bay National Park. A way of life would have been wiped out for the Tlingits of Alaska . . . if we had done nothing.
>
> But we decided to act. Environmentalists from all over the world came together to save the Tatshenshini, led by the people in this room, and they deserve our applause! And while you are nice enough to honor me, what I did was easy compared to the courage of Premier Harcourt. His decision to designate the Tatshenshini-Alsek region as a permanent provincial park was a victory of vision, of boldness, and of statesmanship. It was the victory of people over profit — the kind of short-term profit that leaves us much poorer overall.

When he finished, the vice president turned to shake the premier's hand, who surely deserved it. After that the people in the hall rose and applauded fervently. Together we had all succeeded.

As I stood with all the others and clapped, special memories moved through my mind. I thought back to when Dona saw the river for the first time. Having already spent 18 hard months campaigning to save the Tatshenshini, she had gone down to the shoreline to touch the water and had begun to cry. Even sight unseen this place had become a very important part of her.

More than any other person Dona had made Tatshenshini happen, and the crowd's applause now was also for her. Operating tirelessly and selflessly behind the scenes, she had given me the strength to keep on going. Even in the toughest moments she hadn't faltered. For while I was the strategist, she was the tactician, both on the campaign and in the world together. As she often said, while I might be great at saving the world, I could never find my car keys! And it was true. Thankfully she always kept track of the details. As well, she worked the phones, did research, raised money, was a computer "sysop," and generally kept the show running. In all, Tatshenshini owed much to Dona. And I felt blessed by her presence in my life.

U.S. Vice President Al Gore and B.C. Premier Mike Harcourt
celebrate the preservation of the Tatshenshini.

While the applause continued, I also thought of my other love, my daughter Sheena. I remembered that time when she had stood proudly in my office with a newspaper she had just made. The crayoned headline had read: THE WILD WIDERNESS (*sic*). She was six at the time; now she was already 11. How time had passed in those intense years. Like Tatshenshini's braiding channels, her childhood had been interwoven with those waters. As a result, she was certainly wilderness savvy, having been down the river a couple of times. She had climbed thousands of feet of mountainside to have alpine snowball fights in July. She had walked through flower meadows taller than she. And she had managed to fall asleep in the tent beside grizzly trails, even as bears moved in the brush.

Finally, as the crowd in the hall sat down again and the evening moved toward a close, I recalled all the good times spent running Tatshenshini's wild waves with some of the finest, most dedicated conservationists anywhere, especially Johnny, because he had started this whole thing off.

IN EARLY AUGUST 1995, a year and a half after that Washington celebration, and eight months after Tatshenshini became a U.N. World Heritage Site, I went back on the river. This time there were only six of us: Dona, her son Jesse, Sheena, Alan Young (who had skillfully led the campaign in Yukon), and our boatman, Will. With just one raft on this trip, we would have no margin for error, since there would be no other boat to undertake rescues. If one of us was dumped into the rapids or got washed away in the mile-wide, 32-degree-Fahrenheit water, he or she would drown. If someone took a bad fall or got mauled by a grizzly, medical attention would be days away. So this time, as our little group headed out, the river seemed much larger than before and the land wilder than ever.

Downstream we went, day after day, shooting through rapids, scudding over shallows, deeper into Nature, back toward the Ice Age, on water widening with each incoming tributary. Again we rode that rushing ocean toward the sea.

Again the mountains reached higher and the ice eased lower. And again we reached the heartland of this wilderness to witness two great rivers joining.

Here in the land of rising mountains where the continental plates collided, where glaciers crept forward, where salmon returned upriver and bears came down to feed, at the junction where Tlingit and Tuchone had encountered each other, and where the Tatshenshini and the Alsek combined, once more I was at Confluence, the place of union and of unity.

Sitting in this supreme space, I reflected on all that had happened since my last visit. Surely the spirit of Confluence had inspired us. In fact, the entire campaign for Tatshenshini had been based on a coming together of all those leaders and groups in Tatshenshini International in the countless cities and the capitals in both Canada and the United States. Together, the public – conservationists, rafters, mountaineers, scientists, politicians, civil servants, teachers, schoolchildren and their parents – had helped, each in his or her own way. Like individual rivulets, they had contributed to what became a massive flow, creat-

This team of exceptional conservationists led the continental effort to keep Tatshenshini wild.

ing a pressure for conservation of such a force that it could no longer be resisted.

Then, inevitably, the ice dam burst and the floodwaters of change rushed forth. A torrent of huge proportions swept down the Alsek through the Turnback gorge, washing Windy Craggy Peak clean of the toxic miners' plans and threats of acid-rock or heavy-metal poisons. Down the O'Connor and into the Tatshenshini it surged, sweeping away all thought of bridges, roads, or slurry pipelines. On and on went these cleansing waters, inundating everything as they passed, streaming all the way to the Pacific. Then, as the river subsided in the wake of the flood, calm returned. Sandbars became tracked up again with wildness in a landscape newly preserved, protected for all people, for all the world, for always.

Because this time, unlike before, I now sat at Confluence within the Tatshenshini-Alsek World Heritage Site, in the heart of the greatest international park on Earth, on the banks of North America's wildest river, beside Tatshenshini, the spirit of a vast land.

Nine

Chilcotin Mountains
Living Like an Ancestor

WHEN Great Spirit made this world, He dreamed the land into being. In one special place He envisioned heaven on Earth: a most splendid chain of mountains, the Chilcotins. On their eastern expanse He fashioned the ground gently, rounding the ridges. Clothed in grass, from lowland to the peaks, this territory became home for both bighorn sheep and deer.

Westward, He shaped the alpine crests sharper and ever more impressive until finally they reached so high that the snow never melted and the summits were glazed always with ice. Then, to make the grandeur complete, with deft motion Great Spirit carved three bold trenches and filled them with water to become lakes. Each one He painted with vibrancy: chalk-green Taseko, bright turquoise Chilko, and deep cobalt Tatlayoko. And so that the beauty of this land in all its abundance could be enjoyed, He now gave life to the Tsilhquot'in, the people who would always live here.

Pleased with His artistry, and wishing His work to endure forever, Great Spirit bestowed the stewardship of the Chilcotins upon two god mountains —

T'šil?os and his wife, Eniyud. "Care well for my country," He instructed, "the peaks and long lakes, the animals and people. Tend to the future. Live always like ancestors."

And thus the sacred mountains began their duties together, Lord T'šil?os, massive on the horizon, emblazoned with a glacial sash, and Eniyud, his spirited companion, knife-edged ridges rising to a feisty peak. Together from their lofty setting they watched all the goings-on throughout the length of these ranges. Sometimes, too, they looked northward, gazing out across a great flat plateau that stretched away to the horizon and beyond.

In the winters winds howled around these noble summits, obscuring all in fierce blizzards. During the short summers, with snow melted clear, the alpine flowers would bloom in such color again. Down on the lakes, the bright waters were always swept with waves, whipped up by gusts that jetted through the passes from the distant Pacific.

But despite such idyllic timelessness, T'šil?os and Eniyud had problems. They could never agree on anything. Like so many couples, they argued, endlessly, it seemed. Often the Chilcotin skies would ring with thunder, and lightning flashed as they fought. This was not surprising, given their powerful, proud dispositions. But eventually it became too much for Eniyud. The thought of living out immortality in such close quarters with her husband was unbearable. So one night she just picked up and left.

Heading out at the infinitely slow pace that mountains must move, she made her way west, descending and crossing Chilko Lake. But here Eniyud had to pause. She gave birth to a smaller set of mountains, which she left to live between the lakes of Chilko and Tatlayoko. Before moving on, though, she remembered Great Spirit's instructions, and so, living like an ancestor, she covered the slopes of her children with a small white flower. Its roots looked and tasted like tiny potatoes. Now, she thought, there would always be food here for whoever came by.

Traveling across Tatlayoko Lake to its western shore, the mountain goddess finally reached a point that seemed far enough away from T'šil?os, but still close enough to keep him in view. Midway between, she could also watch over their children, the Potato Range. And so, stretched out across the Chilcotins, this family of immortal mountains attended to their sacred task.

THIS STORY OF T'ŝil?os and Eniyud was the myth the Tsilhquot'in told to explain how their home country had first been formed. Always the people treated these two great peaks with utmost respect. Never point at T'ŝil?os, they warned, or the weather will change for the worse. Since the Chilcotin Mountains and the adjacent plateau experienced some of the coldest winters anywhere in southern British Columbia, this advice was to be taken seriously.

Yet despite the harsh climate, the wilderness grandeur of these mountains was undeniable. As for the Tsilhquot'in, they were a part of this fine place, woven as deeply into the fabric of Nature as their brother, the bear, or sister, the deer. Living a nomadic lifestyle, they followed the animals up into the alpine each summer and out across the timbered plateau in winter. Each fall was salmon season when the runs returned in huge numbers by way of the Fraser Canyon up into the Chilko and Taseko Rivers.

For generations beyond number the Tsilhquot'in lived here in harmony with the land, the animals, and the fish, never taking more than they needed, grateful for what they were given, loving Great Spirit, and leaving health for the future. For these people Great Spirit's instructions were the divine reason for being, the basis of life and of their survival. Always they remembered to think of those yet to come.

And so they lived season by season, one year into the next, from generation to generation. Always life's lessons learned were passed down from the elders to those younger who, upon getting older themselves, continued the tradition. Nor were the old people forgotten when their time to leave was at hand. Rather, their bodies were reunited with the land under the watchful eyes of the god peaks. Then, as their spirits went beyond, their memory of their time on Earth was kept alive. They were revered as the ancestors to those living, the ones who came before.

Thus did timelessness pervade the Chilcotin Mountains – the river of life flowing constantly down through the ages until the day the white men came into the country seeking furs. Unlike the Tsilhquot'in, these new people stayed apart from the land, living within walls at Fort Chilcotin on Puntzi Lake. They wanted the Natives to trade the lives of animals for things: pots, guns, knives, and the like. While these objects were useful, the Tsilhquot'in never got as enamored with fur trading as other aboriginal peoples did. Much to the European traders' frustration, these Natives trapped only enough to barter for the goods they most needed, and little more. Eventually business proved so poor that the white men closed down Fort Chilcotin and moved away.

Later, in the 1860s, when British promoter Alfred Waddington commenced his scheme to build a road up the tortuous Homathko River canyon into Chilcotin country and on to the Cariboo gold fields, the Tsilhquot'in intervened, killing 14 workers. They wanted no part of the colonialists' road and the white man's ways, which would despoil their homeland. This conflict, dubbed the Chilcotin Wars, resulted in the road never being built, nor did the Tsilhquot'in ever formally surrender their land.

Over time, however, a small number of white people did make their way into the country to settle as ranchers. They ran cattle up into the alpine meadows in summer and out onto the plateau through the cold winter months. But the Tsilhquot'in were more willing to accept these newcomers, since they seemed to understand the land and the Chilcotin way better. Putting down roots, the ranchers, too, sought to live in balance with Nature. They learned, as the Natives long had known, that their survival depended on doing so. And in the following decades, Tsilhquot'in Natives and Chilcotin cowboys came to coexist out on the broad plateau under the tall presence of T'śil?os and Eniyud.

THE MYSTIQUE OF Chilcotin country first touched my life the summer after graduating from university. It was 1972, and with the Nitinat Triangle recently saved for inclusion in Pacific Rim National Park, I was offered a short contract by the National Parks Service. The agency wanted me to scout the B.C. interior plateau for potential federal park sites. This assignment was a great one. It required me to poke up back roads in my secondhand Datsun camper truck, exploring the center of the province from the U.S. border to Prince George, 500 miles north. During that time, I saw a lot of territory and found several possible parks. But of all the places I encountered I was most taken by the wild expanses west of the Fraser River.

While the maps referred to the entire region as the Chilcotin, in fact, there were two distinct landscapes. The plateau portion north of the Chilcotin River was formed from lava flows and seemed unendingly flat. A stunted spruce-pine forest grew there, frequently threaded with natural moose pastures. At that time this plateau country was virtually unlogged.

Along the southern verge of the plateau the land rose into a marvelous procession of peaks and valleys – the Chilcotin Mountains. Here I looked down into the dryland canyons of the Fraser and Chilcotin Rivers, an almost unknown part of British Columbia, reminiscent of the cowboy country of the American Southwest. These grasslands were home to the finest herd of California bighorns in Canada. Higher up, the grasslands connected to long, wending meadows that meandered into alpine. On the skyline the high peaks were a mountaineer's delight: T'śil?os, Mount Queen Bess, and magnificent Mount Waddington, the tallest peak in the Coast Mountains and British Columbia's second highest summit, after Tatshenshini's Mount Fairweather.

Penetrating this wildness were three spectacular lakes, each one distinct. In particular, I remember the first time I sat on the beach at Chilko Lake, with its vividly hued waters. Looking down its windswept length, I could see into the core of the range all the way to the distant snowfields. Along the western shore the land rose to the relaxed alpine of the Potato Mountains. To the east, T'śil?os's imposing form dominated, remote, grand and mysterious. I felt as if I had chanced upon Shangri-La.

This wilderness was one that I couldn't forget. Even years later, sometimes late at night as I slipped off to sleep, the view 50 miles down Chilko would drift once more through my mind. But decades would pass before I returned to the Chilcotins. In the meantime I moved north to Smithers where the Babine and Spatsizi regions drew my attention. Still, for all the years I lived in the north, each time I flew down to Vancouver for yet another business meeting, the jet flight path would take me right over the Chilcotins. Each time as I peered down from 30,000 feet to the brilliant waters of Tatlayoko, Taseko and Chilko, I vowed that one day I would work for this land's preservation.

However, it wasn't until the early 1990s, as the epic Tatshenshini campaign moved toward culmination, that I had the chance to make good on my old pledge. Proposals to protect the Chilcotin Mountains had been around for 40 years, but in all that time nothing had been preserved. From the gentle Tyax-Big Creek country in the east to Chilko Lake in the center and the Niut (or Eniyud) Mountains in the west, there were plenty of people and environmental organizations concerned about these mountains, 200 miles north of Vancouver. But translating this concern into on-the-ground protection had been elusive.

One summer, midway through the Tatshenshini campaign, when the strug-

gle was very intense, and with no time off in the past two years, I realized I had to have a break. To ensure that I could get away from my worrying about the Tatshenshini and its Ice Age wilderness, I decided to get to know some different country that I had long wanted to explore. Over the next couple of months I made three different forays into the Chilcotin Mountains.

To start with, Sheena and I went up for a weeklong horseback trip into the eastern part of the range. She was in elementary school at the time and had never been on a horse. Fortunately for her, there was a boy her age, Davey, who had ridden a lot. As they went into the mountains, these two were so involved in being kids that Sheena never stopped to consider that the saddle was someplace new to her. The first time she got up on her horse, she just rode. Before long she and Davey were so preoccupied teasing each other and goofing around that they figured out how to twist around backward in their saddles to make faces at each other, even as their horses were cantering.

This mood was blackened, however, when one afternoon we crossed a steep rock slide area during a thundering downpour. With horses strung out nose to tail across the scree slope, a boulder suddenly washed loose 200 feet above. The rock bounded down the slope and smashed into one of the lead pack animals, breaking its back. The wranglers had to shoot poor Cinnabar on the spot to end the mare's suffering. Then they buried the body so that the grizzlies wouldn't get it. Everyone was pretty shaken up, especially the kids. But thankfully, there hadn't been a rider involved.

Despite this freak accident, the trip turned into a good one. Over the next several days we rode trails through tall meadows of grass and blue lupines. With soft, verdant ridges and smooth alpine passes this was a gentle wilderness. High above the tree line our horses moved steadily. On the Tyax divide we glassed for bighorns and watched mule deer grazing. Peering down into the wetlands at the head of Big Creek, we let our eyes trace a moose trail as it headed out into the far expanse of the plateau.

Later that summer I again looked out on this vista, but from a different location. Farther west, this time Dona and I climbed T'si1?os up to the tight summit where cliffs drop away. There was no question that this spot was sacred. The whirling winds were ferocious, the air energized and charged. A pair of rough-legged hawks were thrown about as they spiraled. I could see why this peak should be treated with ultimate respect, with reverence.

Wedged between the topmost rocks, out of the savage gusts, we saw the sights this god mountain had long observed. Off to our right, in the distance, we could make out the Tyax-Big Creek country where Sheena and I had ridden. Looking south, we saw 30-mile-long Chilko Lake in all its dazzling glory, striking deep into the Coast Mountains. Farther away to the west, bold on the horizon, the queen peak, Eniyud, stood forth, timeless, like her partner Lord T'šil?os. Together, yet apart, still they maintained their joint vigil, guarding the wild lands of the Tsilhquot'in that stretched out between them.

In these past few years on the Tatshenshini campaign, Dona and I had been through tough times together. Like T'šil?os and Eniyud, we, too, had bickered and battled, especially when the stress of our work seemed unbearable. But unlike them, we had found the means to hold together. Through even the most difficult moments we had campaigned, parented, and breathed life closely. Now, huddled up here, just the two of us, we were restored by the Chilcotin magic. Like the hawks lifted high in the mystic mountain's updrafts, how our spirits soared that day on the summit of T'šil?os!

Late in the summer we made one more wilderness journey. This time Sheena, Dona, and I were together for a backpack into the Niuts. However, this trip was almost aborted when the night before departing Sheena learned that a big male grizzly had been sighted where we were headed. Her fears surfaced at the trailhead as we readied our packs.

"Daddy," she said, sobbing, tears streaming down her face, "I'm afraid. I might get eaten by the bear."

Dona and I agreed with her that there were real dangers here and that bears were a part of this wilderness. We left it up to her, though. If she wanted to, we were willing to forget about going into the mountains and would stay down at Tatlayoko Lake instead.

The choice wasn't easy for her. She struggled with her fears for several minutes as Dona and I sat in the midst of our gear, giving her what support we could. Gradually she calmed herself and said, "No, I want to go. Because if I don't, I won't get to see the mountains. And I like being up in them a lot. But we'll have to make plenty of noise, okay? Because I really don't want to get eaten."

We all agreed to this plan and off we went, shouting all the way. Within a mile or two her fears faded as she became immersed in the flowers and in carrying her pack. That day she climbed 3,000 vertical feet. Dona and I were impressed. But while Sheena may have forgotten about the grizzlies, I certainly hadn't. Her fears had set mine in motion, and I thought about what it would be like if she ever got hurt up here. So for the next few days I looked for bears behind every tree.

This final trip for the summer was different again from the two earlier ones. There was a delightful chain of alpine lakes up high. Sheena and Dona went skinny-dipping several times. I summoned up the courage only once and decided, as all parts of me began to shrivel, that the water was definitely too cold for my liking.

On that hike we climbed a peak just north of Eniyud. The goddess mountain, too steep to attempt without rock-climbing gear, was beyond our ability. Still, the ascent we made to our ridge top was long and demanding. Again I was delighted by Sheena's stamina and high spirits.

At the top our little family looked across the next valley to ice-faced Mount Waddington, higher than anything else around. Scanning eastward, I saw the familiar pyramid profile of T'̂sil?os off in the distance where just weeks before Dona and I had crouched by its summit cairn. This time we looked across the Chilcotins from Eniyud's perspective. Straining to see 150 miles to the grassy mountains above Big Creek, I felt as if I was just beginning to know this range.

The more time I spent in these mountains, the greater my desire to help protect them. And the more times I drove the road west from Williams Lake toward the Chilcotins, the stronger my sense of urgency that we had to work fast.

Always rolling by in the oncoming lane was an endless procession of logging trucks. They were hauling out the trees of this region far faster than they could ever regrow. Situated in the rain shadow of the Coast Mountains, at high altitudes (5,000 feet on the plateau and up to 7,500 feet in the Chilcotin ranges), these forests survived in a cold, semidesert ecosystem. The biological productivity was low, which meant that an old-growth spruce typically required 150 years to reach just 12 inches in diameter. Therefore, unlike the giant rainforests of the B.C. coast, regrowth after logging took a very long time in the Chilcotins.

However, one would never know this fact from the convoy of trucks. In recent years the sawmills in Williams Lake had expanded in number and size so fast that their appetite for wood was now double what the forests could sustain. And while the Chilcotins had been virgin territory up to only a few years earlier, a place where cowboys had authored classic books such as *Three Against the Wilderness* and *Grass Beyond the Mountains*, now this beloved frontier was being rapaciously overcut.

By the early 1990s the clearcuts were spreading across the plateau country like a plague. In fact, half of all the trees ever cut in the region had been felled in the previous eight years. Such cutting couldn't last. Fixated on shareholder returns and profits, the companies had a bottom line that was *now*. They wasted little thought for the future; there was no evidence of ancestorship among them.

Moving like locusts, the logging companies surged off the now-ravaged plateau and up into the mountains toward T'ŝil?os and Eniyud. From up in the alpine I could see this tide of destruction approaching, the clearcuts marching ever closer. This vision disturbed me deeply. It tormented me for days during my hikes. Soon, I realized, this wilderness would be no more.

Driving home after such trips, with truck after truck roaring by, I knew the chance for preservation was almost gone. So one afternoon, inbound for Williams Lake on Highway 20, I resolved to make an all-out effort to protect the Chilcotins, once and for all. Over the next hundreds of miles of pavement I formulated my plans. The immediate need was to determine the priority sites for preservation and then bring together in a coordinated effort the people who already cared about the Chilcotins. Once this was done the resources necessary to wage the campaign – monetary, informational, and staff – could then be assembled.

When I got home, I set to work and soon secured initial funding from the World Wildlife Fund. With the Tatshenshini campaign still not finished, there was far less opportunity than I would have liked to focus on the Chilcotins. Nevertheless, given the rate of overcutting under way there, I made a special effort to find time to begin scoping out strategy to save these mountains. I studied the many reports and proposals written over the decades about these mountains by groups such as the B.C. Naturalists Federation, the Federation of B.C. Mountain Clubs, and the South Chilcotin Mountains Wilderness Association, which enabled me to identify the most important wilderness and wildlife ranges. As well, I flew the whole region to field-check this data and then proceeded to chart onto Mylar sheets what I had learned about the region's land-use patterns. Finally, by overlaying different combinations of these maps on top of one another, it was possible to determine the preservation priorities and the most apparent conflicts.

What this mapping research confirmed was that wilderness protection was still achievable for the Chilcotins. Still, I knew the resource companies would stridently oppose any proposal for parks. As always they would want access to all the land and not want anything "locked up." Therefore, a unified citizens' effort to protect the Chilcotins would be required. Since concern for these mountains was long-standing and extensive, I felt the best way to help would be to serve as a catalyst to consolidate this public support. So I set out to meet with conservationists, ranchers, Natives, guide outfitters, and all those who loved this wild place. The overlay maps proved useful in these sessions to explore preservation and campaign strategy options. At meetings convened in community halls or living rooms across the plateau, and also with the longtime provincial Chilcotin Mountains advocates in Vancouver, a cohesive campaign began to coalesce.

With the first grass-roots threads strung into place, what was needed now was someone to work in the region to weave these people and many others into a cohesive web while I did the same at the provincial level. To protect a wilderness of the caliber and scale of the Chilcotins would require a top-down, bottom-up campaign approach, galvanizing the local public as well as selling the issue provincially.

For a long time I had believed the best way to preserve a wilderness system was to work B.C.-wide, linking the larger provincial conservation associations and then connecting them with the rural supporters through regional field organizers. This model was the one long used effectively by trade unions to organize their people locally. So, when a number of the major B.C. environmental groups began in the early 1990s to coordinate their campaigning and fundraising efforts, my priority, as one of them, was to ensure that funding would flow to several regional organizers across British Columbia.

This collaborative effort succeeded and resulted in money becoming available to hire a field organizer for the Chilcotin-Cariboo region. Since I knew that part of British Columbia well, I took the lead on locating the best campaigner for the job. The person I had had my eye on since conducting the Chilcotin grass-roots meetings was Dave Neads. An ardent conservationist, Dave had been a backcountry ranger for the B.C. Parks Branch and now lived in the far plateau country where the Chilcotin Mountains merged with Tweedsmuir Park.

A modern-day homesteader who lived off the grid – his home was powered by solar cells and heated by wood – Dave knew and lived the wilderness better than most. The backcountry house he had built looked straight out to the Chilcotin peaks. Definitely his driveway was the longest, roughest one I had ever seen – an hour's travel by truck in from the nearest logging road; 45 minutes by snowmobile in winter. Dave was as skilled on a computer and working the phone lines as he was haying or packing horses. Tough, disciplined, dedicated, and smart, he had what it took to fight for the land.

Once Dave was on contract he soon began to organize the local conservation movement. Meanwhile I got busy in Victoria. British Columbia by now was ablaze with land-use conflicts. At Tatshenshini, Clayoquot Sound, and the Carmanah and Slocan Valleys, as well as countless other places, conservationists and exploitationists locked horns in battle.

As the government saw it, this was a lose-lose situation. The province's resource markets were under threat of environmental boycott, and jobs were at risk even as the land suffered further from devastating corporate practices. In Premier Harcourt's opinion it was time to act and end the war in the woods. Therefore, he established the Commission on the Resources and the Environment (CORE) to find a middle ground by developing land-use plans which, in accord with the United Nations Brundtland Report's biodiversity target, would preserve at least 12 percent of British Columbia's land base and also identify the areas available for development.

To lead CORE the premier appointed Stephen Owen, the province's former ombudsman. In his earlier position – responding to citizen complaints of government mistreatment – Owen had earned a reputation for integrity and fairness. A lawyer who had worked extensively with Amnesty International, he believed strongly in local public participation as the means to move from land-use confrontation to cooperation. By this he didn't mean some advisory talk-and-log scam, but an honest democratic forum where the public from all walks of life could reach consensus, and which the government then would honor. It was on these conditions that he had accepted the job and to which the premier had agreed. In a province polarized on everything, it seemed that Owen had taken on an impossible task to bring peace to the land.

Because of the sheer size of British Columbia, the CORE process had to focus on regions of a manageable scale. At the outset Owen intended to address the most troubled places: Vancouver Island rainforests and the interior region of the Kootenays. While this plan was a good start, I still felt it critical that CORE should also deal immediately with the Chilcotin-Cariboo. After all, this area was the part of southern British Columbia with the most wilderness left to protect. Yet given the rate of logging, I was concerned that if preservation didn't happen soon, the wild Chilcotin country would vanish.

Therefore, in the weeks after Owen's appointment I pressed the Premier and various Cabinet ministers hard to include the Chilcotin-Cariboo in CORE's initial assignment. And while others might also have pushed this viewpoint, the good news was that the lobby succeeded. As a result, citizen groups, ranging from conservationists to loggers, soon sat down around the CORE tables in three locations to begin negotiations.

Their challenge was to reach agreements that would protect a system of wilderness areas as well as meet employment and economic needs. The critics and pundits laughed. They said that in a place like British Columbia, CORE was a naive, idealistic concept that would never succeed. And, indeed, during the two years that each of the tables met, it looked as if these cynics might be right. Repeatedly the word coming out of the meetings was that the traditional opponents were having difficulty finding much to agree on.

Of the three regions, the prospects were especially bad for the Chilcotin-Cariboo. There the resource companies and chamber-of-commerce types organized the Cariboo Communities Coalition to obstruct, so it seemed, the CORE process entirely. These people looked like they wanted no part of preserving nature. For months they stonewalled, preventing the group around the negotiating table from reaching consensus even on a matter as simple as the region's boundaries. Needless to say, no progress was made on deciding which lands would become parks and which would be open for industry.

To counter this roadblock, the conservationists, under Dave's leadership, stuck to the moral high ground. They tried to explain the urgent need for protection, using satellite imagery to show the extent of the overcutting problem. With ecological data and economic reports they persistently answered the other side's objections and tried to move the talks toward solutions, but to little avail.

Using wildly inflated figures and jobs-versus-environment scare tactics, the resource industry's Coalition warned that if CORE protected land for Nature, thousands of people would be thrown out of work. Yet the government's figures, and certainly our own, showed that the jobs at risk were one-third to one-sixth of those claimed by the companies. It was also evident that such "losses" would be more than offset by gains in value-added manufacturing and better forest management. But this message didn't seem to matter much to the opposition forces. They simply drowned it out.

214

Bankrolled by the resource companies, and with hundreds of thousands of dollars at their disposal, the Coalition hard-liners ignored the facts and deepened fears. Newspapers, radio, and television were swamped with advertising that warned of environmentalist-inspired, economic disaster. Mass rallies were organized and mills gave workers paid time off to attend them. At these events the anti-CORE ringleaders further stirred up the fearful anger of the townspeople.

Now residents who had long been concerned about what was happening to their forests became afraid to speak out. Threats were muttered against them in cafés. For the first time ever in the Cariboo-Chilcotin, people became wary of their neighbors. Mainstreet merchants were pressed into supporting the Coalition's rhetoric whether they liked it or not. The situation was beginning to get ugly.

Provoking hatred, leaders at a Coalition activist-training session gave speeches that labeled environmentalists as tyrants akin to Hitler and Idi Amin. During a local community parade, a Coalition-inspired float featured Stephen Owen's body hung in effigy. And when Owen came to the region in person to explain his findings, an angry mob confronted him with a highway blockade of noisy logging trucks and a hangman's noose.

All the while Dave and his folks bravely continued their work for wilderness in what was becoming an increasingly dangerous situation. One evening the television news showed Dave jostled by a jeering, irrational crowd as he appealed for reason. To his great credit he never lost his temper, nor his courage. Later that night on the phone he told me that even as he had been on camera some thugs behind him had repeatedly and painfully kidney-punched him with low, out-of-sight blows. As I heard his account, my regard for him grew even greater, as did my concern for his safety.

In the meantime, throughout these months, I had devoted myself to the provincial aspects of the Cariboo-Chilcotin environmental effort. I worked strategically to coordinate the campaign with various B.C. and national conservation groups and found myself serving as spokesman in the provincial media, doing interviews to raise public awareness of the wilderness values at

stake. In part this meant countering statements made by public-relations specialists and logging CEOs from corporate head offices.

As always, I worked the halls of the Legislature, often mobilizing conservation lobbying teams in order to meet and surpass the efforts of the other side.
And, finally, I took on the task at the provincial level to ensure that Dave and the
other Cariboo-Chilcotin conservationists had the necessary mapping, computer
analysis, media materials, and whatever dollars could be mustered to allow them
to do their job. As had been agreed at the outset, Dave and I worked in tandem:
he on the regional frontline and me in Vancouver and Victoria.

When Commissioner Owen finally announced his Chilcotin-Cariboo recommendations to the B.C. Cabinet on July 14, 1994, I was there at his Legislature press conference. True to the skeptics' predictions, this CORE group had
failed to reach a consensus. The blocking tactics of the company-led Coalition
had seen to that. Therefore, to provide direction for the government, Owen's
staff had come up with its own plan. The moment I saw CORE's proposed map
I knew we conservationists had serious problems.

Somehow, in order to devise a compromise, the CORE plan presented by
Owen had fragmented our key wilderness proposals in the Chilcotin Mountains and elsewhere to a point where they would be too small to be ecologically
viable. The plan contained a series of small, postage-sized reserves that might
protect flora but not fauna. If CORE's scheme was enacted, wild predators like
grizzlies and wolves, and the caribou, bighorn sheep, moose, and deer they fed
on, would have too little room to roam. They would die out over time. For
Nature not to lose big-time, the environmental forces would have to convince
the government to reassemble our original extensive proposals. To achieve this
goal the acreage from CORE's proposed small reserves would have to be traded
and consolidated into four or five large wilderness areas.

The question was: how could we get the Cabinet to revise CORE's plan to
hold on to the wilderness, especially given the extreme opposition of the
resource companies? It was obvious the other side was even more upset by
Owen's announcement that morning than us. Even the small parks that CORE

proposed made them see red. Judging by their media statements that day, they intended to kill the plan completely.

Watching the Coalition spokesmen give their irate statements to the television reporters, I could almost taste the vitriol and feel the tension rising. I feared that if tempers continued to flare, violence was possible. Never before as a Canadian or a British Columbian had I worried so much about bloodshed. But that day, as I chose my words carefully on camera, in the depths of my heart dread seeped in. Events in the Chilcotin-Cariboo could soon go critical. If they did, communities could be torn apart with hatred and people, especially our people, could get physically hurt.

Like the lead-up to a massive earthquake, the pressure was now extreme. With tempers flaring, both sides were locked into anger and fear, a recipe for disaster. The only way out was to defuse the situation through tough, top-level negotiations, and that didn't mean more CORE-style discussions. After an impasse of two years, these discussions were headed for oblivion, thanks to the destructive tactics of the Coalition hard-liners. What was urgently needed instead was discreet, brokered talks among pragmatists, among those individuals with influence who might be able to find an agreement their respective parties could live with.

To achieve such an objective all sides had to be willing. And somehow a first invisible contact had to be made, but how could that happen? As with the Arabs and Israelis in their most bitter days, there was no trust anywhere. In fact, there weren't any contacts at all, visible or invisible. So just as the Norwegians had enabled the first step toward Mideast peace by secretly getting both enemies in touch, a back channel had to be opened, silently and soon.

I wrestled with how to accomplish this but got nowhere. And then, as so often happens, fate intervened at just the right moment. Unsolicited, a third party phoned to suggest that I get together with a certain forest company CEO who, I was told, might be interested in confidentially exploring possibilities. With nothing to lose and sensing this could lead to the back channel I sought, I acted on the advice. A few nights later I quietly got together for dinner with

Jake Kerr, president of Lignum Forest Products, one of the largest and oldest sawmills in the Cariboo-Chilcotin.

The dinner was a classic power meeting between extremely cautious adversaries. Like two wary wolves circling, Jake and I checked each other out with the smallest of talk while we perused the menu. As we ate, we spiraled subtly closer to the issue we both wanted to discuss, testing each other for trustworthiness while continuing to posture. As the main course moved to dessert, I began to conclude that this fellow was a straight shooter and that there was a possibility of getting something done working with him.

Presumably he was thinking the same thing, for finally, over coffee, we homed in on the Chilcotin-Cariboo standoff and the danger of the situation. Jake had grown up in Williams Lake and he, too, seemed genuinely worried that the land use conflict was close to exploding. He also concurred that if this happened, everyone would lose, perhaps tragically so. And while he wasn't a raving "enviro-lunatic," to use his own words, he also knew that a solution had to be found that would meet enough of the needs of the conservationists and his people, as well.

"Do you think," he asked, "there's any chance for a settlement here?"

"Yes," I said. "But it won't be easy. How about you?"

"I agree."

"Shall we give it a try?"

He nodded, and so did I.

For the rest of the dinner we talked in general terms about how to proceed. We both knew there were no promises that an agreement could be reached. Not only was there a huge gulf between our two sides, but within each camp there was a wide range of personalities and positions to relate to. There was no certainty that Jake or I could convince our people to work together. After all, neither of us could claim to lead, speak for, or control the people we worked with. The best we could do was to try to get our respective allies moving toward a solution and to keep this back channel open between us. As well, we both committed to approaching the premier's office independently. We would seek to have a mediator appointed to help broker a deal. And so by the time the last coffee was gone, the "Prince of Darkness" (Jake's handle for me) and "Jake the Snake" (as I nicknamed him) shook hands and departed.

Our separate lobbies brought results. The government accepted the fact that the CORE plan, as currently written, worked for no one and was opposed by all. Therefore, Grant Scott, an environmentally progressive forester with international experience, was contracted to troubleshoot and broker a deal if one could be found. His assignment looked impossible. The Coalition was spending big money on advertising to kill any chance of preservation and to further incite anti-enviro hysterics. Meanwhile our side was readying a major international counterstrike.

Using contacts and strategies acquired in the Clayoquot and Tatshenshini issues in Washington, D.C., and across the United States, the B.C. environmental movement laid the groundwork for a comprehensive, multi-pronged campaign that would vastly surpass anything British Columbia had ever experienced. While such an action wasn't my preference, it was necessary both for negotiating leverage and as a contingency.

From grim past experience conservationists knew well that any last-ditch talks would only succeed if environmentalists had the muscle to be taken seriously. More probable was the prospect that the Cariboo-Chilcotin CORE process would blow apart entirely. If that unfortunate event happened, it could trigger similar failures in the other CORE regions, thereby halting further preservation. In the event of this worst-case scenario British Columbia's environmental movement would need the means to hit back hard at the resource companies. Otherwise they were likely to use bulldozers to smash through what remained of the province's fragile wilderness.

If this U.S. campaign were to be launched, it would surely set off a series of moves and countermoves by both sides that, in the end, would be disastrous for everyone: workers, conservationists, industry, government, small communities, and the land. Yet we couldn't simply allow the Coalition to tear apart the future of our parks system. Therefore, as every warrior knows when war looms, you must rigorously prepare for the possibility and then hope your credible threat will, in fact, prevent it. Only if that fails must battle be engaged.

Given the economic and political plans our people were readying, and the risk of violence being incited, if events went critical, the damage could be widespread, long-term, and tragic. And so in those late, hot days of summer 1994 British Columbia teetered on the brink of environmental conflagration. Understanding this potential danger, Grant Scott initiated intensive shuttle diplomacy. In a series of confidential meetings with each side he worked to identify what the hot buttons of disagreement were, who the potential leaders capable of eventually swaying their people were, and where possible areas of agreement might lie. Like a B.C. Henry Kissinger, he went back and forth from city to country, union hall to corporate headquarters, eco-office to the Cabinet room over and over again.

Slowly the elements needed for peace began to reveal themselves, and leadership emerged in each faction. In order to move events along Scott now proposed a weekend of pressure-cooker negotiations in Williams Lake. Because of the deep dislike each side harbored for the other, he intended to keep them separate. He would repeatedly move between the camps, carrying proposal and counterproposal in the hope of narrowing the gap toward a resolution. It was a plan that Dave, myself, and our conservationist team were willing to try.

So one October Friday night I flew to Williams Lake. Slipping quietly into town and my hotel, I took care not to be seen either by the local media or leaders from the other side. Due to my high-profile role provincially, I wasn't the most beloved person as far as the Coalition was concerned. I figured news of my presence would only stir up anger and diminish the chance for success, so I decided to confine myself to the building and keep out of view for the weekend.

My first task for the weekend's discussions was to develop a psychological leadership role with the other conservationists. Despite all my work at the provincial level, as an outsider I was still viewed with suspicion by these local enviros. That was par for the course, but now trust had to evolve so I could play out my role of pressuring the CEOs, labor leaders, and premier's staff on behalf of our people in an eventual endgame.

Over the weekend, with Dave's help, I was able to develop the trust needed even as Scott pushed our group harder and harder to make compromises. It was tough for our people to back off on any issue. Each time we gave in meant condemning yet another piece of wild earth to destruction. The only consolation, a seemingly poor one at the time, was that the other side was also losing things dear to it.

The hours in that hot, stuffy hotel room ticked by tediously. We conservationists argued and struggled, each one of us trying to convince the others of where to give or what to hold. The whole affair was agonizing. The sense of responsibility for the future weighed oppressively on our shoulders. We knew the choices we made that weekend would be judged not just by our peers but would affect British Columbians yet unborn. In spite of this awareness none of our people lost their will, or their goodwill toward one another. Instead, there was a common, heroic determination brought on by the countless months under heavy attack. I felt honored to work with these valiant souls.

It was negotiation by exhaustion. Scott kept at us to 4:00 a.m., only to start again after three hours' sleep by 7:00. Each time he returned from the other side we made headway on some critical site only to backslide on another. But with each new offer I sensed a shifting in the psychology of our unseen adversaries as they, too, battled among themselves in their own meeting room. Their hard-liners were losing out. The extremist, fear-mongering rhetoric had gone too far even for their side. By the nature of their proposals, I could discern that the pragmatic progressives, like Jake, were beginning to dominate. For the first time my gut told me an agreement might be possible.

It all came down to Sunday morning, a half hour before many, including Scott, had to depart by plane. Now was the moment of truth. The two parties appeared to be within bridging distance but, as with any negotiations, the last items preventing an agreement in principle were the toughest. Given all the anger, fear, and distrust of the past two years, it was questionable whether a deal could be reached. Endangered wilderness and the prospect of a full-force war in the woods hung by a thread. I could almost feel the Chilcotin Mountains holding their breath and waiting.

And then it was as if an unknown will intervened. Possibly it was the god mountains themselves coming to life. Perhaps, after watching years of destruction, T'ŝil?os and Eniyud seized this critical moment to telegraph that age-old instruction: "Live always like ancestors." Whatever the cause, it was as if time paused. Each side stood back and saw soberly the full costs if talks failed. Both parties reflected on their achievements of the past marathon days. Then suddenly the impossible happened. Fear transformed into faith, and an initial framework for agreement was achieved. Hesitantly and most cautiously, companies, enviros, unions, and government tentatively agreed to give peace a chance.

Uncertainty, insecurity, even reluctance held sway. The next few days required care and precise action. The situation wasn't final yet. Countless details had to be nailed down. Over a two-week period, acting on behalf of the conservationists, I finally met my industry and union counterparts face-to-face for some last pro forma table pounding. There was also a frenzy of brinkmanship in which both sides pressed the premier's staff hard, and thereby each other, for final concessions. But such dramatic moments were only the closing scenes; the main act was over. For the first time ever in British Columbia a regional land-use agreement that comprehensively protected both wilderness and jobs had been successfully negotiated between environmentalists and developers.

For our part we had protected the key wild lands in the Chilcotins, the bighorn sheep and horse-riding ridges of the Big Creek country, the splendid Chilko Lake country with the adjacent T'ŝil?os uplands, the Homathko Valley, and Tatlayoko Lake at the foot of Eniyud. This package was by no means perfect. For instance, places such as the Niut uplands and Taseko Lake could still be threatened. But since we had preserved the most critical forest lands and placed the rest in a special management zone, we were cautiously hopeful that the desecration visited out on the plateau could be contained there.

What was more, the Chilcotins were only one of the large wilderness areas protected by the agreement. In addition, Dave's backyard mountains, the Itchas-Ilgatchuz, home of the largest caribou herd in southern British Columbia, and the equally important wet belt forests of the Cariboo Mountains, were also part of the package. As with the Chilcotins, painful trade-offs had been made in each place. But likely if we hadn't come to an agreement then, the logging companies would have gutted these lands by the time any North America-wide firestorm we might have ignited had a chance to yield results. After such a conflagration, we would have returned from our crusades to find we had won the battle but lost the war. With the wilderness razed, we would have faced paradise lost.

In return for staying their saws and bulldozers in these wild places, the resource industry and unions received agreement from our people that large portions of the region would be open for logging and mining. It was also resolved that part of this commercial land base would be used for higher-intensity tree farming. While more a monoculture plantation than a biodiverse forest, these places would see industry invest, with government assistance, in advanced silviculture – pruning, thinning, fertilizing. The result would be to grow greater volumes of wood per acre faster, thereby compensating for the "loss" of the wilderness forests that had now been protected and those to be stewarded especially carefully in the special management zones. In all, the total package laid the foundation for certainty, in essence, what lands would be preserved and which ones logged. As such it sought to balance the employment needs of those now working with the environmental necessities of those yet to come.

This Cariboo-Chilcotin Land-Use Plan established a precedent in British Columbia for further negotiated settlements. Soon a similar one was concluded in the Kootenays. And even though in the lead-up to that agreement the resource industry imported the hard-line Cariboo Coalition organizers to stir up fears through rallies and advertising, these tactics, in the end, failed there, too. By then the truth was public: peace in the woods was possible.

Indeed, the news of the Cariboo-Chilcotin Land-Use Plan made the front pages across Canada. After hearing for years of the fierce environmental battles at places such as Clayoquot, Tatshenshini, and South Moresby, Canadians now learned with disbelief that a truce had been reached, that both jobs and the environment could coexist. The sense of relief was palpable.

THE FOLLOWING SUMMER in the Chilcotins I took time to explore the middle ground between two old adversaries. I hiked up atop the Potato Range, with T'ŝilʔos on one horizon and Eniyud on the other. As I thought about how these two protectors had learned to find peace, I smiled. Looking down on the Tatlayoko forests that we had recently saved, I realized that in all their time here the Tsilhquot'in had never had the need to preserve wilderness. In fact, like so many Native peoples, they didn't have a word for wilderness. They didn't require one because, unlike the white man whose society had become separate from and which subdued Nature, the Tsilhquot'in had lived within the wild world throughout the ages.

Only a culture with so little care for the land as ours that it would clearcut forests, poison predators, and pave the frontier would differentiate between the world altered by humans and the original Earth. Only Westerners in their systematic eradication of the pristine could have eventually sensed the need to give wilderness a name, and then, once so labeled, rally desperately to prevent its extinction.

How had we come to this place, I wondered. How had our civilization strayed so far from Native traditions, from our own earlier traditions? After all, in the distant past our predecessors had also lived close to the land, just as the Tsilhquot'in did. But that was long, long ago. In the intervening time something had changed in us. Unlike North American aboriginal peoples, European society hadn't been content to stay at one fixed address. Instead, it became restless and always on the move, exploring, colonizing, and exploiting new worlds. Especially after the Europeans arrived in North America, they lost their sense of place, of what it meant to be one with the land and rooted to a single location for generations.

By contrast, what Native peoples learned from living in one place was the consequences of abusing Mother Earth. From experience that could only be gained from staying put through the ages, the Tsilhquot'in and other aboriginal peoples understood that their survival depended on respecting the land. They knew if they exceeded natural limits they did so at their peril. Kill too many animals and next winter you might starve. Take more fish than you need and the runs might decline. So traditional teachings existed that instructed Native society how to live on the land responsibly, holding individual greed in check for the well-being of all.

Since Native peoples remained in one place, the family lineages and all their stories were never lost. Instead, they gained immortality as the wisdom acquired over time – the right way of living and one's place in the world – was passed on and remembered. The First Peoples knew who their ancestors were and what their own responsibilities were to the generations to come. Aware of their history, they took care for the future.

Sadly this wisdom is something our "modern" society has forgotten. For while ours is the Information Age, complete with knowledge workers and people drowning in data, we want sorely for wisdom. Yet without it, how can we learn to live like an ancestor? How can we know what Great Spirit meant?

Wisdom is gained not from study but by living. Generations in the making, it takes a lifetime to learn and to become an elder. But today in our youth-oriented, baby-boom ways we know little about wisdom and are too adolescent to respect it, despite the fact that we now need wise teachings urgently if we are to endure.

To have a tomorrow we must reconnect with before. Our old-timers knew something about the land. They, too, paid their dues and earned their right to be elders. But in our narcissistic, now-fixated ignorance, we have disowned them. And it isn't that they couldn't be good ancestors; rather, it is because we aren't willing to accept what they knew.

In recent times our footloose, childish society in which mobility has created a false sense of abundance – the grass always being greener in the next valley, with valleys believed to be infinite – has grievously wounded our world, and our humanity. With today's technology only amplifying the impact on the land we have traded life for things. In too many once-splendid Chilcotins around Planet Earth we have chipped forests to pulp, trapped out the wolves, slaughtered the buffalo, and forced wild Nature back. All in the name of objects owned, so cold and dead. All in the quest for money, numbers in ledgers, and bottom lines.

Indeed, if we are to have any hope for survival, we must change our ways fast. We must reconnect with our elders and the wisdom they offer. We must rediscover our sense of place. We need to know that our greed, our love of cold, dead things, threatens survival. Again we have to learn what it means to live with heart, to have courage, just as Dave Neads did in the midst of that threatening crowd, or Jake Kerr did when he had dinner with his adversary, or Sheena did as she faced down her fears about grizzlies.

Humans *with* Nature, not against it. That is the meaning of Great Spirit's words, and how the ancestors lived. That is the path we must take to escape our abyss, to become sane once again. Just like T'ŝilʔos and Eniyud, we, too, must obey Great Spirit's commandments. Like those god mountains presiding over the Chilcotins, we must come again to treasure the loving, wild wonder of Creation and to find it also in one another.

Only then will our battles cease and our agreements hold. Only then will the forests, animals, and mountains no longer be mined to exhaustion. And when that happens, once more we will sense the beauty of our place, our heaven on Earth. At last we will redream the world back into being, with visions of wilderness bringing us safely, all through the night.

Hiking with my daughter Sheena in the Chilcotin Mountains.

Epilogue
On the Wilderness Frontline

ONSERVATIONISTS work as saviors of life. Like canaries once kept in coal mines to alert workers of deadly gas, their role in society is to serve as an environmental early-warning system, as humankind's messengers of impending danger. Yet how often have self-serving companies tried to make us believe that it is these citizens who are the menace and not the industrial risks? How often do big corporate powers urge the public to kill the canaries and ignore their message? Up against today's blinkered morality of maximized profits and rates of return, environmentalists are too often vilified for working to save Nature, for enhancing humanity's chance of survival, for improving the world for our children.

Environmentalists aren't recruited; they enlist voluntarily out of concern for the damage they see happening to the planet. They come in with their hearts to counter this heartbreak. As such they aren't much different than most human beings except that they personally commit to make things better. They make a contribution to life on Earth in the same fashion that others help the physically challenged, the poor, and the sick.

Like such social activists, conservationists work for the greater good of the community. In particular, these individuals are the defenders of environmental integrity, beauty, and life. They hold the thin green line for humanity against those vested interests that would exploit Nature and which justify such behavior solely by fiscal performance. For their social concern conservationists consistently endure corporate salvos that are lobbed at them in full fury.

In the post-Cold War era neoconservatives have retargeted their attack from the Reds to the Greens. An unyielding establishment stereotypes, ridicules, and marginalizes environmentalists as being drugged-up, antisocial troublemakers intent on sabotaging society, jobs, and communities. Such slander is painfully ironic since environmentalists give of themselves in the service of all humanity to ensure that our lives and our world will be healthy, not polluted, poisoned, or killed.

There isn't much money in this lifestyle, especially considering the sacrifices required. Indeed, most environmentalists are sustained by bake-sale-type budgets and donate much of their lives at no charge. When they try to raise money, the forces of industrial might often do whatever they can to lean on governments and foundations to dry up support. It is much easier to finance projects that are nonthreatening to the status quo, such as a hospital, a university, or a symphony orchestra, than to save an old-growth forest. But while funding is typically scarce, my experience is that when conservationists acquire money, they know how to stretch a dollar farther than a rubber band and wring it tighter than any efficiency expert.

The work week of conservationists is measured in absurdly long hours over countless weekends year after year with no possibility of overtime, sick days off with pay, or company pension plans. That is what the lifestyle involves. Out of sheer dedication environmentalists often put everything at risk: their employment, their relationships, their well-being.

This choice is freely made. The rewards come from seeing 1,000-year-old red cedars still standing when conventional wisdom predicted they would now be stumps, or marveling at the scarlet spectacle of spawning salmon in a river now spared from the death sentence of a once-proposed toxic mine. The satisfaction for sacrifices made comes from knowing that by personal action wilderness, wild creatures, clean water, and pure air will endure, that yet another special corner of our world will retain its splendor.

Over the years I have spent much time in wild places. In my church of the living land I have sat by rivers and on top of mountains, trying to make sense of my life, trying to figure out how to live. Long ago the wilderness in its wisdom taught me that I do best for myself by working my best for others. That is how I find my fulfillment and reward for my struggles, and that is why, for all its hardships, I am glad I have chosen conservation as my career.

I don't believe that human existence has to be reduced to the bottom line. While money may be an essential consideration, it isn't the essence of being. Humanity is the only species that seems concerned with making a living. All others just get on with life and live. As such I prefer to take much of my payment in parks rather than dollars. My fulfillment flows from the realization that three generations from now some child will come upon a Tatshenshini sandbar and thrill to see grizzlies. And while he or she will never know about me, passing on the treasured wilderness that has enriched my time and life is worth more to me than fortunes.

Just as an Olympic athlete gives everything to go for the gold, I have found that protecting wilderness means putting all of me on the line. It is about seeing the victory and then making it happen. And while that may sound glorious, in fact, it is mostly terrifying. Those who know me well will confirm that often my lifestyle is overwhelmingly stressful. But so be it. As a balance, I have those times of total release when I am once more in the wild country.

Crusading on the environmental frontier is all about fear of failure and inadequacy. What if this wilderness valley is logged through my actions? What if we run out of time and the mine road goes in? What if the funder, the premier, the public says no? What if I act incorrectly or make a misstep? What if the campaign is too hard and I am not tough enough, smart enough, or compassionate enough? And what if I am just not good enough?

These are the recurrent fears of campaigning. They fill up the days and haunt the nights. Each one is scarier than the one before. Every one of them must be faced and stared down. But then, isn't that what life is about, anyway? After all, how else can I grow as a person if not by encountering my fears? How can I succeed if I won't first risk failure? How else do I learn of my personal strengths?

Wilderness campaigning isn't about inhuman perfection; it is about learning how to survive the countless mistakes that I make. It has taught me to keep on trying even after failing miserably. It has helped me to understand how to try to live responsibly and ethically. To save the wild earth requires living today for tomorrow with a memory of the past. It is about living as if your life depends upon it. Because it does.

Therefore, despite all the hard times, I am always aware that I have freely come to be a crusader for wilderness. In this I consider myself lucky because my life has meaning and is rich in experience. By doing what I do I have the chance to demonstrate for myself, and possibly others, that one person can make a difference. Just as those before me have gifted my life through their actions, I now strive to do the same for those who come after me. Always in my efforts I am thankful that I am not alone, that many allies share in this task, this adventure.

For more than 25 years since the first Earth Day I have dreamed of, struggled over, worried about, and exalted in the wild country of British Columbia. And while the various campaigns I have contributed to have focused on one part of the planet, I believe they have a significance that reaches well beyond. They are ecological archetypes because saving wilderness is about much more than lobbying, publicizing, or fundraising. It is about a way of being, of relating to this home we call Earth. It is about the geography of hope.

Like the Amazonian rainforests, British Columbia is one of the few places still fortunate to retain expanses of pristine Nature. Therefore, the wilderness campaigns fought here are on the global environmental frontline. What conservationists protect in British Columbia, we do for the benefit of the whole world. By our actions we serve as environmental custodians for all humanity to enable a future with promise and sanity.

Dona, my partner in wilderness campaigning and life.

So while my passion and skill help to protect wild British Columbia, I believe that what I do is no different than the Greenpeacer in Europe who opposes nuclear power, the Nigerian who opposes disastrous oil-drilling practices, the mother in Chicago who tries to live responsibly by reducing her family's environmental footprint, or you in the choices you make.

I am a believer in the "can do," in getting results on the ground. When I look back at the record of conservationists in British Columbia and elsewhere over the past quarter century, I see how successful we have been. Up against 100,000 years of genetic programming in Homo sapiens to exploit and subdue wilderness for survival, environmentalists have done much to bring humanity to its senses. This we've done in the few short decades since NASA's men on the moon first saw the Earth shining blue and alone in the infinite darkness of space. Not that the job is complete; for, in truth, there is a huge amount yet to do. But just as the Berlin Wall finally fell peacefully against all odds, spelling the beginning of the end of thermonuclear destruction, the preservation of wildness in places like British Columbia signals the dawning of the day when humankind will learn to live in balance with Nature.

For beyond all the other reasons used to justify preservation – the protection of scenic splendors and the pioneer frontier, recreational experiences, wandering space, solitude and freedom, the tourism economy, endangered wildlife and biodiversity – the most important reason for saving the original Earth is that it will guide us homeward. Wilderness shall be the path we will follow to rediscover the Garden of Eden.

Eventually, I believe, humanity will acquire the wisdom to live in peace with all Creation, in mature harmony rather than adolescent domination. When that day arrives, the grace of Great Spirit as preserved in our parks will provide us the means to restore life fully on Earth. As T.S. Eliot once wrote, we will have returned to the place of our beginning and know it for the first time. Then, too, we will understand Thoreau's wisdom. For truly we shall see that "In Wildness is the Preservation of the Earth."

They are magical places: the Chilcotin Mountains, with T'šiľ?os and

Eniyud ever watching; Nitinat Triangle's eternal trees; those Babine River steel-head; the grizzlies and caribou out on the Spatsizi Plateau; the Purcell Mountains, where Art Twomey lies buried; Schoen Valley, with midnight elk grazing; the northern Babine Mountains, homeland of the pioneers; Height of the Rockies' rugged summits; and the mile-wide waters of the Tatshenshini River flowing down to Confluence. All are sacred and divine. Each is now protected, intact, and pristine, five and a half million acres of wildness. As always before and now ever after, the spirit of the vast land I so love.

Wilderness British Columbia is my passion, my life. It is my place on this most precious of planets. Here is home where along with dear friends and courageous companions I have campaigned to pass Nature onward, to save the wild earth. How fortunate I have been to be blessed with this work. How privileged and grateful I feel.

And I thank my Creator in silence, with reverence, for all that has been given. For all that remains. For the mystery and wonder. For the spirit eternal. For life without end. Amen.

Index